LITERARY CRITICISM AND CULTURAL THEORY
OUTSTANDING DISSERTATIONS

edited by
William E. Cain
Wellesley College

A ROUTLEDGE SERIES

Other Books in This Series:

Dialectic of Self and Story
Reading and Storytelling in Contemporary American Fiction
Robert Durante

Allegories of Violence
Tracing the Writings of War in Late Twentieth-Century Fiction
Lidia Yuknavitch

Voice of the Oppressed in the Language of the Oppressor
A Discussion of Selected Postcolonial Literature from Ireland, Africa and America
Patsy J. Daniels

Eugenic Fantasies
Racial Ideology in the Literature and Popular Culture of the 1920's
Betsy L. Nies

The Life Writing of Otherness
Woolf, Baldwin, Kingston, and Winterson
Lauren Rusk

From Within the Frame
Storytelling in African-American Fiction
Bertram D. Ashe

The Self Wired
Technology and Subjectivity in Contemporary Narrative
Lisa Yaszek

The Space and Place of Modernism
The Little Magazine in New York
Adam McKible

The Figure of Consciousness
William James, Henry James, and Edith Wharton
Jill M. Kress

Word of Mouth
Food and Fiction after Freud
Susanne Skubal

The Waste Fix
Seizures of the Sacred from Upton Sinclair to The Soprano's
William G. Little

Will The Circle Be Unbroken?
Family and Sectionalism in the Virginia Novels of Kennedy, Caruthers, and Tucker, 1830–1845
John L. Hare

Poetic Gesture
Myth, Wallace Stevens, and the Motions of Poetic Language
Kristine S. Santilli

Border Modernism
Intercultural Readings in American Literary Modernism
Christopher Schedler

The Merchant of Modernism
The Economic Jew in Anglo-American Literature, 1864–1939
Gary Martin Levine

The Making of the Victorian Novelist
Anxieties and Authorship in the Mass Market
Bradley Deane

Out of Touch
Skin Tropes and Identities in Woolf, Ellison, Pynchon, and Acker
Maureen F. Curtin

Writing the City
Urban Visions and Literary Modernism
Desmond Harding

Figures of Finance Capitalism
Writing, Class, and Capital in the Age of Dickens
Borislav Knezevic

Balancing the Books
Faulkner, Morrison, and the Economies of Slavery
Erik Dussere

BEYOND THE SOUND BARRIER
The Jazz Controversy in Twentieth-Century American Fiction

Kristin K. Henson

ROUTLEDGE
NEW YORK & LONDON

Published in 2003 by
Routledge
29 West 35th Street
New York, NY 10001
www.routledge-ny.com

Published in Great Britain by
Routledge
11 New Fetter Lane
London EC4P 4EE
www.routledge.co.uk

Copyright © 2003 by Taylor & Francis Books, Inc.

Routledge is an imprint of the Taylor & Francis Group.
Printed in the United States of America on acid-free paper.

All rights reserved. No part of this book may be reprinted or reproduced or utilized in any form or by any electronic, mechanical, or other means, now known or hereafter invented, including photocopying and recording, or in any information storage or retrieval system, without written permission from the publishers.

10 9 8 7 6 5 4 3 2 1

Library of Congress Cataloging-in-Publication Data

Henson, Kristin K., 1968–
  Beyond the sound barrier : the jazz controversy in twentieth-century American fiction / by Kristin K. Henson.
      p. cm. -- (Literary criticism and cultural theory)
Includes bibliographical references and index.
   ISBN 0-415-94300-0 (Hardcover : alk. paper)
  1. American fiction--20th century--History and criticism. 2. Jazz in literature. 3. American fiction--African American authors--History and criticism. 4. Music and literature--History--20th century. 5. Musical fiction--History and criticism. 6. African American musicians in literature. 7. Jazz musicians in literature. 8. Music in literature. 9. Race in literature. I. Title. II. Series.
   PS374.J38 H45 2003
   813'.509357--dc21   2002015219

Dale Miller, husband and friend, thanks for the teamwork.
B. Joan Karr Henson and John L. Henson, parents, thanks for believing.
Pyrite, the Golden One, thanks for sanity.

Contents

INTRODUCTION	1
CHAPTER ONE "A sympathetic, singing instrument" Musical Tropes and Cultural Fusion in James Weldon Johnson's *The Autobiography of an Ex-Coloured Man*	11
CHAPTER TWO "A big sensation" F. Scott Fitzgerald and Jazz Anxiety	37
CHAPTER THREE Musical Range Langston Hughes's *The Ways of White Folks*	69
CHAPTER FOUR "Only in the head of a musician" The Powers of Music in Toni Morrison's *Jazz*	87
CONCLUSION	121
NOTES	127
BIBLIOGRAPHY	145
INDEX	155

INTRODUCTION

Literature and the Jazz Controversy

> ...[T]he modes of music are never disturbed without unsettling of the most fundamental political and social conventions.... It is here, then that our guardians must build their guardhouse and post of watch. (333-334)

As the preceding quotation from Plato's *Republic* illustrates, the idea that music and listeners' responses to it can stimulate social disruptions surfaced early in the history of Western thought. Public responses to twentieth-century popular music reveal strong traces of Platonic idealism that encouraged some commentators to categorize European classical music as inherently good, true, and pure and to classify popular forms as debased and threatening to the social order. In particular, vehement reactions to the popular American music of the 1920s, music loosely categorized as "jazz," indicated anxieties about rapid and monumental cultural changes.

Even before the widespread popularity of jazz, the controversy surrounding popular music in America began to emerge with the ascendancy of ragtime. Musicologist Charles Hamm notes several unifying, characteristic assumptions in what he describes as "modernist narratives" surrounding popular music that began to take shape in America concomitantly with the rise of ragtime. I will list these assumptions to establish them as reference points in the discussion of a binary "high/low" discourse in relation to early twentieth-century popular music. According to Hamm, the modernist narratives that were constructed around the dichotomy of "high and low" genres of music include the following:

- The ascendancy of the notion of "musical autonomy," which relies on the conviction that text supersedes context (2). The musical text itself is privileged over its function and reception. This belief is promoted in conjunction with narratives that extol the superiority of the European classical repertory above all other music.

- A narrative developed in response to the prevailing fear that "high" culture was being corrupted and debased by the technological innovations that began to widely disseminate popular culture, particularly in the form of music. Underlying this assumption of debasement is the belief that "the people creating, disseminating, and consuming these mass products are of inferior ethnic, class, or moral stock" (9). This aspect of the narrative not only privileges one genre of music over another; it privileges one group over all others under the guise of upholding standards of aesthetic value.

- A narrative promoted the idea that folk music spontaneously arises as the "authentic" expression of a particular group of people.

- Another narrative supported the belief that classical music is permanent and universal, while folk and popular musics are ephemeral and particular to marginal groups. (2-17)

In conjunction with Hamm's description of modernist narratives of value, considering historian Lawrence Levine's assessment of the role of jazz in the emergence of an American cultural hierarchy helps to further clarify prevalent American attitudes toward popular music in the early twentieth century.[1]

Levine attributes tremendous cultural importance to "jazz," that elastic term for many distinctive musical practices (including ragtime) emerging from African American culture and shaping American (and international) popular music in general. In his insightful and impressively researched *Highbrow/Lowbrow: The Emergence of Cultural Hierarchy in America*, Levine thoroughly documents the ascendancy of the notion of "Culture" (with a capital "C") as synonymous with "refinement" in American society. In a related essay, devoted specifically to the subject of jazz, Levine mentions that the word "culture" was so closely associated with "refinement" that this "was precisely the definition it carried in the single-word definition pocket dictionaries popular at the turn of the century" ("Jazz," 174). This notion of Culture as refinement, Levine argues, sets up jazz as diametrically opposed to "Culture" in public discourse regarding the music. Levine demonstrates that cultural categories such as "high," "low," "highbrow," "lowbrow," and "popular" became fixed in public perception around the turn of the century.

Introduction

In his study of jazz, he notes that at this time, "two older words with new meanings ... came into general usage ... Culture and Jazz ... helped to define one another. That is, they served as convenient polar points, as antitheses" (174). Some of the opposing characteristics that Levine documents parallel and compliment Hamm's observations regarding the modernist narratives that were constructed to support aesthetic and social value judgements. Again, I will list these for the convenience of establishing reference points. According to the established criteria for judgment:

- Jazz seemed a "new" product while Culture seemed "traditional" and the product of the ages.
- Jazz epitomized discord and chaos while Culture was associated with harmony, reason, and order.
- "Natural" musicians "spontaneously" created jazz; Culture was the product of intensive study and training.
- As a participatory art, jazz blurred distinctions between audience and performer. Culture carefully constructed these boundaries, demanding a passive and reverential audience. The performance context of the two was entirely different.
- Jazz also blurred boundaries between composer and performer. Culture exalted the text as sacred and required strict adherence to it, rather than emphasizing improvisational freedom.
- Jazz appeared to be a distinctively American cultural product, and even its harshest critics, who often concomitantly denied its African American sources, acknowledged this. Culture was decidedly Eurocentric. (174-75)

The influence of this hierarchical conception of Culture indicated, according to Levine, America's lingering uncertainties as "a colonized people attempting to define itself in the shadow of the former imperial power" (175). The ascendancy of jazz, however, was

> an expression of that other side of ourselves that strove to recognize the positive aspects of our newness and our heterogeneity; that learned to be comfortable with the fact that a significant portion of our heritage derived from Africa and other non-European sources; and that recognized in the various syncretized cultures that became so characteristic of the United States not an embarrassing weakness but a dynamic source of strength. (175)

The conflict between jazz and Culture in the American imagination was a vital part of the nation's struggle to define itself in the early twentieth century. Certain American writers responded creatively to this conflict, and this book will examine twentieth-century American literature that explores the implications of this jazz/Culture tension and boundary negotiation.

My objective in this study is to explore the symbolic role of jazz in twentieth-century American fiction and the association of the music with cultural "mixing" and the negotiation of boundaries that contributed to the definition of modernity in America. In her article "Debating with Beethoven: Understanding the Fear of Early Jazz," Kathy Ogren observes:

> An examination of the fear of jazz illuminates specific social and political anxieties of Americans in the 1920s; it also establishes a context for understanding the symbolic role played by popular music generally in twentieth-century American culture. (249)

For many people in early twentieth-century America, the emergence of first ragtime and then jazz as American popular music epitomized the abandonment of old values and certainties. Ogren points out that in the 1920s, "For many Americans, to argue about jazz was to argue about the nature of change itself" (7). This study considers music's symbolism in literature with the goal of achieving insight into the implications of that literature and the cultural contexts from which it emerges.

In the work of all four authors in this study, music–particularly music based on or associated with improvisational aesthetics–symbolizes the *process* of culture and the ways that cultural boundaries are continually negotiated. Historian Lawrence Levine defines the concept of culture as process:

> Culture is not a fixed condition but a process: the product of interaction between the past and the present. Its toughness and resiliency are determined not by a culture's ability to withstand change, which indeed may be a sign of stagnation not life, but by its ability to react creatively and responsively to the realities of a new situation. (*Black Culture*, 5)

Levine's definition of culture indicates that cultures are most vital when they are improvisational, an idea affirmed in the fiction of James Weldon Johnson, Langston Hughes, and Toni Morrison. F. Scott Fitzgerald's fiction, as a contrasting example, documents an early twentieth-century American anxiety about improvisational change equating to chaos. An analysis of these writers' representations of various styles of music loosely grouped into the category of "jazz" illuminates some of the complex negotiations involved in the cultural boundary crossing that the music symbolizes.

For each of these writers, music is associated with crossing boundaries that normally structure the social order in a hierarchical manner. How can music act as a source of social disruptions? What makes its form of expression special? Musicologist John Shepherd considers the ways that music, as physical sound, negotiates boundaries, and his observations

Introduction

address the preceding questions about the social role of music. Shepherd writes:

> Sound (and therefore music as text) is the only major channel of communication that actively vibrates inside the body ... the human experience of sound involves in addition to the sympathetic vibration of the eardrums, the sympathetic vibrations of the body [i.e., lungs, sinus passages, mouth, etc.]. Sound is thus felt in addition to being "heard." As a consequence it transcends actual tactile awareness and the *particular* form of erotic awareness at the surface of the body which then finds internal resonance. Sound, however, is in the body and enters the body. (179)

Shepherd's observations indicate that social contact can be achieved through musical contact, and that it is precisely the material vibrations of timbre and the body's role as a sympathetic resonator that can break down the dichotomies of inside/outside and self/other. Shepherd argues that music achieves this effect because it expresses signification "through purely abstract and tactile dimensions" (91), while language is essentially reified and denotative (93).

Shepherd's comments do not simply restate the old cliché that music is a "universal language." He asserts that music can transcend cultural barriers, *not* because, as is often argued, it creates a type of universal language beyond cultural coding, but precisely because it does encode "culture-specific realities in a way that escapes the prison of denotative and referential modes of signification" (271). This book considers various literary uses of the musical–representations of music that impact themes, tropes, characterization, narrative structure, and language. Shepherd's warning about the distinctions between music and language are important to bear in mind in any literary-musical study, but music also has metaphorical and aesthetic properties that some writers have creatively employed to alter the range and style of their fiction.

Cultural theorist Simon Frith, who studies the implications of popular music, examines the special relationship to identity that music can have. Frith argues that "pop tastes do not just derive from our socially constructed identities; they also help to shape them" (276). Frith's comment suggests one of the ways that music can evoke social changes by playing a part in the fluid and overdetermined construction of identity. Certain writers have seized upon this aspect of popular music and have utilized it through characterization. Of course, when we think about popular music's progressive powers to incite change, we are simultaneously confronted with its failure to break through stultifying conventions and stereotypes. Ralph Ellison, a great advocate of the powers of music, exposes this corollary phenomenon in his one of his essays on the character of American culture, "The Little Man at Chehaw Station." Ellison asks:

> What, by the way, is one to make of the white teenager who, with a transistor radio, screaming a Stevie Wonder tune, glued to his ear, shouts racial epithets at black youngsters trying to swim at a public beach—and this in the name of the ethnic sanctity of what has been declared a neighborhood turf? (21)

Ellison implies that the notion of "ethnic sanctity" among Americans is absurd in a nation that is—by its very definition—culturally "mixed." Interestingly, he chooses music as his metaphor for cultural amalgamation, but why, he asks, does a social awareness and a sense of justice fail to necessarily accompany what appears to be an unthinking kind of cultural appreciation?

Frith's response to this dilemma might be that the music does not create a utopian social environment, but it can, in some cases, enact a utopian vision. Frith writes that:

> ...musical identity is both fantastic—idealizing not just oneself but also the social world one inhabits—and real: its is enacted in activity. Music making and music listening, that is to say, are bodily matters; they involve what one might call *social movements* ... music gives us a real experience of what the ideal could be. (274)

In this sense, also bearing Ellison's observations in mind, American popular music can enact the creative potential of a multicultural society. In this story of pop music in America, we might also include Andrew Ross's admonition that although there exists "everyday, plagiaristic, commerce between white and black musics," nonetheless, "it is important to remember that this *overexchanged* and *overbartered* record of miscegenated cultural production everywhere bespeaks a racist history of exploitation exclusively weighted to dominant white interests" (68). Still, in addition to these economic and political realities, music also has the power to be a socially disruptive force, and individuals respond to this fact in conflicting (and sometimes conflicted) ways—as an analysis of the literature included in this study clearly indicates. While acknowledging the limitations of music as a cultural product, we might still consider the use these writers make of music's potential to disrupt binary oppositions upon which stereotypes often rely.

John Shepherd's analysis of the sympathetic resonation that accompanies the experience of music illustrates one way that music can potentially disrupt binary oppositions that are embedded in an ideology of absolute difference. Simon Frith explains both the sources and the ramifications of this musical phenomenon:

> [T]he dominant forms [of popular music] in all contemporary societies have originated at the social margins—among the poor, the migrant, the rootless, the "queer." Anti-essentialism is a necessary part of musical experience, a necessary consequence of music's failure to register the separations of body and

mind on which "essential" differences (black and white, female and male, gay and straight, nation and nation) depend. (274)

Each of the four writers included in this musical-literary study engages with the musical phenomenon that Frith describes. These writers symbolically employ various styles of music in their narratives to represent the implications of popular music's anti-essentialist potential in different ways.

In each chapter, I approach an analysis of particular musical allusions and more general references to or incorporations of musical styles with an awareness of the importance of historical specificity. Although I am admittedly seeking connections among disparate works that rely upon musical tropes to communicate ideas about culture, I am also alert to the importance of recognizing difference. I hope this project demonstrates that, when studying representations of music in fiction, an interdisciplinary approach that includes research in music history is valuable. When I use vague terms such as "ragtime," "jazz," "blues," and "popular" and "classical" music, I try to provide an explanation for what these terms specifically mean with the context of each particular literary text. To discern what use these texts make of music, it is important to pay close attention to the kind of music to which they refer.

This book explores the ways that four twentieth-century novelists use musical tropes to engage with public debates over the tendency of popular music to negotiate social boundaries more fluidly than other modes of expression. The 1920s debate over the meaning of jazz is central to this study, but my analysis also extends beyond the reaches of this controversy to consider earlier conflicts regarding the popularity of ragtime. I will argue that a concentrated analysis of musical tropes in the fiction of the writers included in this study–James Weldon Johnson, F. Scott Fitzgerald, Langston Hughes, and Toni Morrison–suggests that cultural "mixing" is one of the crucial preoccupations of modernist thinking and that this central concern still has resonance, particularly in contemporary American fiction.[2]

Beyond the Sound Barrier begins with an analysis of James Weldon Johnson's *The Autobiography of an Ex-Coloured Man*. This novel, first published in 1912 and reissued in 1927, predates the 1920s jazz controversy and anticipates it with its intervention in a less heated but still significant debate over the social implications and aesthetic value of ragtime music. I interpret Johnson's early, groundbreaking work as, in part, a novelistic meditation upon the implications of popular music in America. Johnson's novel employs musical tropes to dismantle certain aspects of binary thinking. *The Autobiography* suggests that in early twentieth-century America the concept of "race" could only be *lived* according to the dichotomy of "black" or "white," although individual and cultural identity could be *understood* in terms of "black and white," and music provides the novel's central trope for an exploration of this phenomenon.

F. Scott Fitzgerald's representations of popular music, which reveal aspects of American literary modernism that sometimes go unnoticed or at least unspoken, provide the topic for chapter two. Fitzgerald's musical tropes suggest an anxiety over the cultural amalgamation that permeates American modernism and that gives it a distinctively, internationally recognizable "American" style. Chapter two analyzes Fitzgerald's allusions to jazz-influenced popular music and reassesses his role as the spokesman for the "Jazz Age."

Chapter three considers the role of music in three stories from Langston Hughes's 1933 collection, *The Ways of White Folks*. Hughes uses music as a trope for social boundary crossing and explores its powers and its limitations as a cultural force for social change. In "Home," the protagonist tries to use his musical talent to escape the realities of a hierarchical social system defined by race and class, but he is ultimately and fatally unable to do so. In "Rejuvenation through Joy," the implications of the jazz controversy are humorously and satirically addressed through the story of a charlatan who sells the "joy" of jazz to a wealthy white audience. Cultural ownership of music is the focus of "The Blues I'm Playing," in which the protagonist defends her right to play the blues against the demands of her wealthy white patron. In each of the stories, music is the intersection at which white and black culture meet and engage in conflict. Through these stories, Hughes examines a central component of the jazz controversy by revealing the ways that debates over aesthetic value can often be a cloaked method for debating about race and even for promoting racial stereotypes.

By considering 1920s jazz and blues from a late twentieth-century perspective, Toni Morrison uses musical tropes to unravel modernist intellectual knots resulting from a dichotomized approach to the concepts of race and culture in American life. For Morrison, music represents an aesthetic statement that is culturally distinctive *and* fluid in its manipulation of boundaries. Jazz provides her with a particularly effective trope to approach the concept of cultural amalgamation because of the immediate, physical ways that music crosses boundaries.

Chapter four explores the ways that Morrison's *Jazz* portrays the relationship between particular musical styles and the idea of community. Morrison's novel emphasizes the profound, widespread cultural impact of African American music and its capacity to articulate and reinforce cultural distinctiveness. Morrison uses musical tropes to dismantle the binary oppositions that constrained some modernist approaches to understanding the implications of this music. Through its musical tropes, *Jazz* also suggests that the music and fiction that embraces its aesthetic priorities can promote individual and communal healing. The novel redefines the meaning of the jazz age and

Introduction

the implications of the controversy that the music inspired.

The notion of music's power to symbolically express meaning in a more abstract and simultaneously more physical way than language can enters the fiction of all four writers in this study. Rather than avoiding a mode of expression that communicates in significantly different ways than their own chosen medium of written language, these authors take up the idea of music's tendency to blur boundaries and explore the ramifications of this effect. While their language definitely has different effects than music does, all of these writers are interested in and engaged with the aesthetic priorities of the music they incorporate into their writing. This study focuses on the ways that music widens the scope of their narrative symbolism to communicate ideas about the implications of cultural amalgamation.

The novels and short stories included in this study are concerned with what might be very loosely classified as "popular" music because it quite literally appealed to a fairly large and diverse audience in the early twentieth century and was considered "low" culture or "lowbrow" by the cultural elite. In several instances, the narratives explore the connections and conflicts between popular and "high" cultural forms. The representations of the music vary according to the time period and social circumstances of the setting. For example, in James Weldon Johnson's *The Autobiography of an Ex-Coloured Man*, the popular music of the day is ragtime, and Johnson explores its intersections with the classical music of "high" culture. F. Scott Fitzgerald's *The Great Gatsby* and *Tender is the Night* most often allude to jazz-influenced songs from musical comedies that were vaguely grouped under the heading "jazz" in the 1920s. Langston Hughes's collection of short stories, *The Ways of White Folks*, incorporates jazz, blues, and classical music to explore the concept of range in a musical and philosophical sense, exposing the narrowness of stereotypes. Toni Morrison's *Jazz*, set in 1926, alludes to the jazz and blues emerging from a distinctively African American urban cultural context in the 1920s, but the novel also alludes to the whole history of African American music and its role in modernizing America.

All of these representations of music imply that music has a special relationship to identity. The portrayal of music in these novels and stories suggests that music somehow provides one of our significant sources for self-definition and that music can also contribute to the ways that we are socially defined. Again, Simon Frith's work on popular music helps to explain this sociomusical phenomenon:

> For the best part of this century, pop music has been an important way in which we have learned to understand ourselves as historical, ethnic, class-bound, gendered, national subjects. This has had conservative effects (primarily through nostalgia) as well as liberating ones. What music does (all music)

is put into play as sense of identity that may or may not fit the way we are placed by other social forces. Music certainly puts us in our place, but it can also suggest that our social circumstances are not immutable (and that other people–performers, fans–share our dissatisfaction). Music is not in itself revolutionary or reactionary. It is a source of strong feelings which, because they are socially coded, can come up against common sense. (276-277)

Frith's comments suggest that music and listeners' responses to it can have either disruptive or conservative social repercussions, and the fiction included in this study explores both of these possibilities. In each of these texts, popular music is depicted as tremendously influential in shaping the characters' experience of their world. The music often functions in complex ways because it embodies contradictions without reducing them to absolute dichotomies, thus enabling the characters (and the narratives themselves) to delve into ambiguity instead of accepting simple answers to difficult questions.

According to Frith, the implications of popular aesthetic forms are not self-evidently obvious simply because they are popular. The popular can require the same kind of analytical, interpretational expertise that "high" art forms demand, but the popular is generally discussed in different terms. Frith asserts that some popular art is difficult and challenging and that this characteristic makes it interesting and attractive to its audiences because "the 'difficult' appeals through the traces it carries of another world in which it would be easy" (20). Frith concludes, "The utopian impulse, the *negation* of everyday life, the aesthetic impulse that Adorno recognized in high art, must be part of low art too" (20).

Popular music has been a powerful social force in twentieth-century America, and, in its vast range of styles, it continues to be a defining feature of twenty-first century American culture. The narratives featured in this study engage with music as a social force in various ways, but they all explore the potential of music to offer a "negation of everyday life" that suggests alternative ways of understanding and ordering the world. These narratives bring the popular into the literary realm of the "high" and use musical tropes to negotiate boundaries that may seem to be rigid and absolute but which prove to be mutable and tenuous. In all of these novels and stories, music appears as an indication that binary oppositions and the old certainties that derive from them are artificial and socially constructed, although the depictions of this realization and its implications vary significantly.

CHAPTER ONE

"A sympathetic, singing instrument"
Musical Tropes and Cultural Fusion in James Weldon Johnson's *The Autobiography of an Ex-Coloured Man*

Recounting the story of his life, the narrator of James Weldon Johnson's *The Autobiography of an Ex-Coloured Man* depicts his early development as a musician in terms of his proficiency with written forms and his skill as an improviser. By the age of seven, he can play by ear, and he knows all the notes in both clefs, but he "prefer[s] not to be hampered by notes" (9). He takes lessons and later studies "the theory of music" (40), but his childhood music teacher has "no small difficulty at first in pinning [him] down to the notes" (9). He listens to his mother play Episcopal hymns "from the book" (7) and old spirituals "by ear" (8). She sings, and he interrupts "by chiming in with strange harmonies" (8).

As a child prodigy, the ex-coloured man distinguishes himself not just with technique but also with the emotional impact of his interpretations. He writes:

> Very early I acquired that knack of using the pedals, which makes the piano a sympathetic, singing instrument, quite a different thing from the source of hard or blurred sounds it so generally is. I think this was due not entirely to natural artistic temperament, but largely to the fact that I did not begin to learn the piano by counting out exercises, but by trying to reproduce the quaint songs which my mother used to sing, with all their pathetic turns and cadences. (27)

This passage suggests that the ex-coloured man evokes a distinctive expressive and vocal sound from the piano, a sound influenced by African-derived cadences of his mother's "quaint songs." He develops his own style, not by playing written music as "counting out exercises" but by the methods of oral tradition. He uses the "pathetic turns and cadences" of the music he hears his

11

mother sing to transform a traditional European instrument from a "source of hard or blurred sounds" into "a sympathetic, singing instrument."

The Autobiography of an Ex-Coloured Man often raises questions about how its protagonist can fuse the elements of his multivalent cultural identity. Music serves as a trope in the novel for a kind of fusion or coherence that allows contradictions to coexist. The ex-coloured man's musical style, like his cultural background and his parentage, fuses "black" and "white." The beauty of his musical style–his transformation of something "hard or blurred" into something "sympathetic, singing"–highlights the tragedy of the novel. According to the rules of the racially divided society in which he lives, the ex-coloured man is denied the option of fusion; he must stay within one boundary or the other. He must limit his identity to "white" or "black" only. In the face of the social realities, the ex-coloured man's expertise in two musical traditions illustrates the actual fluidity of boundaries that are conventionally represented as rigid and immutable.

In terms that parallel the portrayal of the ex-coloured man's approach to musical expertise, Ralph Ellison once described his own youthful musical ambitions. Ellison asserts that

> there wasn't always this division between the ambitions of jazz musicians and the standards of classical music; the idea was to master both traditions. In school the classics were pushed at us on all sides, and if you danced, if you shared any of the social life of the young people, jazz was inescapable; it was all around you. And if you were a musician you were challenged by its sounds and by the techniques required to produce them...Such men as [trumpeter Icky] Lawrence and [bassist Walter] Page–and there were several others–had conservatory training as well as a rich jazz experience and thus felt no need to draw a line between the two traditions. Following them, our ideal was to master both. (9-10)

Johnson's ex-coloured man enacts the principle of "master[ing] both traditions," by fusing them to create a stylized coherence from his dual cultural heritage. The ex-coloured man's pivotal encounter with ragtime music seems as if it presents the opportunity to merge his expertise with oral and written forms and with improvisational and standardized approaches. Faced with the brutality of a white lynch mob whose murderous impulses are legally sanctioned, however, the ex-coloured man acquiesces to the binarism of a society divided by racial categorization, and he renounces his youthful ambitions.

Initially published anonymously in 1912, *The Autobiography* stands as the first novel to use jazz–specifically ragtime as an early and a particular facet of the blues-jazz matrix–as an integral trope.[1] The narrator's musical inclinations serve as the earliest introduction we receive to his most salient characteristic– his tendency to move across boundaries and to resist definition according to conventional binary categories. Although we know from the beginning that he eventually chooses "white" as his self-defining category, the title also indicates that he is an "ex-coloured" man, a term that mocks the impossibility of any such category in a society racially delineated according to the "one-drop" rule and legally segregated.[2]

Despite rigid social categorizations based on "race," according to the ex-coloured man's "true" account we must concede that he is simultaneously "white" and "black."[3] Much of what readers might consider separate and even oppositional the narrator proves to be contained within his complex and seemingly contradictory identity. Most often, Johnson engages the trope of music to convey this idea of accommodating contradictions without reducing them to dichotomous oversimplifications. In the novel, ragtime music epitomizes the concept of boundary crossing and elaborates upon the notion of "passing" in a way that heightens our understanding of both the distinctiveness of African American culture and the artificiality of categories of "race."

Ragtime can be understood as central to the novel, because, as a historical study of the music reveals, it crossed boundaries of race and class in ways that symbolize the complex "crossings" in which the narrator engages. Consequently, this chapter begins with an analysis of ragtime's history. Four sections organize the chapter, and each addresses a particular facet of the musical tropes in Johnson's novel. The first section examines the historical background of ragtime as a musical form and as the subject of academic inquiry and compares these versions of the music with Johnson's portrait of it. The second section analyzes the relationship between ragtime and classical European concert music within the early twentieth-century discourse on the binary nature of "high" and "low" culture and considers how Johnson's novel responds to and participates in this discourse. Section three evaluates how ragtime, as a facet of African American oral traditions, fits into Johnson's artistic objective to historically document African American expressive cultural practices and the impact of those practices on "mainstream" America.[4] In section three, the challenges of "transcription" are addressed in relation to the music and to Johnson's writing. The fourth and final section explores Johnson's international perspective and considers the connections between his writing and certain formal innovations in music and literature that followed his work.

NOTES ON THE HISTORY OF RAGTIME

Ragtime music, which the narrator first encounters in New York–the urban American center of cultural amalgamation–has a history that parallels and contributes to the development of the novel's boundary crossing themes. Ragtime is a musical art, like the ex-coloured man himself, liminally situated within divergent cultural traditions and crossed lines of descent, mocking artificially constructed categories that strive to contain its overdetermined identity within neatly demarcated lines of "purity." In ways that also parallel the experiences of the ex-coloured man, the music's history reveals the alienating loss of cultural identity that can accompany wholesale incorporation and assimilation into the "mainstream" and can be part of the achievement of "legitimacy." A closer look at the history of ragtime in the United States reveals the ways that Johnson uses the music to symbolize the triumphs and the hazards of class and racial boundary crossing in early twentieth-century America.

Ragtime is considered by most commentators to be a culturally amalgamated art. As Rudi Blesh and Harriet Janis note in their study of ragtime, "With this music the wires of dark and white America crossed and the vital currents were flowing back and forth" (13).[5] In his influential history of jazz, Marshall Stearns describes ragtime as a music that, because it was heavily influenced by European styles, was able to break new cultural ground and introduce other Americans to African American musical styles. According to Stearns:

> Ragtime developed a wider and more influential fusion of European and African musical elements than ever before. It began with such a large component of formal European characteristics that (although it absorbed more and more of the African rhythmic complexity during its twenty year popularity) it was never able to go the rest of the way and incorporate the bittersweet mood of the blues. Ragtime remained cheerful, pianistic in concept, and predominantly European. But just because of this, ragtime spread farther—and thinner—than any preceding wave of Afro-American music, carrying with it an elementary but basic introduction to new rhythms. (148-49)

Ben Sidran argues, in a similar fashion, that the "watered-down rhythmic aspect of [ragtime] was perhaps the core of its appeal to whites" (27). Amiri Baraka also sees ragtime as a kind of "basic introduction" that was superseded in musical importance by the cultural separatism of blues musicians and their audiences. For Baraka, ragtime, unlike blues, represents "a premature attempt at the socio-cultural merger that later produced jazz" (148).

Baraka finds in ragtime the crossing of cultural "wires" similar to those described by Blesh and Janis: "Ragtime was a Negro music, resulting from the Negro's appropriation of white piano techniques used in show music. Popularized ragtime, which flooded the country with songsheets in the first decade of the century, was a dilution of Negro style ... [illustrating the] hopelessly interwoven fabric of American life where blacks and whites pass so quickly as to become only grays!" (110-11). Like Baraka, musicologist Edward A. Berlin associates the rise of ragtime with musical theater (what Baraka calls "show music"). Berlin points out that "among ragtime's sources and early settings were the minstrel-show and vaudeville stages" (*Reflections*, 24).

Johnson himself along with his brother Rosamond and their partner Bob Cole began their artistic careers in musical theater, and they knew first hand the influences of ragtime music in this business. Johnson's ragtime tropes in *The Autobiography*, however, do not condemn the "interwoven fabric of American life" to which Baraka refers. Instead, Johnson's incorporation of music into the novel allows him to use signs of cultural amalgamation for his own purposes. Johnson's portrayal of music in *The Autobiography* is not a naïve paean to an idealistic vision of cultural "unity in diversity" in early twentieth-century America. The novel explores and enacts the ways that the negotiation of boundaries in American culture can provide material for artistic creations that are not simply ornamental but that may inspire change on individual and social levels.

Stylistically, one of the most unconventional aspects of the novel is its flaunting of generic boundaries between written and oral / language and music that Johnson takes up again in his formalistically innovative *God's Trombones*. As Eric Sundquist points out:

> The establishment of an African American cultural poetics had to demonstrate the continued presence in America of an African culture where speech and song more closely approached each other on the continuum of cultural sound, where the vocalized "talk" of drums and rhythmic instruments was paramount and where *nommo*, the power of the word in its oral dimension, governed human interaction to a far greater degree than in the Western tradition. (*To Wake*, 385)

Johnson's writing, particularly in the way it uses musical tropes to negotiate the modern Western boundaries between oral and written, is a crucial part of the development of the African American cultural poetics that Sundquist describes.

In his extended analysis of *The Autobiography*, Sundquist calls our attention to the language of the text as it constructs this African American cultural poetics. He notes the convoluted complexity of "the seemingly simplest prose of *The Autobiography of an Ex-Coloured Man*, in which fictive autobiographical narrative, cultural essay, historical allegory, and signifying parody are intertwined" (*Hammers*, 4). Sundquist describes the quality of Johnson's language as "brittle" and "chameleonlike," noting that it assumes these characteristics as it deftly combines "fiction and cultural analysis" (6). Sundquist's adjectives are excellent descriptions of Johnson's prose. Johnson's language seems brittle because it is stretched to its breaking point with a self-conscious awareness of its immutability and its silence in print. It is also like a chameleon in its resistance to both "color" hierarchies and the static medium of print—changing colors, resisting full self-exposure, camouflaging its intent to dissolve boundaries considered to be sacred. The language of Johnson's novel often pretends to be straightforwardly simple in keeping with Johnson's decision to first publish the book anonymously so that it would seem "true." The musical themes undermine the seeming simplicity of the language and clue us to its multivalence.

Consider, for example, the differences between the description of the event that inaugurates the ex-coloured man's decision to "pass" as a white man–his witnessing of a white mob burning a black man alive–and the descriptions of the sermons and spirituals at "big meeting" (173), which immediately precede the murder scene. At "big meeting," a religious and social function, we are introduced to the preacher, John Brown, who delivers his sermons as "tone pictures" (176) in which meaning never supersedes sound. John Brown's performance convinces the ex-coloured man that "eloquence consists more in the manner of saying than in what is said" (176). Another person who greatly impresses the ex-coloured man is Singing Johnson, who acts as "a leader of singing, a maker of songs, a man who could improvise at the moment lines to fit the occasion" (178). With his depiction of Singing Johnson and the music he improvisationally composes by relying on his "memory and ingenuity" (180), Johnson attempts to render "that elusive undertone, the note in music which is not heard with the ears" (181). Through language and characterization Johnson works to capture the emotional impact of music–its power, as he asserts in another context, as "the touchstone ... the magic thing ... that by which the Negro can bridge all chasms."[6]

Yet these lovely descriptions of the music, the sermons, and the people who create them are immediately followed by the narrator's detached account of brutal mob violence arising from racial hatred and legally sanctioned murder. The "chasm" it is necessary to bridge in this case seems to be an insurmountable obstacle. The tone of the narrator's description of the murder is reportorial, or, to recall Sundquist's term, "brittle":

> Fuel was brought from everywhere, oil, the torch; the flames crouched for an instant as though to gather strength, then leaped up as high as their victim's head. He squirmed, he writhed, strained at his chains, then gave out cries and groans I shall always hear. The cries and groans were choked off by the fire and smoke; but his eyes, bulging from their sockets, rolled from side to side, appealing in vain for help...Before I could make myself believe that what I saw was really happening, I was looking at a scorched post, a smouldering fire, blackened bones, charred fragments sifting down through coils of chain; and the smell of burnt flesh–human flesh–was in my nostrils. (187)

The first phrases are abruptly clipped ("oil, the torch;"). The verbs sound as harsh and contorted as their meaning implies, almost in onomatopoetic fashion ("squirm," "writhe," "strain," "bulge"). The last sentence is the longest, suggesting the lingering impression of witnessing such a sight and covering the last sensory response–internalization of the murdered man into the bodies of all present through the scent of his burned body.

In addition to its "brittle" language and alternating phrasing, the impact of the passage results in part from its juxtaposition with the music and "tone picture" sermons that precede it. One of Johnson's most famous assertions is that "[t]he final measure of the greatness of all peoples is the amount and standard of the literature and art they have produced."[7] By juxtaposing "the arts and tricks of oratory" (175) and the "elusive undertone" (181) of music with the brutal violence that leads to the question, "Have you ever witnessed the transformation of human beings into savage beasts?" (186), Johnson suggests the costs of an unjust and hypocritical society. We are shown art that establishes "the greatness of a people," then we witness the arbitrary yet legal murder of a man who, though unnamed and unknown, could have been any member of the big meeting or even Singing Johnson himself. The narrator is astounded that America, "the great example of democracy to the world, should be the only civilized, if not the only state on earth, where a human being would be burned alive" (188). The novel implies that while the narrator's decision to become an ex-coloured man is cowardly and morally weak, it is not inexplicable in the face of such brutal conditions.

The tragedy of the novel becomes the fact that the narrator cannot find a way to merge his emotional response to the music of Singing Johnson with his response to witnessing the murder. He cannot historically and experientially contextualize his own music in such a way that will allow him to express the coexistence of these two realities–the coexistence of "black and unknown bards" with charred and blackened bones. His manuscripts are "yellowing" (211) because he has renounced his affiliation with African American identity *before* the work of dismantling racial categories has been accomplished. Particularly through its musical tropes, the novel enacts the idea that race is a social construction, but the novel also implies that being ex-coloured is not a viable option until one can be ex-white as well–until the ideological construction of whiteness has been revealed and dismantled.[8]

RAGTIME, CLASSICAL, AND THE BINARY RULES OF "HIGH" AND "LOW" CULTURE

An analysis of *The Autobiography*'s relationship to the early twentieth-century American discourse on popular music reveals the methods the novel employs to negotiate socially constructed boundaries and thus to open the way for formal innovations in music and literature that followed it. Any novel that relies on popular American music as an integral theme owes a certain debt (directly or indirectly) to *The Autobiography of an Ex-Coloured Man*.[9] If we do not recognize the entrenched nature of cultural categories of value in early twentieth-century America, then we are apt to read Johnson, from an early twenty-first century perspective, as less revolutionary than he actually was. Johnson opened a space, albeit an ambiguously framed one, for popular music in the literary realm of "high" culture.[10]

Within this specific historical context, then, we can appreciate the tremendous social pressures that Johnson, as one of the earliest jazz advocates, confronted. One of the striking aspects of the written descriptions of ragtime music in *The Autobiography* is that these passages reappear almost verbatim in Johnson's preface to *The Book of American Negro Poetry*, an anthology he edited that was published in 1922. The ex-coloured man's narrative documents the African American origins of the music, just as Johnson himself does in his 1922 Preface. This documentation work establishes the music as a distinctive feature of African American expressive culture that provided the post-colonial nation as a whole with an identity separate from the oppressive dictates of European value.

By noting that ragtime "appeals universally" (100) and that "not only to the American, but the English, the French, and even the German people find delight in it" (100), the ex-coloured man establishes the "originality" of the music–the quality upon which "universal appeal" depends. In other words, the ex-coloured man and Johnson (in his Preface) directly assert that African American music is the wellspring of originality in American culture, and, while this originality is culturally specific, it also transcends the boundaries of culture and nation to appeal to divergent groups of people. This music frees America from its purely imitative (and colonially subservient) relationship with European culture. The description endows the music with early twentieth-century legitimacy through its reference to European appreciation, "proving" its value by citing European recognition of its merits. Why, then, does the ex-coloured man and Johnson (in his Preface) couple these grand assertions with the condescending disclaimer that the African American innovators who produced this independent music "knew no more of the theory of music than they did of the theory of the universe, but were guided by natural musical instinct and talent" (99)?[11] Why do the narrator and the author assert, "Now, these dances which I have referred to and Ragtime music may be lower forms of art, but they are evidence of a power that will some day be applied to the higher forms" (Preface, xv)?[12]

Musicologist Charles Hamm and historian Lawrence Levine's descriptions of early twentieth-century high/low discourse offer guidelines by which we might address these questions.[13] The only point raised by both Levine and Hamm that Johnson's novel and his nonfiction writing supports is the idea that "popular" music, including "jazz" in its multifarious forms, somehow comes naturally to "untrained" musicians who spontaneously produce it, thus making it a "lower" form of musical expression. Even this assumption, however, is qualified by the ex-coloured man's description of the extraordinary technical ability of "the club's" ragtime pianist. Johnson's references to "trained" musicians indicate primarily their ability to read and write music, a skill that allows these musicians to protect their claims to their own artistic innovations. In a musical sense, this stance is a similar kind of advocacy of empowerment and resistance through literacy that earlier African American authors promoted in slave narratives.

Rather than acquiescing to propagation of "high" cultural values, the ex-coloured man specifically addresses what Berlin refers to as "the great ragtime debate," which can be understood as a facet of the high/low discourse.[14] According to Neil Leonard, "the ragtime controversy ... lasted until the 1920s when it became part of the larger battle over jazz" (103). The ex-coloured man's direct commentary on the ragtime debate resurfaces in Johnson's 1922 Preface, indicating Johnson's personal involvement with the terms of the argument. The ex-coloured man claims that in spite of ragtime's "universal" (87) appeal and its "world-conquering" (87) influence, authorities still dismiss the music in its homeland. "In Paris they call it American music" (87), he proclaims, but "highbrow" Americans still condemn it.

In the following passage, the ex-coloured man takes on the American musical Establishment:

> American musicians, instead of investigating rag-time, attempt to ignore it, or dismiss it with a contemptuous word. But that has been the course of scholasticism in every branch of art. Whatever new thing the *people* like is pooh-poohed; whatever is *popular* is spoken of as not worth the while ... In spite of the bans which musicians and music teachers have placed upon it, the people still demand and enjoy ragtime ... Anyone who doubts that there is a peculiar heel-tickling, smile-provoking, joy-awakening charm in rag-time needs only to hear a skilful performer play the genuine article to be convinced. (100-101, italics in original)

The musicians and music teachers to whom the ex-coloured man refers represent the elite factions of American society who strove to establish homogenous and immutable standards of aesthetic value. "The people," however, as the ex-coloured man points out, enthusiastically embraced ragtime, as the tremendous success of the sheet music industry demonstrates (Berlin, *Ragtime*, 123). This split between "highbrow" and "lowbrow" can be traced back to the early history of the arts in America, a post-colonial country that looked to its former imperial ruler for definitions of refinement.

In his study of the reception of ragtime, Neil Leonard observes that, "Art music was imported from abroad and superimposed uncomfortably on our [American] culture" (104). This music was not "popular" in the literal sense– most people did not like it. Perhaps because it was presented to Americans in a decontextualized way, European classical concert music did not speak to most Americans' experience of the world. Ragtime, and the jazz that followed it, however, seemed to spring from their own soil. The rhythms of the music captured the energy and spontaneity of a culturally amalgamated, rapidly industrializing and urbanizing nation. Supporters of ragtime often appealed to its characteristic Americanness as evidence of the music's value. Prominent music critic Hiram K. Moderwell writes in a 1915 *New Republic* article:

> As you walk up and down the streets of an American city you feel in its jerk and rattle a personality different from that of any European capital. This is American. It is our lives, and it helps to form our characters and conditions our mode of action. It should have expression in art, simply because any people must express itself to know itself. No European music can or possibly could express this American personality. Ragtime I believe does express it. It is today the one true American music. (qtd. in Berlin, *Ragtime*, 51)

Despite such support for popular music, the powerful contingent of the cultural elite was still committed to refining Americans' boorish inclinations. According to Neil Leonard:

> Autocratic conductors like Theodore Thomas and members of the Damrosch family were trained in the idealism of German romanticism, which regarded music, in its highest forms, as the most spiritual of all the arts. These zealots set about to bring uplifting symphonic music in uncompromising programs to frequently indifferent and sometimes hostile audiences ... The prevailing feeling about the ennobling nature of art music is aptly illustrated by Theodore Thomas's statement, "The man who does not understand Beethoven and had not been under his spell has not half lived his life. The masterworks of instrumental music are the language of the soul and express more than those of any other art. Light music, popular music, so called, is the sensual side of the art and has more or less devil in it." (104-105)

Thomas's comment served as the epigraph to his 1905 autobiography. In his statement, Beethoven is the particular composer who is set in opposition to the debauchery and even the satanic corruption of the popular in music, which, in 1905, would have been predominantly ragtime. It is especially poignant, then, that Johnson juxtaposes (in a nonhierarchical fashion) Beethoven and African American vernacular music in *The Autobiography*.

Turning points in the ex-coloured man's life are always marked in the novel by his performance of or his experience with music. The first major occasion of this sort is when he plays Beethoven's *Sonata Pathetique* after his mother's death. The second occurs when he hears a German man play his ragtime theme in "classic" form. The third is when he listens to spirituals at "big meeting," just before he witnesses another man burned alive by a lynch mob, and the fourth time he plays Chopin's *Thirteenth Nocturne* for the woman who will later become his wife. These events chart a course of change in the ex-coloured man's perspective, and no one music is elevated above the rest. They all signify different things, but they signify in similar ways. Each musical reference highlights an equally significant event. To appreciate the implications of this juxtaposition requires knowledge of the controversy surrounding the practice of merging the "popular" or the "folk" with the "classics."

The ex-coloured man engages in a practice called "ragging the classics," which he claims to have invented (115). "Highbrow" music critics held this practice in great contempt in the early twentieth century, but the proliferation of ragtime instruction manuals and sheet music transcriptions of "ragged classics" countered their disapproval.[15] The ex-coloured man mentions, in particular, the popular appeal of his ragged version of Mendelssohn's "Wedding March" (115). Berlin observes that "of all classical composers, Mendelssohn, the darling of turn-of-the-century piano teachers, was the most frequent target for ragtime parody; versions of the *Wedding March* are innumerable..." (*Ragtime*, 70). The popularity the ex-coloured man claims is substantiated by historical evidence. He notes that his playing helped increase the number of "slumming visitors," or white patrons, to "the club," indicating the crossover appeal of ragging the classics (115). He concludes that ragtime affords him more success and recognition "than [his] playing of Beethoven or Chopin could ever have done" (115). Here his classical expertise does not make him a better or more "refined" musician than his ragtime accomplishments; his ragtime skills make him a popular musician. While the ex-coloured man's comments on ragtime music do advocate the need for "higher" forms in addition to popular music, they also serve as a subtle critique of the musical elitists who promoted European concert music over all other genres.

According to Berlin, "The main lines of the offensive against ragtime were: (1) ridicule; (2) appeals to racial bias; (3) prophesies of doom; (4) attempts at repression; and (5) suggestions of moral, intellectual, and physical dangers" (*Ragtime*, 40). Leonard observes that attacks on the music were often expressed in terms of the "fear of contagion" (106). Leonard cites classical pianist Edward B. Perry's warning in the conservative *Etude* magazine that ragtime must be treated "like a dog with rabies, with a dose of lead. Whether it is simply a passing phase of our decadent art culture or an infectious disease which has come to stay, like la grippe and leprosy, time alone can show" (106). In a critical climate such as this, Johnson's defense of ragtime appears much more revolutionary, especially his coupling of ragtime and classical music on equal planes of importance to the narrative structure.

Johnson's particular choices of classical allusions to Beethoven and Chopin are also striking. At the height of his youthful idealism, just before he embarks on his hapless journey to Atlanta University, the ex-coloured man plays Beethoven's *Sonata Pathetique*, one of the German composer's very early works. This sonata, according to Beethoven biographer Maynard Solomon, helped establish Beethoven as a composer rather than solely a performer and "achieved a wide sale, inaugurating competitive bidding by music publishers for his future works" (60). The piece is not an expression of pitiful wallowing in sorrow, but instead suggests a tone of resignation in the face of suffering.

Unlike Beethoven, whose overtly political music condemned the corruption of the revolutionary-turned-dictator, Napoleon, Chopin was the darling of French court. By juxtaposing these two composers, Johnson may be suggesting the ex-coloured man's vacillation between committed idealism and self-indulgent materialism. On the occasion of meeting his white, southern aristocrat father, the ex-coloured man pleases him with his performance of a Chopin waltz. He also wins the favor of his future wife by composing music for her "in a more or less Chopinesque style" (201). The climactic moment in their courtship occurs when he declares his love for her while playing the "Thirteenth Nocturne," a composition which, in the context of the narrative, evokes an association with another "thirteenth"–the Thirteenth Amendment to the Constitution, which abolished slavery in 1865.

The narrative clearly indicates that the narrator betrays the constitutional "thirteenth" by capitulating to the sentiments that he attributes to the musical "thirteenth." His decision to embrace the ideology of whiteness is epitomized by his commitment to strive for "a white man's success; and that, if it can be summed up in any word, means 'money'" (193). His perception of his love interest represents the blindness of this ideology. He perceives her, in her appearance and dress, as "the most dazzling white thing [he] had ever seen" (198). Interestingly, it is the musical quality of her voice that attracts him, a quality he hears as "tones of ... passionate colour," which in conversations are "low, yet thrilling, like the deeper middle tones of a flute" (198). The woman as an individual is not the problem; in fact, the representation of their shared melodramatic tendencies suggests a real affinity between her character and the ex-coloured man's. The problem arises from a social structure that is so starkly delineated according to categories of race that the ex-coloured man is forced to choose one component of his identity over all of the others. This choice, cemented by his selection of a white marriage partner, leaves him with desiccated "yellowing manuscripts" (211). It is not "white" identity, which is part of the ex-coloured man's experience from the beginning, but rather the ideology of whiteness, to which he sells his "birthright" (211), which is his claim to an amalgamated cultural identity.[16]

The novel implies that music could have been the means for accommodating and integrating the various aspects of the narrator's identity into a fluid, improvisational coherence. His abandoned manuscripts, however, indicate the renunciation of this musical/political project. Through his musical tropes, Johnson suggests that an overdetermined identity, such as we now associate with a *post*modern condition, is the experience of the narrator who cannot fit into the rigidly defined categories of race in America.[17] Aldon Nielson argues that the novel is a narrative enactment of "the instability, the impossibility of American racial definition" (174). He locates the novel's crowning irony in the *impossibility* of being "ex-coloured" in America and concludes that the novel is "among the most profound texts in America's racial history because it exists in a state of suspension between racial realms of cognition" (173).

One of the ways that the novel enacts this suspension is in its negotiation of the tensions between oral and written modes of expression. Brent Edwards has noted the importance of music to facilitate this negotiation in Johnson's writing. Edwards observes: "In Johnson's work on poetics, there is almost never a description of a direct transmission from the oral to the written: almost always, the figure of music intercedes. Music as a metaphor seems a necessary mediating element in the process of linguistic transcription" (588). Why music? Perhaps because, as Eric Sundquist points out, "The problems of transcribing black language and black music are not, in fact, separable in the evolution of African American culture" (*To Wake*, 310).

THE CHALLENGE OF TRANSCRIPTION

In the conclusion of his discussion of the ragtime debate, Berlin writes: "A question that was not raised in the magazine debates, but which must have occurred to at least some composers who experimented in this direction, is whether ragtime could be transferred to a 'higher form' without, in the process, losing its singular spirit" (56). Kathy Ogren observes that in both the arguments against ragtime and in the jazz controversy, "the participatory and improvisational characteristics of the music are often the salient features acknowledged by fans and foes alike"(16). How could one retain these features in the European "classical" forms, which dictated the ascendancy of the written text and required sharp divisions between composer, performer, and audience?

Johnson's article, "Now We Have the Blues," written on the occasion of W. C. Handy's publication of his anthology of notated music, *Blues*, indicates Johnson's critical awareness of the problems (and perhaps the impossibility) of documenting "undiluted" folk culture by means of *conventional* "high" cultural forms. Johnson has suffered at the hands of some critics who have focused on his "cultural elitism" and who have claimed his allegiance to "white," Eurocentric standards of value.[18] While certain class prejudices in Johnson's writing are undeniable, a consideration of his negotiation between oral and written modes of expression indicates that he valued both African American vernacular culture and the idea of the fusion of forms and the fluidity of identity in a multicultural society.

Within the context of his historical milieu, Johnson sought ways to document African American cultural contributions that were rapidly being absorbed into the national identity. Johnson knew that any documentation would change the vernacular style, but he also knew that vernacular materials had already changed conventional, official forms in ways that had not been adequately acknowledged. These alterations were glaringly apparent in "American" music marketed as "white"—music that would have remained overly attached to its European-derived elements without its African American influences. Johnson's writing suggests that white and black America must recognize their cultural fusion so that the nation could begin the long, painful, and arduous process of dismantling ideological construction of race upon which the nation had been built.

Johnson worked closely with his brother Rosamond throughout his life, first in the musical theater along with Bob Cole, and then later collaborating on their two collections of notated spirituals. Rosamond, like the narrator of his brother's novel, was trained in two schools of music. He attended the New England Conservatory in Boston, and he also understood the nuances of African American folk music and helped to infuse the musical theater team's popular songwriting with this style. The Johnson brothers wrote what is popularly known as the "Negro National Anthem," "Lift Every Voice and Sing," and the team wrote over two hundred popular songs, mainly for musical comedies, including their very well known, ragtime-inflected hit, "Under the Bamboo Tree."[19] Marie Cahill introduced this hit to Broadway audiences with her performance of the lead in *Sally in Our Alley* in 1902 (Peterson, 303). The Cole and Johnson brothers' team achieved recognition and financial success, often by bringing versions of African American musical styles such as ragtime to audiences of "white-oriented" musicals.[20]

Johnson knew well from his early experience as a successful professional musician that artistic "ownership" could be difficult to assert and defend.[21] Cultural capital could be easily misappropriated. In Johnson's history of New York, *Black Manhattan*, he records the artistic and social achievements of African Americans, ensuring the existence of documentation. In this history, he tells a story about Bob Cole's break with the white managers of the Troubadours, an African American theatrical group. Johnson writes:

> Not reaching a satisfactory agreement, [Cole] gathered up the music he had written and walked out with it. This action led to his arrest, and he was haled into court. Before the magistrate he declared: "These men have amassed a fortune from the product of my brain, and now they call me a thief; I won't give it up!" However, as is usual, the stronger side won. (101-102)

Johnson ultimately concludes that the course of events amounted to a triumph because Cole formed his own theatrical group and produced "the first Negro show to make a complete break from the minstrel pattern" (102). It is clear from this passage that the fact that Cole's music was *written* allowed him to declare ownership. Even if an unjust court system ruled against him, he was able to walk out with his music, leaving the exploitative managers with nothing substantial. Johnson's comments indicate some of the reasons for his emphasis on the written, despite its shortcomings, as a form of documentation, and they also shed light on some ragtime artists', such as Scott Joplin's, emphasis on publication.[22] Johnson's own writing can be understood as another means of "scoring" the music.

Ragtime achieved popularity before the recording industry had come into its full bloom, so publication of notated scores was the primary means for the documentation of ownership. Many Americans had pianos in their homes, and published ragtime music swept the nation near the turn of the century.[23] Late twentieth-century accounts of the music often refer to it as almost an entirely written form, involving little or no improvisation. Like many of the commentators who followed their lead, Blesh and Janis, in their early study, base their interpretations of ragtime upon the evidence provided by sheet music and piano rolls (4-6). Schafer and Riedel's definition of the music is typical of the predominant critical perceptions of ragtime:

> Ragtime is a black musical form developed and brought to maturation between 1890 and 1910. It is rooted in several musical traditions, all vital in the flow of folk and popular urban musical culture of the late nineteenth century. Basically it is a formation, an organization of folk melodies and musical techniques into a brief and fairly simple quadrille-like structure, written down and designed to be played *as written* on the piano. It is formational music, as distinct from improvisational music. In a sense, ragtime composers served as folk collectors or musicologists, collecting music in the air around them in the black communities and organizing it into brief suites or anthologies which they called piano rags. (5, italics in original)

This definition fits the ex-coloured man's ragtime style, but it does not account for the clearly improvisational elements of the "ragtime" he learns from the pianist at "the club" in New York.[24] In Johnson's portrait of the music, it is both "formational" and "improvisational;" it is a product of cultural amalgamation that is not dominated by its European influences. In this sense, Johnson's novel offers us important historical information about the music in performance that is sometimes overlooked in academic accounts of its style.

Marshall Stearns describes ragtime as a "largely notated music in the European tradition of written composition" (141). Although Stearns recognizes that improvisation must have been employed by skilled pianists who provided (in performance) "an endless variety of rhythmic suspensions, unusual accents, and between the beat effects" (143), he still bases the conclusions he draws about the music *as a whole* on his analysis of written scores. Jazz critic Guy Waterman takes a similar approach by defining ragtime music as written music produced according to "the method of concert composers" (Williams, 13). While he concedes, "It is probably true that ragtime pianists indulged in improvisation," he maintains that since "we have no written record of the manner in which it was done," we must "view ragtime *solely* as a composed music" (13, italics in original). Of course a "written record" of improvisation is a contradiction in terms; only a recording approaches documentation of the form. Other music critics, however, also base their interpretations of ragtime as virtually non-improvisational on the absence of "written records." According to respected jazz critic Martin Williams, "A very few ragtime scores survive which include written variations. In performance, spontaneous variations, or at least decorative embellishments and fills, were sometimes made, but variation is not essential to this music" (22). There seems to be little evidence for these assertions about the early history of the music, and contemporary accounts of ragtime openly refute the idea that it was *solely* a written form.

Johnson's and J. A. Rogers's contemporary accounts of late nineteenth and early twentieth-century ragtime challenge the more recent characterizations of the music as only a written form. Their accounts seem more closely aligned with Berlin's assertion that "virtually every professional ragtime pianist improvised, and was expected to do so…" (*Reflections*, 23). Jazz historian Burton Peretti also notes a combination of aesthetic impulses: "In the Southwest–including Missouri, Arkansas, Oklahoma, and Texas–ragtime resulted from a stimulating convergence of black syncopation and white musical notation" (42). Johnson's ex-coloured man attributes both southwestern and deep southern roots to the music, when he explains that it "originated in the questionable resorts about Memphis and St. Louis by Negro piano-players…" (99).

The ex-coloured man cites Chicago as the place where the popularity of the ragtime blossomed, an assertion that probably refers to the mass audience for the music at the Chicago World's Fair, known as the World's Columbia Exposition, in 1893.[25] He then notes the movement of the music to New York where the early ragtime musicians' "improvisations were taken down by white men, the words slightly altered, and published under the names of the arrangers" (99). The ex-coloured man goes on to observe, however, that since this time "a number of coloured men, of not only musical talent, but training, are writing out their own melodies and words and reaping the reward of their work. I have learned also that they have a large number of white imitators and adulterators" (100). In its account of the history of ragtime, which echoes Cole's story in *Black Manhattan*, *The Autobiography* suggests that improvisational techniques must be combined with substantial documentation in order to prevent outright theft. Once the record is established, imitation becomes a matter of artistic influence, but before this foundation set, the artist is vulnerable to exploitation.

In this sense, the narrator's assertion that the ragtime innovator from whom he learns his art is "just a natural musician"(101) who plays "by ear alone" (101) is not necessarily a derogatory comment. The ex-coloured man's account of ragtime's background can be understood, within its historical context, as a cautionary tale about the dangers of theft when music remains unrecorded and unnotated. While the narrator's praise of ragtime music is laced with the language of primitivism, his reference to the player's technique is a straightforward account of virtuosity:

> It was music that demanded a physical response, patting of the feet, drumming of the fingers, or nodding of the head in time with the beat. The barbaric harmonies, the audacious resolutions, often consisting of an abrupt jump from one key to another, the intricate rhythms in which the accents fell in the most unexpected places, but in which the beat was never lost, produced a most curious effect. And, too, the player–the dexterity of his left hand in making rapid octave runs and jumps was little short of marvellous; and with his right hand he frequently swept half the keyboard with clean-cut chromatics which he fitted in so nicely as never to fail to arouse in his listeners a sort of pleasant surprise at the accomplishment of the feat. (98-99)

Clearly this unpredictable music demanded expert improvisational skills. According to Berlin, whose studies of ragtime engage *The Autobiography* as a source for the historical documentation of the music, "The ragtime [in Johnson's novel] is described in great detail, suggesting a music that is far more sophisticated and technically demanding than the published ragtime that has come down to us" (*Ragtime*, 48). Berlin cites Johnson's portrayal of ragtime as evidence for the idea that ragtime, at least in its early history, was a complex and largely improvisational music.

Like Johnson, J. A. Rogers, whose essay on jazz is included in Alain Locke's 1925 anthology *The New Negro*, refers to ragtime as an improvisational art whose creation relied upon, in part, the manipulation rhythmic intricacies rather than upon compositional regularities of classical form. Rogers defines ragtime as the "direct predecessor of jazz" and describes the creators of this music, "the earliest jazz makers," as "itinerant piano players" who did not read music and who knew "nothing of written music or composition" (218).[26] A glaringly apparent contradiction exists between these accounts of ragtime innovators as skilled improvisers who did not read music and critical definitions of the ragtime as a solely written form of music. One source of the confusion is the scarcity of recorded performances, since the recording industry did not fully emerge "until after the effective demise of the ragtime idiom" (Sidran, 29). Also as ragtime-style music grew in popularity, the term "ragtime" quickly became applied to any kind of popular music in order to increase sheet music sales.[27] According to Berlin, "Public acceptance of ragtime, as shown by the enormous increase in commercial publications in 1899, was coupled with the gradual absorption of its name and style into the mainstream of American popular music" (*Ragtime*, 123). Hasse also notes that the term was "widely applied to songs that were not syncopated or were only slightly syncopated" (4).

The popular conception of ragtime music as defined by syncopation began fairly early in the music's history. In the 1908 edition of *Grove's Dictionary of Music and Musicians*, "Rag Time" was defined as "a modern term, of American origin, signifying, in the first instance, broken rhythm in melody, especially a sort of continuous syncopation" (qtd. in Berlin, *Ragtime*, 11). Most late twentieth-century studies also cite the defining feature of ragtime as "syncopation" or a rhythmic emphasis on the typically weak beats. Blesh and Janis note syncopation as the defining distinctive characteristic of the music and attribute it to the music's African American sources:

> The really unique thing about ragtime when it appeared was the way the pianist opposed syncopations (or accents on the weak and normally unaccented second and third beats of the measure) in his right hand against a precise and regularly accented bass ... Continued syncopation is deeply stimulating and exciting, and European masters seem always to have been wary of it ... The use of this driving, exciting propulsiveness in the most complexly developed ways is ... a commonplace in the music of Africa and the Americas ... it is used by the Afro-American to transform all of our [national] music. (7)

Isaac Goldberg, who published the first book length survey of American popular music in 1930, cautions against overly hasty and generalized application of the term "syncopation" as a definition of ragtime. According to Goldberg, "Into the definition must go something of the *rubato*, the nonchalance, the uncertainty of accent that characterize the ragtime player; something of the glorious indifference to precise pitch ... Syncopation alone–the regular dislocation of regular rhythmic accent–is as orthodox as the common triad" (143).

Johnson's reference to "intricate rhythms" (99) parallels Goldberg's account of a kind of polyrhythmic complexity and harmonic inflection that cannot be adequately notated according to a European scalar system. This is one of the great dilemmas the ex-coloured man must face in his desire to dismantle binary categories while preserving distinctively African American cultural traditions. How can he document in conventional forms "intricate rhythms" (99)? How can a static print medium capture "that elusive undertone, the note in music which is not heard with the ears" (181)? While syncopation fits the paradigm for documentation, traditionally African American musical approaches to rhythmic flexibility and harmonic variation do not.[28]

The tendency to play with the time signatures and rhythms of a written composition is a musical habit of the ex-coloured man that corresponds to Goldberg's description of the ragtime player. The ex-coloured man writes: "I have never really been a good accompanist because my ideas of interpretation were too strongly individual. I constantly forced my *accelerandos* and *rubatos* upon the soloist, often throwing the duet entirely out of gear" (29). These rhythmic effects are subtle and seemingly irregular. Straight syncopation, however, is easily notated, as Stearns explains, "the left hand plays a heavy 2/4 rhythm, much like the march from which it is probably borrowed. The right hand plays eight beats in the same interval, but accents every third beat, an effect that may well have been taken from the minstrel banjo" (142). In this description we have the conjoining of European- and African-derived influences that comprise ragtime in "its simplest form" (142). As Stearns also points out, complex rhythmic variations that were not notated could be improvised within this regular form, but much of the published sheet music followed this rather formulaic approach (143). Here, too, the history of ragtime mirrors the ex-coloured man's experience with the difficulties of documenting oral cultural practices within a written form.

By the end of Johnson's career, he had written popular music, scores of essays and articles, and *The Autobiography*. He had collected an anthology of African American poetry and two books of spirituals (with his brother Rosamond). He had made his own transformation of sermons into verse in *God's Trombones* and had recorded history in *Black Manhattan* and in his own autobiography, *Along This Way*. All of this was done in addition to his other work as a consul, a political activist and leader of the NAACP, and an educator. By the end of his career, one imagines that he must have felt confident that he had achieved his personal goals for the documentation of African American culture and its far-reaching influences. At the time he wrote *The Autobiography*, however, early in his writing career, perhaps he felt more uncertain about his documentation objectives. This uncertainty is reflected, in part, in the characterization of the ex-coloured man in association with ragtime music.

African American musical traditions have had a long and complicated history in this country, and some of the obstacles encountered and the victories achieved by the music that Johnson documented are still with us today. As the twentieth century emerged, many Americans and Europeans were finding alternatives to traditional, European-influenced "high" culture and alternative ways to be and to sound "modern" by looking to African and African American culture as a source of style.[29] Often music provided a crucial entry into "other" cultures for fascinated "outsiders." As Tricia Rose points out in her seminal study of rap music, "many black musics before rap (e.g., the blues, jazz, early rock 'n' roll) have also become American popular musics precisely because of extensive white participation; white America has always had an intense interest in black culture" (4-5). Rose goes on to observe that this participation does not necessarily indicate the music's movement away from its focus on "black pleasure and black fans" (5). The process does, however, always include, in addition to appreciation, "white appropriation and attempts at ideological recuperation of black cultural resistance" (5). Johnson, who some late twentieth-century readers condemn as bourgeois, was well aware of the musical and political realities of American life as articulated by Rose. At his particular historical moment, his knowledge of the dangers of appropriation led him to the promotion of the written, despite its seemingly inevitable limitations.

Johnson's essay "Now We Have the Blues," which appeared in the *New York Amsterdam News* in 1926, offers us insights into why he so often uses musical metaphors to mediate between oral and written traditions—why music makes language a vital and powerful agent of social change for him. Johnson's musical metaphors indicate his awareness that American literary dialect conventions (for language) and the European notational system (for music) both presented obstacles to historically accurate and artistically innovative documentation strategies for African American vernacular cultural practices. To erode the limitations placed on him as a writer, he used linguistic constructions of music to break the constraints of dialect conventions.[30]

In this article, he stresses the importance of "the record" being "written" for African Americans as the premier creators of American folk art (389). He expresses his approval of the documentation of the spirituals, certainly with Du Bois in mind, and the preservation of folk tales. He approves of Joel Chandler Harris's collection of the "Uncle Remus Stories" primarily because Harris, by fixing them in print, "made them a permanent part of American literature," and because Harris clearly identified their "exclusive Negro origin," rather than claiming that he had invented them himself. The implication is that, even if the record is distorted, it is written, and it is something upon which to build and perhaps to improve.

Johnson laments the fact that African American dance forms and secular music had not, at that point, experienced similar fates. Aside from Vernon Castle's public admissions of his debts to African American dance forms, Johnson notes the "Negro influence" on American dance had been obscured as these dances increased in popularity. The secular musical traditions also suffered from unattributed imitation and out and out theft:

> The early blackface minstrels simply took such Negro songs as they wished and used them. The first of the so-called Ragtime songs to be published were set down by white men who affixed their own names as the composers. In fact, before the Negro succeeded in fully establishing his title as creator of his

> secular music the form was taken away from him and made national instead of racial. It has been developed into the distinct musical idiom by which America expresses itself popularly and by which it is best known. For a while it was absolutely divorced from the Negro; and there was much publicity discussion as to which of the white jazz band leaders was entitled to the credit of originating the instrumental form. But the tide has set in the other way. The record with regard to Negro secular music is now being written, and may some day be as firmly established as it is in the case of the Spirituals and the plantation stories. (389)

Johnson views Handy's efforts to notate the blues as a positive step toward combatting the kind of theft he describes in the preceding paragraph, although he certainly does not see Handy's project as unproblematic.

Johnson observes, with his own practical knowledge as a composer of music, that Handy's work records the music "as closely, perhaps, as our present system of notation permits" (390). This kind of understatement and emphasis on the positive while making useful correctives is characteristic of Johnson's prose style, designed to educate through example, encouragement, and constructive criticism.[31] In this case, he wants the project of written documentation, particularly in the area of African American musical traditions, to continue. He knows that both his own writing and Handy's anthology are useful contributions to this effort. He also believes that Handy's efforts "perhaps" fall somewhat short because they rely for documentation on a European twelve tone chromatic scale ("our present system of notation") to record music heavily influenced by African music's "blue" notes (or inflected harmonics) and other tonal and rhythmic elements that find no corollary in the European scalar system.[32] Thus Johnson regrets that there are not more examples of "the true, undiluted folk blues" in Handy's collection and that Handy did not even include his own "Memphis Blues" (390). Johnson's final comment praises the book's intent to document, "despite any shortcomings" (391).

This article was published just a year before Johnson's *God's Trombones* at a time when he was probably putting the finishing touches on the latter work. Johnson must have been particularly aware at that moment that new forms were necessary to render Aframerican expressive culture in print, since *God's Trombones* is perhaps the most formally innovative writing in his repertoire.[33] In 1927, the same year *God's Trombone's* was published, *The Autobiography* was reissued, this time under Johnson's own name.

DOCUMENTATION AND INNOVATION

Johnson stands as an important figure not just in the history of literature but also in the history of jazz. Johnson's metaphorical use of music to help launch the dismantling of ideological constructions of race contributed to the formal innovations derived from blues and jazz that followed in the work of Harlem

Renaissance writers such as Sterling Brown, Langston Hughes, Zora Neale Hurston, Claude McKay, and Jean Toomer.[34] These innovations firmly established African American literary history as inseparable from African American musical traditions, and sometimes, later, the influences of the literature identifiably crossed back over into the music. While the younger generation of Harlem Renaissance writers and those who followed their literary influence did not call for "higher forms" to express a jazz sensibility, perhaps, in part, they did not feel compelled to do so because Johnson had already documented the early stages of jazz history as predominantly shaped by African American innovations. Through *The Autobiography* and his other writing, Johnson had been instrumental in the establishment of jazz as a crucial aspect of American culture that emerged from a distinctively African American context. In his fiction, his essays and articles, and his collections of spirituals, he preformed several kinds of "transcription" of the music, and this documentary work has had far-reaching effects.

By the time the Renaissance movement was in full swing, Johnson had already asserted the originality and the international appeal of African American art forms drawn from oral traditions. In part through musical metaphors, Johnson had helped eradicate dialect conventions and helped free African American literary voices from the constraints of these conventions, while many white modernists still remained trapped within their limitations.[35] Johnson opened the way for the writers who followed him to establish their voices in new ways, to dismantle traditional narrative structures, and to deterritorialize language, often through the influence of jazz and blues aesthetics.[36]

Johnson's visionary, international perspective contributed to his capacity to create spaces for formal innovations. The formal innovations that followed Johnson's groundbreaking work can be seen as part of what Lawrence Levine describes as the fundamental *process* of culture, as opposed to the static notion of "Culture" as synonymous with "refinement." Levine writes: "Culture is not a fixed condition but a process: the product of interaction between the past and present. Its toughness and resiliency are determined not by a culture's ability to withstand change, which indeed may be a sign of stagnation not life, but by its ability to react creatively and responsively to the realities of a new situation" (*Black Culture*, 5). Johnson understood the dynamics of this process because he was invested in both the historical specificity of African American culture and the relationship of those particularities to a global context.

Coupling these two kinds of knowledge contributes to the broadest perspective—one that Gayl Jones describes in her study of the influence of oral traditions on African American literature. Jones demonstrates how oral modes of expression have allowed writers to free their voices, and she places this characteristic of African American literature within the frame of world literatures seeking similar objectives. Jones criticizes a failure to acknowledge that:

> the problems of the freed voice apply not only to African American literature and criticism, but to all the world's literatures and criticisms: European versus American, Anglo-American versus Chicano, French Standard versus French Creole, Canadian English versus Canadian French, Russian versus Estonian, and so on. One sees it in the dynamics of every national literature vis-à-vis another. The voices of the less powerful group, "the other," always must free themselves from the frame of the more powerful group, in texts of self-discovery, authority, and wholeness. (192)

Johnson, because he approached boundaries and the constraints of convention from a global perspective, was able to document cultural and historical specificity by situating particularities in relation to broader trends. Johnson's *New York Age* editorials offer the best overview of his global perspective. In this writing, as well as in *The Autobiography*, we witness Johnson pushing democracy away from hypocrisy and toward the ideal language of the Constitution. These editorials reveal his knowledge of an impressively vast array of subjects, and they demonstrate his personal investment in political action coupled with artistic achievement.

The 1917 piece, "Under the Dome of the Capitol," illustrates his undaunted optimism and his attempt to inspire his audience to positive action. He proclaims, "the basic spirit of America is democracy, and though that spirit is often thwarted it is constantly struggling forward and will finally prevail" (215). In the same year, writing on the occasion of the Russian Revolution, Johnson makes connections between the experiences of African Americans and Russian American Jews in "Russian Democracy and the Jews." Here Johnson cautions against hasty optimism: "For a great part of the world the word 'democracy' is a fetish. But the American Negro has been disillusioned. He knows from experience that a despised people can be deprived of their rights, oppressed and down trodden in a democracy just as effectually as under the worst form of autocracy" (235). His knowledge of international politics strengthens his critique of injustices at home and abroad.

In other editorials Johnson, who campaigned vigorously for the Dyer Anti-Lynching Bill that was defeated in the Senate in 1922, exposed the hypocrisy of a U. S. policy that demanded democracy in Germany while legally condoning lynching and oppression within its own borders. In 1919 he criticized the British Parliament's approval of the Irish Home Rule bill that did not allow for a truly independent Irish government and expressed admiration for Irish patriots who, in spite of obstacles, "kept up the fight" (240) by continuing to resist British imperialism. In the same year in "The Japanese Question in California," Johnson objects to California Senator Phelan's hysterical proclamation that the Japanese population must be contained before they overrun the white race in the state. The editorials illustrate Johnson's knowledge of and political engagement in the fight against national and international totalitarianism and oppression. On the basis of this writing alone, Johnson must be understood as a politically engaged pragmatist, rather than an idealist who simply believed that "art" alone would produce social justice by uniting the talented elite of all races.

His editorials and his novel strive to dismantle the hierarchical system of value inherent in the construction of social and cultural boundaries. While Johnson did call for the stylization of African American vernacular modes of expression, he did so primarily for the purposes of documentation and international recognition of the value of African American culture. Some formal innovations that followed his work were, in part, a response to his call. His fusion of classical and vernacular musical forms set a precedent for other works that followed and challenged the binarism of early twentieth-century distinctions between "high" and "low" culture. In this sense, Johnson can be viewed as taking for the literary tradition the early, tentative steps that jazz musicians took in strides.

Historian Lawrence Levine describes the revolutionary artistic approach of jazz musicians in terms that correspond to Johnson's portrayal of what the ex-coloured man *could have* accomplished had he not renounced his youthful ambitions:

> In their refusal to be governed by the categorical orthodoxies that prevailed, in their unwillingness to make absolute distinctions between the vernacular and classical traditions, in their insistence that they were just attempting to play *music* and just wanted to be accepted as musicians, in their determination to utilize the *entire* Western tradition, as well as other cultural traditions, jazz musicians were revolutionizing not only music but also the concept of culture. ("Jazz," 187)

Despite his reliance on the modernist discourse regarding "higher" and "lower" cultural forms in *The Autobiography*, Johnson depicts an artist whose conflation of various musical traditions challenges the prevailing, early twentieth-century conceptions of "culture" and of "race."

Almost a half a century after Johnson first published *The Autobiography*, another artist who shared some of Johnson's ideas about the transformational powers of art was gaining widespread recognition. Like Johnson, jazz saxophonist and composer John Coltrane had a global perspective that allowed him to be simultaneously deeply aware of and engaged in historical and political realities and to situate those realities within a larger context. According to Coltrane biographer Eric Nisenson, "Coltrane's study of African and other non-Western music was a mainstay in bolstering his belief that the purpose of music transcends that of mere entertainment, and can actually socially transform its listeners" (112).

In 1961, Coltrane recorded four different live versions of his composition "Spiritual" performed with his band at the Village Vanguard.[37] In his biographical and critical study of Coltrane, jazz scholar Lewis Porter mentions that Coltrane's source of inspiration for his "Spiritual" came from a transcription of an old spiritual documented in Johnson's collection. According to Porter: "On page 140 of *The Book of American Negro Spirituals*, originally published in 1925, one finds the song that Coltrane called 'Spiritual,' in the same key of C minor and with the same first and second strain. It is a melody for 'Nobody Knows de Trouble I See...'" (206). This example indicates the importance of Johnson's documentation project.

Coltrane said of the first recording of "Spiritual": "I like the way it worked out. I feel we brought out the mood inherent in the tune. It's a piece we'd been working with for some time because I wanted to make sure before we recorded it that we would be able to get the original emotional essence of the spiritual."[38] Is this what the artistic aspirations of the ex-coloured man might have sounded like? Coltrane did not describe his artistic process as transforming "raw" materials into a "higher" form of expression, but then he was not working within the milieu of the early twentieth century.

Listening to the post-bop reconfigurations of a melody taken from African American sacred musical history illuminates the objectives of Johnson's documentation project. Each distinctive performance of "Spiritual" within a group context articulates Coltrane's definition of his own spirituality as an amalgamation of religious influences and documents his relation to the history of African American musical (and religious) traditions. True to the larger jazz and blues tradition, Coltrane creates a bridge between the individual and the communal, the present and the past in his "Spiritual." According to improvisational style, not only does he create it, he continually recreates it. In addition to the four versions of "Spiritual" on these Vanguard recordings, as his comments about "working with" the piece suggest, he also certainly played "Spiritual" a number of times in unrecorded performances. Drawing on the oral tradition of improvisation that is absolutely central to jazz, Coltrane, responding to the collective improvisations of the other musicians in his band, created the composition anew each time he played it. As Coltrane and his band improvised, they preserved the past–the history of the music and the communal history that it expresses–and they simultaneously reconstructed the past in relation to their own, particular present moment (again and again). Here, in a representative example of jazz performance, is an enactment of the strategies for documentation and artistic accomplishment that Johnson sought and helped to develop. The dynamic jazz balance between documentation and performance suggests the connection between Coltrane and Johnson and the traditions in which they were both invested in terms of individualized expression and communal affiliation.

Both of these artists engaged dynamic forms of expression to dismantle artificial boundaries, while recording the distinctive history of African American cultural practices. Perhaps this is the sort of endeavor to which Ralph Ellison referred when he described the jazz artist's improvisational mode of expression as "a definition of his identity: as individual, as member of the collectivity and as a link in the chain of tradition" (234). We do not have to view the formal innovations that followed Johnson's writing and his own technical experimentation *God's Trombones* as diametrically opposed to his documentation work; we can instead consider them, in their differences and their similarities, as complimentary artistic endeavors. By deconstructing binary oppositions in part through his exploration of musical idioms, Johnson helped pave the way for other artists to transform traditional forms into "sympathetic, singing instrument[s]."

CHAPTER TWO

"A big sensation"
F. Scott Fitzgerald and Jazz Anxiety

THE 1920s JAZZ DEBATE

"'If you read the papers,'" Jay Gatsby's orchestra leader proclaims before his performance of *Jazz History of the World*, "'you know there was a big sensation'" (50). The "sensation" that the papers report is part of the cultural debate over jazz in the 1920s, a debate taken up by F. Scott Fitzgerald's *The Great Gatsby*. Throughout his writing, Fitzgerald's musical references engage in this argument over the implications of the new music. Popular, jazz-influenced music plays a special role in Fitzgerald's fiction as the consummate sign of modernity, as his famous historical designation, "the Jazz Age," indicates. Fitzgerald's representation of popular music can be described as a portrayal of jazz anxiety arising from the cultural amalgamation that the music and, symbolically, modernism itself represents. Fitzgerald's fiction depicts this music as "a big sensation" that enthralls its audiences and signals sweeping social changes. His musical allusions also anxiously suggest that beneath the surface of the music's frivolous gaiety lurks the presence of violence and chaos, which threatens to erupt at any moment.

A similar anxiety underpinned anti-jazz sentiments in the press and in popular magazines in the 1920s. As Kathy Ogren points out in her seminal study of the 1920s jazz controversy, "For many Americans, to argue about jazz was to argue about the nature of change itself" (7). Ogren demonstrates that jazz was associated with World War I because the music was (in part) disseminated by jazz players in military bands. Jazz was also linked with speed, industry and urban life and was related to jagged nerves and neuroses (Ogren,

143-44). "Jazz," in all of its various forms, marked the passage to the new, uncertain values that were replacing what many people revered as the old, stable ones.[1]

In keeping with 1920s accounts of jazz in the popular press, Fitzgerald's jazz references reflect his conflation of the music with a whole worldview—a rebellious, free-spirited attitude toward life in which young people, especially privileged ones, indulged. These attributes not only set this generation apart from the more conservative one that preceded it; they also helped to set American culture apart from European standards of value and taste. In the journalistic attacks on jazz, the music is described as diametrically opposed to classical European standards and is often equated with drunkenness, debauchery, unbridled sexuality, primitivism, and insanity.[2] These negative associations resonate in Fitzgerald's musical references, but his writing, in a more complex sense, aligns the music with an irrepressible desire to express the unspeakable. Fitzgerald's representations of popular music suggest that the music symbolically alludes to struggles for power and domination that always lie beneath the polished public veneer of individuals and societies.

MODERNITY AND THE *JAZZ HISTORY OF THE WORLD*

In the published version of *The Great Gatsby*, little remains of a long section from the manuscript describing the fictional musical composition that Fitzgerald titled *Jazz History of the World*. Critics have speculated on sources for the composition and have analyzed the published and deleted versions of the scene to conclude that the composition illustrates Fitzgerald's allusion to "white" jazz.[3] I will argue, however, that this and Fitzgerald's other "jazz" references suggest that "jazz," as *popular* music, always blurs the boundaries between "white" and "black" and between "high" and "low" culture.

In the revision process from the manuscript to the revised and rewritten galleys, the majority of the passage in which Nick offers his impressions of the *Jazz History of the World* is gradually stripped away. In the deleted versions of Nick's musical experience, the composition and its improvisational playing upon multiple themes articulate a version of the meaning of *history* that Nick is unwilling and unable to fully accept. The rest of the novel explores this version of history as a series of "tribal" conflicts, but the deleted passage does so by extending the anti-jazz sentiments in the newspapers to link the new music with the notion of history as a pointless and chaotic struggle for domination. In his long description of the music, Nick reveals the real "danger" jazz represents. The music—in its improvisational freedom that embodies the very essence of change—tells a version of history in which the oppressed will inevitably overthrow their oppressors.

The deleted account of *Jazz History of the World* is highly significant because it is never really erased from the novel or from any of Fitzgerald's allusions to the popular music of the 1920s. The implications of this music surface like the series of "interruptive notes" that Nick hears in Tostoff's composition, notes that "colored everything that came after them, until before you knew it they became the theme…" (*Galleys*, 36). Nick's description of these "interruptive notes which colored everything that came after them…" (*Galleys*, 36) is strikingly similar to Tom Buchanan's reference to "The Rise of the Colored Empires by this man Goddard" (*Gatsby*, 13), which is probably an allusion to Lothrop Stoddard's *The Rising Tide of Color* (1920). Like the music that "*colored* everything," Stoddard argued that "colored races" everywhere posed a serious threat to the continued existence of the white race. Tom summarizes "Goddard's" argument: "'It's up to us, who are the dominant race, to watch out or these other races will have control of things'" (13). Tom's synopsis closely parallels the gist of Stoddard's *The Rising Tide of Color* as well as Nick's impression of the implications of *Jazz History of the World*. According to Nick's interpretation of this musical composition, the music, like Stoddard's and "Goddard's" books, suggests that the "dominant race" and Western classical order are being seriously challenged.

The musical threat to order in *The Great Gatsby* arises from "a series of interruptive [sic] notes that seemed to fall together accidentally and colored everything that came after them until before you knew it they became the theme and new discords were opposed to it outside" (*Manuscript*, 55).[4] As the deleted passage makes clear, in the improvisation that Nick hears as unpredictable and "accidental," the music has undeniable social implications. Nick's disconcerted response to the music does not result merely from incomprehension and aversion to the aesthetics of the music. The aesthetic foundations of the music derive from the social realities of "history," which the music expresses as a struggle for domination that ultimately amounts to a "purposeless and sardonic"(55) cycle, and Nick responds to this idea in the music.

Jazz History of the World is, above all else, a history of the world filtered through an early twentieth-century American lens. The composition began in the novel's manuscript as Les Epstien's *Jazz History of the World* and then in the galleys went from being Vladmir Epstein's composition to being the work of Vladmir Tostoff. What possibly began as an allusion to Jewish Tin Pan Alley songwriters first took on a Russian influence and then became a joke ("tossed off"), thus becoming increasingly removed from the realities of American cultural amalgamation. Events such as the Red Scare, the Sacco and Vanzetti trial, the Johnson-Reed Immigration Act of 1924 (that placed severe restrictions on Asian and southeastern European immigration), and the wide circulation of books like Madison Grant's *The Passing of the Great Race* (1916) and Stoddard's

The Rising Tide of Color (1920) are just a few examples that indicate the degree of social unrest present in early twentieth-century America. Each of these events suggests the ways that the constructed categories of "ethnicity" and "race" complicated the definition of "American." The deleted version of *Jazz History* enters the 1920s discourse on "race" through its corollary debate over the meaning of "jazz." Traces of Fitzgerald's previous drafts' exploration of popular music's role in the social hierarchy remain in the published version of the *Jazz History* scene. An analysis of the deleted passages, therefore, provides insights into the implications of Fitzgerald's representations of popular music in *The Great Gatsby*.

In the manuscript Nick observes the orchestra members' condescending attitude toward the music, as if it were "a little below them after all" (54). Nick also notices the confusion and the rapt attention of the guests who remain still "for about fifteen minutes … except to laugh now and then in a curious puzzled way when they came to the end of a movement" (54). Gatsby himself has requested this piece that the musicians think may be "a little below them after all," which indicates the tenuousness (and even fraudulence) of Gatsby's position in the social hierarchy. It is apparent from this passage that the music is not the standard fare for a 1920s jazz orchestra because no one "stirred" (54); they are not dancing. The public performance of *Jazz History* at Carnegie Hall had caused a "big sensation," according to the orchestra leader and the newspapers. Apparently *Jazz History* represents a commercial success, even if this success is based primarily upon its shock value.

In the manuscript, Nick describes the music in vivid detail:

> It started out with a weird, spinning sound that seemed to come mostly from the cornets, very regular and measured and inevitable with a bell now and then that seemed to ring some distance away. A rythm [sic] became distinguishable after a while in the spinning, a sort of dull beat but as soon as you'd almost made it out it disappeared–until finally something happened, something tremendous, you knew that, and the spinning was all awry and one of the distant bells had come alive and it had a meaning and [sic] a personality somehow of its own. (*Manuscript*, 54)

Nick clearly seeks some consistency in the music–something to grasp that will offer up meaning. "Meaning" is the only word crossed out of this paragraph. Perhaps it is eliminated to emphasize that Nick is hearing a lot of sounds that strike his ear as discord, but the one thing he cannot discern in the music is "meaning."

The piece begins with "spinning" that is "very regular and measured," but as it becomes increasingly improvisational and "awry," Nick desperately searches for continuity and linearity (or meaning) dependent upon the Western musical traditions of tension and resolution:

> That was the first movement and we all laughed and looked at each other rather nervously as the second movement began. [new paragraph mark] The second movement was concerned with the bell only it wasn't the bell anymore but ~~two instrum wi~~ [sic] a muted violin cello and two instruments I had never seen before. At first there was a sort of monotony about it–a little disappointing at first as if it were just a repetition of the spinning sound but pretty soon you were aware that something was trying to establish itself, to get a foothold, something soft and persistent and profound and next you yourself were trying to help it, struggling, praying for it–until suddenly it was there, it was established rather scornfully without you and it ~~stayed there~~ [sic] seemed to lurk around with complete self-sufficiency as if it had been there all the time. (54-55)

In this paragraph Nick recognizes the "personality" of the music that he refers to at the end of the preceding paragraph. The music takes on human qualities of persistence and self-sufficiency, and it is ultimately scornful–almost as if it were an anxious description of Gatsby's rise to power and financial success. Nick and the rest of the audience are made strangely nervous by the music, and their anxiety appears to arise from a lack of understanding and familiarity. The listeners do not know how to respond at first except by laughing, but after they are lulled by a deceptive monotony, the music asserts itself. As it gains independence, it takes on a sinister quality and seems to "lurk" with its "self-sufficiency." Nick's description implies that, through the unpredictability of improvisation, the music has deceived its audience by seeming chaotic and incoherent, when in fact it represents a self-defined entity.[5]

In the fourth deleted paragraph, Nick shifts from personifying the music to describing it as a historical force:

> I was curiously moved and the third part of the thing was full of an even stronger emotion. I know so little about music that I can only make a story of it–which proves I've been told that it must have been pretty low brow stuff–but it wasn't really a story. He didn't have lovely music for the prehistoric ages with tiger-howls from the trap fishing up with a strain from Onward Christian Soldiers in the year two B. C. It wasn't like that at all. (55)

Here Nick uses the popular early twentieth-century term "low brow" to rank the music in a cultural hierarchy structured, in part, according to the principles of the pseudo-science of phrenology. Nick wants the music to be like a "story," and classifying it as such would confirm its "low brow" status. Despite his desire to classify what he hears, the music is not "really a story" to Nick because he cannot put it in linear narrative order; it just keeps spinning. The non-narrative music also seems non-chronological to Nick because it does not move from references to prehistoric hunting sounds to the anthem of Christian soldiers; it does not fit his established understanding of "history."

As Nick perceives it, the improvisational *Jazz History* is entirely unpredictable:

> There would be a series of ^interruptive^ [sic] notes that seemed too fall together accidently [sic] and colored everything that came after them until before you knew it they became the theme and new discords were opposed to it outside. But what struck me particularly was that just as you'd get used to the new discord business there'd be one of the old themes rung in this time as a discord until you'd get the ghastly sense that it was all a cycle after all, purposeless and sardonic until you wanted to get up and walk out of the garden. It never stopped—after they had finished playing that movement it went on and on in everybody's head until the next one started. Whenever I think of that summer I can hear it yet. (55)

In its nonlinearity, the music seems random and disjointed, but its most shocking effect is the "ghastly" realization it evokes that "it was all a cycle after all, purposeless and sardonic." Experiencing this realization through the music is most disconcerting because it is inescapable: "It never stopped … I can hear it yet." History in this passage is as "tossed off" as "jazz" is. It is cyclical, and yet it is meaninglessly incoherent. It mocks an observer/listener like Nick who would attempt to make sense of it.

Jazz History alludes to history without attempting to offer any meaning. In fact, it substitutes "personality" for meaning, calling to mind the priorities of an emerging celebrity culture. The distinctively American music becomes, in this episode, the global sign of modernity—an expression that articulates world history as "purposeless and sardonic." Fitzgerald's increasingly radical revisions of the *Jazz History* episode indicate his attempts to grapple with the post-war American discourse on race and nationalism through musical allusions. These deletions reveal that at the site of music Fitzgerald struggled to represent issues that complicated the definition of American modernity. Popular music seemed to fluidly negotiate boundaries in ways that indicated modern changes by threatening the old social order that was based upon the idea of a cultural hierarchy.

Most of the songs to which Fitzgerald alludes in his fiction arise from the commercial venues of hit Broadway shows and Tin Pan Alley song factories. Jazz historian Burton Peretti offers a context for Fitzgerald's popular music that considers this music in relation to the jazz tradition. According to Peretti:

> … Fitzgerald, and most other white commentators of the twenties used the word "jazz" to designate the highly visible and popular dance music—a derivative of ragtime and popularized by Paul Whiteman, Ted Lewis, and Tin Pan Alley—that displaced the more sedate popular music after 1919. This music syncopated mildly, rarely used the blues or swung, and it almost never stressed improvisation, and so it is rarely considered part of the great jazz tradition.

It is important to note, as Peretti does, that most of the music to which Fitzgerald refers is more properly described as *jazz-influenced*, rather than as *jazz per se*. Still, we should not too hastily dismiss the complex implications of "influence."

In 1920s America, technological developments facilitated the phenomenon of mass culture. Radio, the phonograph, and the recording industry disseminated popular music to a mass audience. African American musical traditions from work songs and spirituals to blues and ragtime had been shaping "mainstream" American music long before the 1920s, but in the twenties technology dispersed to a mass audience emerging musical developments in the form of jazz and urban blues. Fitzgerald's pervasive use of popular music references suggests that he was aware of the impact of this music on American culture. In his 1931 essay "Echoes of the Jazz Age," Fitzgerald associates "jazz" (in every sense of the term) with "a state of nervous stimulation, not unlike that of big cities behind the lines of war" (16). Fitzgerald's musical allusions suggest that all types of "jazz" signal the violent repercussions of rapid social changes and shifts in power structures in American society.

Most often Fitzgerald refers to a type of jazz-influenced popular music that seems to encapsulate the escapist desires of a certain class of Americans. Musicologist Christopher Small aptly describes the style of music to which Fitzgerald's fiction most often alludes. Small points out that these American popular songs of the twenties

> suggested a world that was essentially adult, glamorous, sophisticated and moneyed, with sentiments that were free-floating, ready to attach themselves to any listener and cover him or her with stardust, lifting the hearer, for the duration of the song, into a world of glamour and opulence, as represented not only be the lyrics but also by the rich harmonies and lush orchestrations....(279)

This is the kind of music played by Paul Whiteman's orchestra, which was famous for its "lush orchestrations." This ornate, composed music was referred to widely as "jazz," as the title of Whiteman's autobiography, *Jazz*, indicates.

In jazz historian Peretti's account of Fitzgerald's conception of popular "jazz" as opposed to "the great jazz tradition," Peretti mentions bandleader Paul Whiteman as a purveyor of "highly visible and popular dance music," music that should be distinguished from the "real" jazz tradition. Whiteman, who undoubtedly has the most ironic name in the history of jazz, was famous for what he called "symphonic jazz." He sought to "refine" the music for "polite" consumption. His concert titled "An Experiment in Modern Music" was held at Aeloian Hall in 1924, and George Gershwin's "Rhapsody in Blue," the closing number, was a huge success. Whiteman described his own objective to "exhibit legitimate scoring as contrasted with the former hit and miss effects which were also called 'jazz'" (*Jazz*, 99). In other words, the concert aimed to redefine "jazz" as a scored, rather than an improvised music. Whiteman's *Jazz* indicates that he believed he had performed a valuable social service by bringing "jazz" out of "the district" (the turn of the century

Storyville brothels of New Orleans) and into the elite (and financially promising) world of a New York concert hall.

Whiteman, who was schooled in the classical tradition and played with the Denver Symphony before forming his own jazz orchestra, emphasized the value of written composition or scored music rather than improvisation. This emphasis alone clearly sets his music apart from one of the central characteristics of what has now been established as the jazz tradition. Whiteman's "Three O'Clock in the Morning," which appeared as the waltz finale of the *Greenwich Village Follies* of 1922, sold over a million copies of sheet music and 3.5 million disks in that same year.[6] This tune is described in *The Great Gatsby* (set in 1922) as a "neat, sad little waltz of that year" (110). This allusion indicates not only that Fitzgerald used popular music to define a historical moment but also that Fitzgerald did associate "jazz" with the likes of Whiteman and other jazz-influenced musicians who were entering the profitable field of the new popular music. This was one type of music that Fitzgerald referred to as "jazz," but there were others, too.

In her study of Fitzgerald's use of popular music, Ruth Prigozy (with valuable thoroughness) cites most of the musical references in Fitzgerald's fiction. She argues that his musical references suggest that Fitzgerald was "simultaneously enchanted and repelled by the excesses of the jazz age—and by jazz itself" (61). In order to make sense of the simultaneous enchantment and repulsion that mirrors aspects of the 1920s jazz debate we must consider the history of this popular, jazz-influenced music and its relation to the concept of an American cultural hierarchy. A major source of the contradictory attraction and repulsion to which Prigozy alludes adds up to an unresolved tension or jazz anxiety that is closely linked to anxieties regarding the tenuousness and arbitrariness of the cultural hierarchy in American society.

POPULAR MUSIC AND CULTURAL HIERARCHY

The kind of boundaries that had been clearly established in Renaissance Europe tended to erode in a technologically accelerating democratic culture. Still lingering in the American Victorian sensibility, however, were traces of early modern aesthetic values that were founded upon hierarchical notions of difference. According to musicologist Charles Hamm:

> Early in the modern era, a distinction developed in the Western world between the music of the elite classes, comprising both classical ("high" art) music and the less technically demanding genres of the bourgeois parlor, and that of the people, encompassing both folk and popular music (as these two terms came to be used in the twentieth century). Classical music, preserved in musical notation and performed by professionals for passive audiences, was understood to be universal and eternal, with a single repertory serving for the entire (Western) world. The music of the people, created and passed on

chiefly in oral tradition, often in a participatory environment, was taken to be regional and ephemeral. (3)

The viability of this ideology was seriously shaken in the modernist era, particularly in the United States. Jazz, with its African cultural influences, relied on what musicologist John Miller Chernoff describes as "perhaps the most fundamental aesthetic in Africa: without participation there is no meaning" (23). As this music and the dances that accompanied it gained popularity, the musical hierarchy of culture began to erode.[7] The influences of jazz mingled with all forms of American popular music and changed the characteristics of popular styles.

As 1920s technological developments including film, radio, phonographs, and the recording industry began to disseminate popular music widely, the absolute distinctions between "high" and "low" began to blur. Music emerged in a way that appeared threatening to many of the guardians of "high" culture. Hamm notes, "The elite had not been concerned with the 'inferior' cultural products of the lower classes as long as they were contained within their own cultural spaces; but with the development of the new mass media–radio, phonograph, film–they moved out of this space and became available to the entire population"(8). In Fitzgerald's fiction and in certain enclaves of American society, tensions regarding the blurring of high/low boundaries signaled the demise of a social hierarchy that could be defined according to categories of cultural value.

Historian Lawrence Levine has extensively studied and documented the emergence of distinctions between "highbrow" and "lowbrow" culture in America at the turn of the century.[8] He has also addressed the role of jazz in the stratification of American culture.[9] He points out that, according to an early twentieth-century structure of value, "jazz" and "culture" were set up as diametrical opposites. For example, the prevalent thinking associated jazz with discord and culture with harmony. While jazz was considered something simple and spontaneous, culture was thought of as complicated and learned through rigorous study and application. Jazz involved audience participation, culture invited passive contemplation. Jazz was ephemeral–a passing fad–and culture was universal and timeless.

The construction and maintenance of a cultural hierarchy served to define "value" and authority in a society that was less rigidly structured according to social class than most European nations. Social divisions could be preserved, for example, because anyone (including Fitzgerald's pre-Gatsby, Jimmy Gatz) could make a fortune through bootlegging, but that same individual might reveal his lack of "breeding" by preferring *Jazz History* to Beethoven. Levine argues that as jazz developed and gained popularity, it began to cross boundaries and blur hierarchical distinctions in American culture. The music became a definitively American cultural product. According to Levine:

> In their refusal to be governed by the categorical orthodoxies that prevailed, in their unwillingness to make absolute distinctions between the vernacular and classical traditions, in their insistence that they were just attempting to play *music* and just wanted to be accepted as musicians, in their determination to utilize the *entire* Western tradition, as well as other cultural traditions, jazz musicians were revolutionizing not only music but also the concept of culture. ("Jazz," 187)

The history of jazz indicates that, in the early twentieth century, although social realities still dictated inequality and segregation, the old cultural hierarchy was disintegrating, and Fitzgerald's fiction explores the some responses to its demise.

In *The Great Gatsby*, Fitzgerald places his criminal hero close to popular music to establish his ambiguous position in the social hierarchy. In a section describing the adolescence of James Gatz that Fitzgerald deleted from the galleys of the novel, fifteen-year-old Gatz channels his desires through the popular music he hears. His emotional response to the music is serious, despite the superficiality of the music itself, and it amounts to a kind of misreading. According to this passage, his fleeting dreams match the ephemerality of the popular music, but in his youthful exuberance, he fails to detect the commercial cynicism of the Tin Pan Alley song factories:

> The part of his life he told me about began when he was fifteen, when the popular songs of those days began to assume for him a melancholy and romantic beauty. He attached to them reveries as transitory as themselves, and attributed deep significance to melodies and phrases set down cynically in Tin-Pan Alley. (*Galleys*, 163)

These songs, "set down cynically" as they may be, begin to shape the character of young Gatz by offering up a picture of the world as an entertaining fantasy:

> For a while these reveries provided an outlet for his imagination, reflecting with their contemporary glamour the gaudy universe in which he believed. They were a satisfactory hint of the unreality of reality, a promise that the rock of the world was founded securely on a fairy's wing. (*Galleys*, 163)

This passage, except for the description of the songs "reflecting with their contemporary glamour the gaudy universe in which he believed," remained in the published novel. Only the direct reference to popular music was deleted, dissociating Gatsby's reveries from their source in popular music. Perhaps this direct reference placed Gatsby too close to the "lowliness" of popular culture by making him a product of popular music, rather than a consumer of it.

Gatsby, as he is in this deleted passage, is identified with popular music in the rest of the novel, but in a more detached, ambivalent style. He, like Jim

Powell in Fitzgerald's 1923 story "Dice, Brassknuckles, and Guitar," is depicted as a "Jazz Master," rather than as mastered by jazz. Dance orchestras set the tone for his parties, and even in a more private moment at home, his "boarder" and occasional pianist, Ewing Klipspringer, plays "The Love Nest" and "Ain't We Got Fun" for Gatsby, Daisy, and Nick. Immediately after these song references, however, Nick notices in Gatsby's expression what appears to be a trace of "faint doubt ... as to the quality of his present happiness" (97). The assertion of lovers' idyllic seclusion in the one song and perpetual "fun" in the other mirrors and threatens to expose "the colossal vitality of [Gatsby's] illusion" (97). Gatsby's response to the music is a mixture of pleasure and doubt, as if the music forebodingly hinted that the moment of joy was transitory and tainted–a "boom" that would inevitably be followed by a crash of epic proportions. The music captured the frenzy of ecstasy on the brink of despair.

"Jazz," for Fitzgerald, for his peers, and for much of America, served as a kind of catch-all term for everything new and modern. In 1925 Fitzgerald referred to his "Dice, Brass Knuckles and Guitar" as "Exuberant Jazz in my early manner" (*Life in Letters*, 121). "Jazz" emerged as a slang term with sexual connotations (like rock n' roll decades later), and many different styles of American popular music were widely referred to as jazz. The term was associated with a distinctive Americanness that had been forged into fast, urban sophistication out of the "raw" materials of "down home" folk practices. The new music helped to establish American cultural independence from Europe as well as national and international markets for American cultural capital. In "Echoes of the Jazz Age," Fitzgerald records his impressions of the prevailing attitudes of the twenties. He cites 1922, the year in which *The Great Gatsby* is set, as the year that marked "the peak of the younger generation" (15), one generation younger than his own. After that year, he claims, the social upheavals became more generalized and less of a matter of youthful rebellion. The result was "[a] whole race going hedonistic, deciding on pleasure" (15). Interestingly, in the twenties "race" and "nationality" often were used as interchangeable words, as if nations could be defined by their monoracial character and as if those who were outside of the dominant race had no claim to nationality. This usage, therefore, linguistically constructed "American" as white and Anglo-Saxon.

Still, Fitzgerald places an interracial cultural product, commercial jazz, at the center of the 1920's hedonistic movement. "The word jazz in its progress toward respectability has meant first sex, then dancing, then music" ("Echoes,"16), Fitzgerald asserts, and this observation indicates that he knew the changes in the implications of the word as it moved from folk expression to urban entertainment. His remarks also suggest an awareness of the lack of "respectability" with which the word "jazz" still resonated in post-twenties

American culture.

In the same essay, Fitzgerald refers to "bootleg Negro records with their phallic euphemisms [that] made everything suggestive" (18), and this reference conjoins these records with other social trends that Fitzgerald categorizes as debauched. Mitchell Breitwieser, in one of the few essays to carefully analyze Fitzgerald's references to jazz-oriented music, asserts that the inclusion of "bootleg Negro records" in this essay demonstrates "an awareness of the African American origin of the music and of the diminishment of the music endemic to mainstream recording" (59). Breitwieser delves into unexplored territory by even questioning the reference's implications, since scarce critical attention is paid to the historical contexts of Fitzgerald's musical references.

Within "Echoes of the Jazz Age," however, a breathless and whirling paragraph conflates the reference to these prohibited (from a white listener's perspective) records with extramarital affairs, "erotic plays," and celebrity scandals exposed by the tabloids (18). Fitzgerald lists contemporary events that illustrate "the universal preoccupation with sex [that] had become a nuisance" (18). In conjunction with the affairs, the plays, and the celebrity scandals, the mention of these bootleg records, which we may assume from recording history are blues records marketed on "race" labels, *does* indicate an awareness of the cultural wellspring of the music, as Breitwieser claims.[10] It *does not*, however, indicate a lament over any kind of "diminishment," whether from mass marketing strategies or anything else.

The records are part of the "nuisance" that Fitzgerald describes in this paragraph. According to Fitzgerald, the records are implicated in a larger social trend toward debauchery. This paragraph, with its condemnation of blues records as part of a sex-crazed, "low" cultural "nuisance," reflects Fitzgerald's conservative tendencies. He does not use jazz references either to celebrate a release from Victorian morality or to criticize the colonization of African American musical traditions.

POPULAR JAZZ AND "MIXOPHOBIA"

Fitzgerald's use of popular jazz complicates his portrayal of class and national identity by making the issue of racial identity unavoidable. The jazz anxiety depicted through Fitzgerald's musical allusions often arises from the interracial quality of American popular music and corresponds to what Werner Sollors (in a tongue in cheek tone) describes as "mixophobia" or "amalgaphobia" (10). The confusion over whether one's "culture" is learned or is biologically inherited (on the basis of racial categories) ruptures the surfaces of Fitzgerald's jazz allusions like the "interruptive notes" in Tostoff's *Jazz History*. The influence of jazz on popular music in general suggests that cultural practices are accessible through learning and imitation. Since this jazz-influenced popular music became integral to the image of "American" identity in the 1920s, it illustrated that, on a cultural level, America was mixed like Ralph Ellison's striking metaphor of "optic white" paint.[11]

In the 1920s jazz controversy, a particularly extreme anxiety about the "crossover" appeal of this new music occurred when the music was either a type of orchestrated dance music or a parody of jazz called novelty or "nut" jazz. These 1920s versions of jazz are most often associated with white performers and white audiences, but, of course, racial identity did not necessarily determine a musician's style.[12] A reference to Lady Caroline Sibly-Biers's song, "There Was a Young Lady from Hell," in *Tender is the Night* (1933) epitomizes "nut" jazz in Fitzgerald's fiction (269). "[A] fair-haired young Scotsman" whose orchestra is called "The Ragtime College Jazzes of Edinboro" accompanies the aristocratic British woman in her drunken performance (269). This reference and others seem to imply that the musical boundary crossing has occurred solely on the level of social class. This type of cultural "transgression," however, is also inextricably bound up with images of racial crossing that complicate the representation of American class structures in Fitzgerald's fiction.[13]

Kathy Ogren, in her study of the jazz controversy of the 1920s, offers brief comments on Fitzgerald's musical references that censure Fitzgerald and some of his white contemporaries for their denial and ignorance of the aesthetic value of African American culture. According to Ogren:

> Fitzgerald's use of jazz and its performance is perhaps the literary equivalent of "nut jazz." The music is important as a novelty that provides humorous touches or atmosphere...none of these writers [Fitzgerald, Carl Van Vechten, Vachel Lindsay] showed a particular interest in developing the fictional potential of black musical performance. These perspectives in white primitivist writing presented a marked contrast to Harlem Renaissance innovators like Langston Hughes and Claude McKay, who believed black culture could be used as both a theme and language representing a modern vision. (151)

The major difference Ogren examines is the contrast between writers who use jazz aesthetics as a model for stylistic innovation for language and narrative structure and writers who allude to the music as a kind of backdrop–particularly in order to conjoin "primitivism" with non-Anglo racial categories. She goes on to observe that "there is very little accurate depiction of jazz performance in Fitzgerald's fiction" (149).

Fitzgerald's writing certainly represents jazz differently from the writing of McKay, Hughes, and other Harlem Renaissance poets, novelists, and essayists. Fitzgerald's fiction primarily alludes to a different *style* of twenties "jazz" than, for example, that which Hughes evokes in a poem such as his "The Weary Blues" or in his depiction of Benbow's dance band in his novel *Not Without*

Laughter. In McKay's novel, *Home to Harlem*, the dance bands at the Harlem clubs that Jake frequents do not play orchestrated music like *Jazz History of the World*. McKay's and Hughes's music is highly blues-inflected and improvisational; it emerges from and–in performance–remains situated within a distinctively African American cultural context.

Fitzgerald does also use "jazz" differently from Van Vechten, however, a distinction that Ogren does not make. Popular jazz does not necessarily symbolize "primitivism" in Fitzgerald's fiction, and it is certainly a different style of music than that portrayed by Van Vechten who was familiar with, for example, the music of blues singer Bessie Smith and jazz innovator Louis Armstrong. Fitzgerald knew much more about Paul Whiteman's orchestra than Harlem rent parties. Van Vechten established himself as a privileged guest in some Harlem social circles, and through his friends and acquaintances he situated himself in relation to African American cultural practices differently from Fitzgerald. Fitzgerald's exposure to "jazz," based on the specific allusions in his fiction, must have come primarily through the popular venue of musical comedies and society dances with well-known orchestras who incorporated jazz flourishes to make their music sound "modern." Fitzgerald's use of the term "jazz" evokes some confusion in a late twentieth-century context, and in retrospect, we might conclude that he would have been more accurate if he had called his and his peers' experience of the 1920s the "Jazz-Influenced Age."

Despite the validity of most of Ogren's assertions, the popular music in Fitzgerald's fiction is more than just a "novelty that provides humorous touches or atmosphere" (151). Fitzgerald's musical allusions are a vital part of his depiction of a culturally amalgamated America, and the anxiety that accompanies this portrayal of the national character offers interesting insights into the social climate of early twentieth-century America. Fitzgerald's exploration of American class structures is well documented, but scant attention has been paid to the ways that his use of popular music indicates a preoccupation with issues of race and the ways that racial identities complicate the class system. A consideration of the history of various jazz styles reveals some of these complications.

In the 1920s, "jazz" emerged as a multivalent term that encompassed a range of musical styles and alluded to a whole worldview or lifestyle. The term "jazz" and the styles of music that accompanied it moved from being located in southern African American cultural practices (such as New Orleans street parades and rural, "jook joint" blues performances) to being the markers for a new conception of black and white northern, urban modernity.[14] In this shift, despite the attempts of some performers and promoters to extricate the music from its African American cultural base, traces of "blackness" remained and profoundly influenced the nascent national identity.[15]

Jazz-influenced popular music as a symbol for the interracial character of American culture appears prominently in the final deleted paragraph from Fitzgerald's manuscript version of the *Jazz History* episode. Here Nick declares: "The last was weak I thought though ~~the audi~~ [sic] most of the people seemed to like it best of all. It had recognizable strains of famous jazz in it–Alexander's Ragtime Band and the Darktown Strutters Ball and [a] recurrent hint of The Beale Street Blues" (55). W.C. Handy's 1919 composition, "Beale Street Blues," although it is deleted from this section of the manuscript does appear later in the published novel. Along with the other two songs mentioned in this reference, the "Beale Street Blues" allusion emphasizes the popularity among the diverse guests at Gatsby's parties ("most of the people seemed to like it best of all") of the new, culturally amalgamated music.

In the published version of the novel, Handy's composition resurfaces in the description of Daisy's romantic remembrances of her girlhood in Louisville, Kentucky. Daisy matures in an "artificial world … [where] orchestras … set the rhythm of year, summing up the sadness and suggestiveness of life in new tunes" (151). Popular music constructs the meaning and emotional tone of life in Daisy's youthful world. At the society dances, "All night the saxophones wailed the hopeless comment of the *Beale Street Blues* while a hundred pairs of golden and silver slippers shuffled the shining dust" (151). The slippers that stir enchanted dust are "golden and silver," indicating the wealthy status of the dancers and alluding to Daisy's nostalgia for what she remembers as a fairytale existence. The saxophones, however, contradict these images with their "hopeless comment," and this "wail[ing]"despair is articulated specifically through Handy's composition, "Beale Street Blues," the same piece mentioned in the deleted *Jazz History* scene. Whether Daisy and her peers acknowledge it or not, "hopelessness" permeates the boundaries of their idyllic, southern, "white girlhood" (20), and the music that fills their lives comments upon that underlying despair. The "shining dust" that encircles the privileged dancers appears in contrast to the oppressive poverty and hard labor in the "valley of ashes" (23-24) and the "foul dust [that] floated in the wake of [Gatsby's] dreams" (2). These other "dust" images allude to oppression based on race and class that sullies the idealism of the American Dream.

A brief consideration of the historical background of W. C. Handy and his music reveals the significance of the "Beale Street Blues" allusion. Some recent jazz critics have condemned Handy as a "sellout" who Europeanized (or "whitened") blues, but many of his contemporaries respected him as a successful member of the African American musical community.[16] James Weldon Johnson recognized the importance of Handy's musical contributions and acknowledged the difficulties Handy faced in attempting to document blues music according to the European scalar system.[17]

Musicologist Christopher Small applauds Handy for notating blues and thus making a vital oral tradition available to a vast audience of black and white listeners:

> It was Handy who, by systematizing the blues inflections and harmonies, and devising ways of notating them, made themavailable to popular-song composers ... Moreover, it was through the medium of Handy's published versions that many black musicians made their first encounter with blues; even so great a performer as Willie "The Lion" Smith [a renowned Harlem stride piano player] confessed that that was how he had first encountered the style and the culture. (266)

To argue that blues or jazz remains truly and authentically "black" *only* by remaining orally transmitted folk expressions is to oversimplify the diverse aspects of African American culture.[18] This "authenticity" argument, which Small refutes in his assessment of Handy's music, also implies that when African American artistry asserts a profound influence on mainstream culture by becoming "popular," then it necessarily no longer expresses the component of its identity associated with "blackness." According to this perspective, the music can be stylistically either "black" or "white" but not both.

In the deleted *Gatsby* passage, Nick's impressions of the music follow the line of argumentation that privileges the idea of cultural "purity." The popularity of the music and its tendency to mix black and white make it "weak" (55), according to Nick's sense of cultural value. Nick categorizes the other songs mentioned alongside "Beale Street Blues" in this passage, "Alexander's Ragtime Band" and "Darktown Strutter's Ball," under the same heading of "famous jazz" (55). "Alexander's Ragtime Band" was published in 1911 by Tin Pan Alley songwriter Irving Berlin, and the song marked the end of the ragtime craze, "although it brought about a brief revival of interest in the music" (Southern, 330-31). This composition and its tremendous popularity illustrate the profound impact of ragtime on mainstream American culture.[19]

Shelton Brooks published "Darktown Strutter's Ball" in 1917. Brooks also worked as a theater musician and played piano and sang in Harlem nightclubs (Southern, 351). According to music historian Eileen Southern, Brooks' songs "pointed to black folk styles" (510) but were recorded and marketed as popular music. Like Handy, Brooks had no qualms about mixing musical genres to create the effect he, as a musician, desired. Handy, who with his orchestra would perform a historical survey concert at Carnegie Hall (a kind of "History of the Jazz World") in 1928, was interested in demonstrating "the variety of black music from folk to symphonic" (Southern, 445). Handy blended jazz elements with elements of the European symphonic tradition.

Obviously, each of the three songs cited in this musical reference is culturally "mixed." They are what Nick describes in the published version of the novel as the "yellow cocktail music" (40) that emanates from Gatsby's parties, and the adjective "yellow" becomes particularly striking when considering the implications of this idea of racial "mixing." Although these three "famous jazz" songs were deleted from the manuscript of *The Great Gatsby*, "recurrent hint[s]" (55) of their aesthetic and social implications remain in the published novel and in Fitzgerald's other fiction, suggesting the linguistic difficulties of writing a "raceless" account of American music in a pervasively or perversely racialized nation.

In this historical context, the issue of race permeated both Fitzgerald's musical allusions and the jazz controversy in the media. The sweeping popularity of jazz seemed to call into question what "whiteness" really was, and if in fact, "American" really equated to "white." Anxious attempts to reinforce the idea of racial difference appeared in the allusions to "scientific" racism that underpinned the condemnation of jazz in the mainstream white press. At the same time, some conservative African American music critics condemned the music for perpetuating stereotypes and for presenting an "undignified" image of black identity.[20] Commentators in white publications often relied upon stereotyped images of blackness to discredit jazz aesthetics. The use of polyrhythms and the manipulation of the European-derived twelve tone chromatic scale (resulting in "blue" notes), both of which are practices that derive from African musical traditions, were denounced in jazz not as stylistic devices but as symbols of "barbarism" and threats to "civilization."

For example, in a *Ladies' Home Journal* article titled "Does Jazz Put the 'Sin' in Syncopation?" one writer claims:

> Jazz originally was the accompaniment of the voodoo dancer, stimulating the half-crazed barbarian to the vilest deeds. The weird chant, accompanied by the syncopated rhythm the voodoo invokes, has also been employed by other barbaric people to stimulate brutality and sensuality. That is has a demoralizing effect upon the human brain has been demonstrated by many scientists. (Faulkner, 16)

The music is tied to a biological conception of culture and is condemned based on an ethnocentric fear of miscegenation that is underpinned by appeals to pseudo-science.[21] The writer makes no attempt to provide a legitimate critique of the music's stylistic attributes. This notion of culture-as-biology also seeps into Fitzgerald's allusions to popular American music and hints at "the troubling suspicion that whatever else the true American is, he is also somehow black."[22]

This "troubling suspicion" is particularly evident in Nick Carraway's characterization of Gatsby, who is, metaphorically, somehow both "black" and "white." Nick sets himself apart from Gatsby based on the American approximation of "gentry." At the very beginning of his story, Nick describes his family as consisting of "prominent, well-to-do people" who comprise "something of a clan" (2). Nick's father imparts to him a sense of noblesse oblige that amounts to a sort of nonjudgmental tolerance for people to whom "the fundamental decencies" have been "parcelled out unequally at birth" (1). Nick's great uncle, whom the family says Nick resembles, "sent a substitute to the Civil War" (2-3), while he made his fortune in the hardware business. This small detail of the family history suggests that "fundamental decencies" may be, in fact, quite ambiguously defined. Throughout the novel, Nick tries to separate Gatsby's "fundamental decencies" and his characteristically American optimism and vitality from his criminal business practices and sketchy past, evoking a metaphorical association with Nick's own family history and with American history in a more general sense.

As Nick and Gatsby cross the Queensboro Bridge on their way to Manhattan, Nick realizes, "Anything can happen now that we've slid over this bridge … anything at all…'" (69). The bridge into modern, urban America initiates the "crossing" imagery that becomes the prevailing motif in the episode. This episode conveys Nick's anxiety about the culturally amalgamated character of Gatsby and of America itself as Gatsby represents it. In Nick's mind, Gatsby is suspiciously intertwined with the idea of crossing boundaries, and he symbolically mingles with the "outsiders" on the bridge.

On the bridge, Nick observes a funeral procession of southeastern Europeans with "tragic eyes and short upper lips" (69), and he happily imagines that seeing Gatsby's beautiful car is a highlight of their "somber holiday" (69). Nick accords to Gatsby's overt display of wealth the status of the American Dream that draws immigrants to seek its promise. In his somewhat derogatory and homogenizing physical description of the southeastern Europeans, however, Nick attempts to distance them from himself and from Gatsby, who has also avidly pursued an American dream of material wealth. Nick and Gatsby then cross Blackwell's Island, the name of which, in this context, symbolizes both African American upward mobility and, as an island, isolation from wealthy, white "society." Nick notices that they are "*passed*" (69, emphasis added) by a limousine "driven by a white chauffeur in which sat three modish negroes, two bucks and a girl" (69). The white driver represents a shift in the power structure, while the word "modish" suggests a *nouveau riche* sense of fashion, and the derogatory and dehumanizing term "bucks" implies Nick's progressively panicked attempts to distance people in passing cars from himself and especially from Gatsby. Somehow, the wealthy, "modish negroes" threaten Nick more aggressively than the southeastern Europeans.

In Nick's mind, Gatsby is as almost as closely associated with "passing" (and in his romance with Daisy with "crossing") as the African American motorists on the bridge into urban America. Later, in the climatic scene at the Plaza

Hotel, Tom reveals his knowledge of Gatsby's feelings for Daisy, and in his tirade he proclaims that, "[n]owadays people begin by sneering at family life and family institutions, and next they'll throw everything over and have intermarriage between black and white" (130). The hypocrisy of his argument renders it absurd, since it is the adulterous Tom himself who "sneers" at "family life," and Nick describes Tom's ranting as "impasssioned gibberish" (130). Nonetheless, Nick's response to the "modish negroes" and their closeness to Gatsby reveals some traces of anxiety in Nick's mind, too, regarding the Daisy/Gatsby alliance as some kind of forbidden miscegenation.

The "modish negroes" pass Gatsby and Nick on the bridge, implying both "passing" for white and surpassing the racing white motorists. Nick proclaims at this moment that he "laughed aloud as the yolks of their eyeballs rolled toward us in haughty rivalry" (69). Dehumanization immediately follows what Nick experiences as unsettlingly close interracial contact. Nick's egg image (neither East Egg nor West Egg but barnyard egg) of "yolks" for human eyes renders the other motorists' "haughty rivalry" absurd and enables Nick to simply laugh and declare that anything can happen. He believes, after witnessing the spectacle of African American "haughty rivalry," that the "anything" that could happen includes "[e]ven Gatsby" (69). The possibility of racial "crossing," which is also enacted through the interracial character of American popular music, makes anything seem possible to Nick, as if what he once imagined to be the prevailing social order has been completely overthrown.

Gatsby is an "outsider," who is, as Tom Buchanan describes him, "Mr. Nobody from Nowhere" (130). In Tom's claim that Gatsby's pursuit of Daisy is akin to "intermarriage between black and white" (130), the novel implies that culture (read: social class) and biology (read: race) are interconnected in the construction of the social hierarchy. Gatsby's association with both black identity and popular music can be interpreted in relation to Ralph Ellison's description of the ways that white Americans, in the quest to define identity, have historically tended "to seize upon the presence of black Americans and use them as a marker, a symbol of limits, a metaphor for the 'outsider'" ("What," 110-11). Golf pro Jordan Baker "murmur[s]" in response to Tom's proclamation about "intermarriage," that "'[w]e're all white here'" (130), but the portrayal of both Gatsby and popular music in the novel suggests that Jordan's faint assertion may not be true, according to Tom and those who share his social status. From the perspective of those of the top of the social hierarchy (like Tom), a democratic kind of social mobility is really the same thing as the eradication of the color line. The culturally amalgamated character of America that its popular music symbolizes refutes the ideological construction of "whiteness" as a separate cultural identity that is primarily negatively defined by being "not black."

Fitzgerald's musical references, like his portrait of Gatsby, engage in the larger modernist intellectual debate over whether we learn or biologically inherit our cultural identities. This debate complicates Fitzgerald's explorations of social class and the system of racial injustices underpinning the prosperity of the "boom years." Similar to Nick's ambivalence and confusion, aspects of Fitzgerald's writing affirm the notion of "culture" as an elite birthright, yet his preoccupation with popular music makes the existence of acquired, fluid, interracial American identities impossible to ignore.

"DICE, BRASSKNUCKLES AND GUITAR": MUSIC LESSONS

One of Fitzgerald's early short stories, which he later described as "[e]xuberant Jazz in my early manner" (*Life in Letters*, 121), offers insight into the way Fitzgerald used allusions to popular music to explore the boundaries between the ideas of "culture" as a biological inheritance and as a learned practice. Through its representations of "jazz," "Dice, Brassknuckles and Guitar" (1923) depicts an "Africanist presence," " the black Hugo" (239), who functions as "body-servant"(238) to the protagonist Jim Powell.[23] The term body-servant implies that Hugo exists only to personally attend to Jim. The archaic associations of the term align Jim and Hugo (from Tarleton, Georgia) with a bygone era of chivalry and slavery, evoking connections with the "old South." Jim heads north to play the innovative capitalist entrepreneur and begins his own kind of "finishing school" among the Southhampton young elite. He describes his venture as "a sort of Academy" (245). His business card reads "JAMES POWELL; J.M./ 'Dice, Brassknuckles and Guitar,'" and he tell his love-interest, Amanthis, that the J. M. stands for "Jazz Master" (245). The story presents Jim as white "master" of the vernacular idioms associated with black culture as well as the veritable "master" of Hugo, who follows him faithfully and unquestioningly.

Jim, as headmaster of the jazz academy, teaches society girls to protect themselves with "debutante's size" (246) brass knuckles, just in case their drunken gentlemen escorts pass out and leave them unprotected in dangerous cafés. When Amanthis asks him if the guitar is also used as a defensive weapon, Jim is appalled at the thought. He teaches the debutantes to play and vows that after only two lessons, "you'd think some of 'em was colored" (246). There is something about the music that has not just crosscultural appeal but that actually turns "white" into "black." Hugo teaches a course in "southern accent," and Jim observes, "Some of 'em even want straight nigger–for song purposes" (247). Apparently Hugo is expert enough on all southern accents ("Georgia, Florida, Alabama, Eastern Shore, Ole Virginian") to fulfill his students' requirements, and he can teach "straight nigger," which, according to the story's formula, transcends regional or state boundaries and is the necessary accent for music (247).

"Straight," in this case, may mean free from white influences and, therefore, separate and distinct or "unmixed." Still, Hugo can teach the young elites the "ethnic secrets" of this music, indicating, in a Boasian fashion, that these musical secrets are culturally, rather than genetically, transmitted.[24] Jim also has the ability to help the privileged class "pass" for "colored" after giving the girls only two guitar lessons. The details imply that music is a vehicle for cultural passing in the minstrel tradition, donning "blackface" to entertain a white audience with the performance music which reveals the "secrets" of black culture. Mastering "jazz" in this story, however, means more than just learning techniques for minstrel entertainment.

At this "Jazz School" one can earn a degree defined as "Bachelor of Jazz," which includes not only a knowledge of the music but also self-defense/street fighting expertise (brass knuckles) and financial/street hustling expertise (dice). Thus, the school offers instruction for survival in a hostile environment, something for which, ultimately, this privileged class of "students" has little need, since the story suggests that money and power insulate them from most hostile threats. The story implies that they come to the Academy primarily to satisfy their voyeuristic curiosity. Jim and Hugo are equally exotic to them and, albeit to different degrees, Jim and Hugo are both outside of the boundaries of their exclusive social parameters. Their interest has its limits: "Polite to, or rather, fascinated by [Jim] as his pupils were from three to five, after that hour they moved in another world" (249). They are curious, but they maintain the aloof detachment that is an attribute of their privileged rank. After *mastering* "jazz," they can easily move back into a world in which money and social status shelter them from the social realities that jazz encompasses and expresses in a musical form.

They exclude Jim from their parties, and a defiant pupil named Van Vleck eventually challenges Jim's authority.[25] Van Vleck demands that Jim call him "sir" and tells Jim that he is "just a servant" (250). Associations with Hugo arise immediately, since in the beginning of the story Jim and the narrator identify Hugo as Jim's "body-servant." Hugo and Jim attempt to carry on after the incident but after a short while they are shut down by the fashionable and irate Mrs. Clifton Garneau and Mrs. Poindexter Katzby. These pillars of the community accuse Jim of serving alcohol and running a morphine den, and, worst of all, Mrs. Katzby exclaims, "'[Y]ou have colored men around! You have colored girls hidden! I'm going to the police!'" (251). The ladies' accusations suggest that they fear racial "mixing" even more than alcohol or morphine. For these society ladies, Jim, Hugo, and the music that they teach all embody the threat of miscegenation. With complete confidence that they have the Law on their side, the women evacuate the debutantes and the gentlemen and leave Jim and Hugo alone in the room.

With his face in his hands, Jim finally turns to Hugo as a companion, an ally. "'Hugo,' he said huskily. 'They don't want us up here'" (252). At this moment, suddenly and utterly unexpectedly, Hugo, the professor of southern accents, is rendered silent. At this narrative moment when we might anticipate the bonding of Hugo and Jim against the exclusion faced by both of them (they don't want *us*"), Hugo disappears, and Jim's call for empathy is answered by Amanthis instead. Amanthis appears from nowhere after the narrator has informed us that Jim "was alone with Hugo in the room" (252). Amanthis comforts Jim, and in a line that prefigures Nick Carraway's feelings for Gatsby tells Jim that he is "better than all of them put together" (252). At the end of the scene Jim turns to Hugo, who is still conspicuously silent, and orders him to "'[s]weep up and lock up'" (253).

Just when we might expect the impoverished, isolated southern white to bond with his similarly situated black companion, Jim re-assumes the role of authority in order to align himself instead with the lovely, lazy flapper character. It is as if Jim, at the moment he becomes truly aware that "society" is out of his reach, turns to Hugo, but almost without skipping a beat his loyalty and his hopes are shifted to Amanthis. He thinks Amanthis is striving for entrance into the higher echelons of society just as he is. As it turns out, Amanthis has been fooling Jim by masquerading as a "poor" girl who stays in a boarding house. She is actually a debutante who is "coming out" (256) in the fall. The dance from which they are both excluded turns out to be a party given in Amanthis's honor, and Jim is allowed to fulfill a dream there by leading Rastus Muldoon's Band from Savannah "[j]ust once" (255). Afterwards, Jim and Hugo retreat south in Jim's dilapidated car. Hugo is pushed further out into the margins of the story so that Jim can tentatively and temporarily enter the upper reaches of the social hierarchy.

This rather awkward narrative design results from the story's attempt to cautiously approach the issue of racial boundary-crossing and then retreat from it. We are left with a silent Hugo who, by the end of the story, exists as nothing more than a southern "accent." The fears regarding "dangers" of the music and its relationship to racial crossing are simultaneously satirized in the depiction of the prissy society mothers and reinforced in the silencing of Hugo. Jim, Hugo, and the society mothers know that learning the ethnic/aesthetic secrets of the music means dismantling the idea of race as biological inheritance and entertaining the idea of race as cultural practice. This intellectual and social shift is ultimately too much for the story (and perhaps, Fitzgerald may have suspected, for the 1923 *Hearst's International* readership) to handle. In this story racial "mixing" is bound up with both class boundary crossing and music. Jim and the social elite get culturally close to Hugo through his teaching of the music, but when Jim wants to advance socially he must distance himself from Hugo and become the "jazz master"–the bandleader who claims the music as his own. Jim's appropriation of the music amounts to a denial of "miscegenation," by anxiously reasserting whiteness. Similarly, in Fitzgerald's 1933 novel, *Tender Is the Night*, jazz music symbolizes miscegenation and is also linked with the most "universal" of taboos–incest.

TENDER IS THE NIGHT: TABOO MUSIC

In *Tender Is the Night*, Nicole Warren's incestuous relationship with her father is the "dark secret" of the novel and the horror that induces Nicole's schizophrenia. The corruption that arises from within Nicole's own family and suggests the distorted reality of the American social ideal. Werner Sollors has demonstrated that in the tradition of interracial literature the themes of miscegenation and incest have been frequently intertwined. For some writers, the linking of the two themes can dramatize "the denial of kinship that is inherent in a biracial organization of the world" (318). For others, "miscegenation is the true horror of any radical ethnocentrist, and incest is the metaphor through which this horror can be (partly) expressed, for there is a general, widely shared sense of *that* taboo" (320). Through Nicole's character, particularly in her association with popular music, the themes of miscegenation and incest are linked in *Tender Is the Night*, and the novel expresses an underlying anxiety about both.

In *Tender Is the Night*, when the young, fragile Nicole meets Dr. Richard Diver at the Zurich clinic, she is closely aligned with the popular music of 1918, the year in which the episode is set. Nicole refers to four songs from musical comedies that were popular that year, two songs that were Tin Pan Alley hits, and one unpublished but widely known song in a blues style that Nicole says "[her family's] cook at home taught ... to [her]" (135).[26] The songs Nicole names are unfamiliar to Dick, although she unquestioningly assumes that he knows them and has danced to them in Paris. Nicole assumes that these are songs every American must know–even expatriate Americans.

In this episode, Nicole embodies music and actually exists as music. While she awaits Dick's arrival at the clinic, "She walked to a rhythm–all that week there had been singing in her ears, summer songs of ardent skies and wild shade, and with his arrival the singing had become so loud she could have joined in with it" (132). She plays records for Dr. Diver, seeking a connection with him through the music. Like music itself, which produces sympathetic resonation in the bodies of its listeners, she anticipates "a beat of response, the assurance of a complimentary vibration in him" (135). For the young Dr. Diver, Nicole and the music express the essence of American culture from which he has detached himself. Nicole and Dick listen to the songs in Zurich, but "[t]hey [are] in America now" (134) because the music epitomizes American culture.

In the Zurich clinic episode, the narrator describes Nicole's music as "thin tunes, holding lost times and future hopes in liaison" (135). This description of Nicole's prized records as "thin tunes" equates the music with her fragile psychological condition induced by her devastating past and her tenuous hopes for recovery. On a more general level, the songs symbolize hopeless despair burdened by history coupled with a prosperous nation's illusory optimism. Nicole and America share a past tainted by abuse and exploitation, and both have a fervid, yet naïve hope that the future will be as bright and effervescent as the songs proclaim. The adjective "thin" indicates this naiveté as well as alluding to a hierarchical conception of culture. According to some modernist conceptions of "high" culture, if the songs are "low" and popular, then they are fleeting, flimsy, and lacking real substance.

The songs Nicole names are "Hindustan," "Why Do They Call Them Babies," "I'm Glad I Can Make You Cry," "Wait Till the Cows Come Home," "Good-by Alexander," and "So Long Letty" (134-35). "So Long Letty" was published in 1915, "Wait Till the Cows Come Home" in 1917, and the other songs were published in 1918, so their selection suggests a concern with historical accuracy and a sense that the songs capture the essence of a particular historical moment. In Fitzgerald's musical allusions, popular tunes often serve as the definitive sign for a particular year. All of these songs except "Hindustan" and "Why do They Call Them Babies" debuted in musical comedies.[27] In fact, musical comedies are the source of the majority of Fitzgerald's musical references.

Many of the popular songs from this era, especially those from musical comedies, suggest that vitality, youthful exuberance, and romantic love last forever, despite the undeniable reality of their ephemerality. As Dick speaks with Rosemary on the phone, he hears "Tea for Two," the hit from the 1925 musical comedy *No, No Nanette*, as "little gusts of music [that] wailed around her" (94). Later, when he thinks of Rosemary, Dick nostalgically plays "Tea for Two" on the piano (169). In this song, the leading lovers imagine a simple but blissfully happy life together, isolated from all external interference–"*Alowown*" (94). Songs like "Tea for Two" with their maudlin lyrics contradict Fitzgerald's portrayal of the convoluted nature of Dick and Rosemary's emotions and the hopelessness of their romance. Fitzgerald repeatedly juxtaposes the sappy idealism of these popular songs with the unflattering depiction of characters' human weaknesses. Fitzgerald's characters desperately and despairingly hope for the idyllic existence that the popular songs' lyrics promise, and this blind optimism appears in his fiction as a particularly

American type of illusion.

Fitzgerald's writing often reflects traditionalist anti-jazz sentiments, yet the music simultaneously symbolizes the characters' genuine desires to express the unspeakable. Their self-deluded dreams lurk just beneath the superficiality of the songs' romantic sentiments, and the realities beneath these illusions constantly threaten to break through to the surface. Fitzgerald's characters repeatedly attribute to this music the emotions that they cannot articulate through language. The songs take on a different significance when the listeners' personal experiences are projected into them. Dick thinks of Nicole and "the dishonor, the secret" when the orchestra plays "Poor Butterfly," "a tune new enough to them all" (151). "Poor Butterfly" was the tremendously popular hit from the musical comedy *The Big Show* in 1916 and, as such, could be classified with Nicole's records as a "thin" tune. According to that system of classification, it is fleeting, sentimental, and popular, yet for Dick at that particular moment it represents all that is unspeakable in Nicole's experience of incest and insanity.

All of the major characters in *Tender Is the Night* have close ties to popular music, but, as a musician, Abe North's connections are the most direct. When Abe is introduced in the novel, he is already beginning a descent into dissipation, but Nicole remembers past times when "he'd be in the library with a muted piano, making love to it by the hour…" (99). The vitality that Abe derived from and projected into the music has inexplicably disappeared. Dick believes that "[s]mart men play close to the line because they have to–some of them can't stand it, so they quit" (99). Dick considers Abe's drinking his way of quitting life on the edge, quitting the kind of life that creativity and brilliance demand. Nicole, however, notes that all artists "don't seem to have to wallow in alcohol" (99). She wonders, "Why is it just Americans who dissipate?" (99). Neither Dick nor the novel ever explicitly answers this question, but both the characterization and the narrative itself anxiously allude to the exploitative aspects of American society hidden beneath the surface of prosperity and the leisure of entertainment. The specter of exploitation lurking in democratic American ideals evokes the characters' impulses to question the escapist pursuits (like popular music and alcohol) that seem to lead to dissipation.

Nicole's experience of popular music that could hold "lost times and future hopes in liaison" (135) directly parallels the effect of alcohol on the novel's debauched musician, Abe North. For Abe, "The drink made past happy things contemporary with the present, as if they were still going on, contemporary even with the future as if they were about to happen again" (103). The music and the alcohol produce inebriation that skews the characters' sense of time and reality. Both intoxicants are aligned with escapism, but *Tender Is the Night* suggests that, even during what Fitzgerald described as the "expensive orgy" ("Echoes," 21) of the boom years, the absence of historical complicity, present accountability, and future consequences is offset by a grim and underlying knowledge that escape is futile.

The murder of Jules Peterson alludes to a connection between this characteristically American dissipation and the nation's history of exploitation based upon racism. Peterson's close association with Abe, the novel's drunken musician, suggests the ways that American music highlights the tenuousness of racial and class boundaries. The violent deaths of Peterson and North imply that "crossing" can be deadly. During the course of events, Abe goes from being implicated in what he calls a "race riot" (98), to being the indirect agent of Peterson's death, to *becoming* Peterson in a metaphorical moment of social boundary crossing.

The significance of this crossing is accentuated by Abe's role in the novel as a musician with aspirations to compose music for Broadway.[28] In the novel, Abe is poised on the edge of social boundaries and eventually falls into the "gray" area of interracial social contact. He is clearly depicted, as a musician and an alcoholic, as an "outsider." In the Roulstons's survey of Fitzgerald's artistic development they note that "two opposing ideas that Fitzgerald seemed quite able to retain were ethnic and social snobbery and sympathy for victims and outsiders, provided they were sufficiently attractive or plucky" (52). As Abe becomes increasingly entangled with Jules Peterson, however, he symbolically moves from this sympathetic "outsider" status to nonexistence.

Robert Forrey and Bryan Washington have shown that Fitzgerald's African American characters are beyond being "outsiders;" they are caricatures.[29] As caricatures, Fitzgerald's African American characters often serve as a marker for the furthest point beneath the social hierarchy. Yet the obvious conjoining of American music with racial identity implies that, despite narrative attempts to suggest otherwise, "blackness" is an essential element of American identity. Portraying Jules Peterson as a caricature and then coupling him with Abe North becomes a strangely labored attempt to dissociate the music from blackness by ritualistically murdering this component of its identity.

What makes the African American characters in Fitzgerald's fiction stand out so prominently to contemporary readers is his reliance on stereotypes for a quick dismissal of their individualized complexity. The gaps in this shorthand strategy of characterization are particularly striking in Fitzgerald's fiction because they stand in stark opposition to his other methods of characterization. For example, although Nicole is in many ways a "type" as a wealthy American, flapper-style woman, readers are not allowed to dismiss her too easily. The damage she has suffered and the strength she struggles to maintain mark her as distinctive. She is a crumbling social *ideal*, and she is still on the grand scale. She is a "viking madonna" (32), and as both a conquering pagan and a Christian saint, she encompasses the history of Anglo-Saxon culture. The complexity of Abe's character is similarly enhanced by the focus on him as a potential social ideal, regardless of the fact that his potential is ultimately unrealized. Abe has a "noble head" (16) and "the high cheekbones of an Indian, a long upper lip, and enormous, deep-set dark golden eyes" (7). He is a strong American type in the tradition of the frontier romance, and he is counted among the good swimmers on the Diver's beach (8).

In contrast to Abe's "noble" appearance, Peterson is described as a "little man with…insincere eyes that, from time to time, rolled white semicircles of panic into view…" (107). Peterson's seemingly legitimate concerns are strangely diminished by the narrative reliance on racial stereotypes. Abe believes that he has initiated a "race riot" (98), but after Peterson is murdered on Rosemary's bed, Dick dismisses the whole affair as "only some nigger scrap" (110). This episode implies a complex array of racial crossings, and one of the most significant of these is the fact that the "nigger scrap," despite Dick's nervous protestations, is not separate from any of the novel's central characters. They are all implicated in the events and the consequences surrounding Peterson's murder.

The irony of Peterson's position as a shoe polish manufacturer is evident, since he metaphorically "blackens" the white characters in the blackface tradition of the minstrel show. Everyone except Abe is most concerned with the *stain* directly linked to Peterson's *blood* on Rosemary's bed and indirectly linked to the possibility of scandal. The whole event is sexually and racially charged with implications of miscegenation.[30] The hotel manager's name, McBeth, further emphasizes "blood" and its associations with genetics and purity. He and the central characters are left with Peterson's blood on their hands (recalling Lady Macbeth) and with murder on their consciences. Peterson's "scrap" becomes Abe's "race riot," which in turn implicates Dick, Rosemary, and Nicole in the affair. This moment marks a turning point in the narrative as Dick begins his descent into dissipation and isolation from "society."

Abe precedes Dick in his descent into what Fitzgerald describes in "Echoes of the Jazz Age" as "the dark maw of violence" (20) that seemed an inevitable accompaniment to frivolity and debauchery and that "happened not during the depression but during the boom" (20).[31] When Abe becomes consumed with his alcoholism he appears to be a man "who has lost all inhibitions, who will do anything" (107). The indeterminacy of "anything," in Abe's case, is a threatening rather than a liberating freedom. The anarchic "anything" of which Abe is capable is represented by his "entangling himself with the personal lives, consciences, and emotions of one Afro-European and three Afro-

Americans inhabiting the French Latin quarter" (106) during the course of events preceding Peterson's murder. Abe's identity as a musician extends the implications of his "entanglement" and boundary crossing.[32] His name (both as Lincoln and as North) aligns him with the northern side of the Civil War, and his association with a "prominent Negro" (106) restaurant-owner named Freeman further emphasizes these connections.

The narrative tone in the Peterson episode exudes a kind of willful detachment that at times trivializes the events of the episode with sarcasm. Peterson is "rather in the position of the friendly Indian who had helped the white" (106), a description that draws upon one system of American racial mythology in order to reinforce another. Abe has spent the past day surrounded by "unfamiliar Negro faces bobbing up in unexpected places and around unexpected corners, and insistent Negro voices on the phone" (106). The disembodied, "bobbing" heads and demanding voices lend an air of farce to both the course of events and the concerns of the individuals involved in Abe's "race riot" (98). Strangely, these events are absolutely central to the development of the novel, thus anticipating serious treatment. In other words, the narrative tone seems incongruous with the subject matter.[33] The Peterson episode prefigures Abe's murder and Dick's collapse, and it immediately precedes Nicole's first narratively depicted "crack-up."

Peterson appears as Abe's double in the episode. Both North and Peterson make careful attempts at etiquette that somehow fall short of the mark. Abe enacts "the exquisite manners of the alcoholic that are like the manners of a prisoner or a family servant" (102); his social performance implies restraint and an inferior social status.[34] Peterson's speech reveals the "precise yet distorted intonation peculiar to colonial countires" (107); he, too, attempts to be "correct" from a position of inferiority. Rosemary is "revolted" (107) by Abe's "dirty hands" (107), another image that suggests that Abe's contact with Peterson has sullied him. Peterson is as unkempt as Abe at this point. As he checks to confirm that Peterson has no pulse, Dick notices, in an oddly detached way, that Peterson's shoe is "bare of polish and its sole [is] worn through" (110). Despite his profession as a shoe polish manufacturer, Peterson has failed to attend to the upkeep of his own shoes. Abe has also neglected his musical profession, and his sole/soul is metaphorically "worn through." Most strikingly, when Rosemary first glimpses Peterson's body on her bed, "she ha[s] the preposterous idea that it was Abe North" (109). Later, Abe is beaten to death in a New York speakeasy and just "manage[s] to crawl home to the Racquet Club to die" (199). Abe does not survive the interracial world of New York jazz and alcohol venues but manages to retreat to the symbolic marker of white boundaries–the Racquet Club–crawling like a wounded animal. The imagery suggests that Abe's racial crossing has precipitated a death as debased and violent as Peterson's own.

In addition to foreshadowing Abe's death, the Peterson episode directly relates Nicole's breakdown to Peterson's murder through the symbolism of blood. Nicole conflates the ideas of Peterson's blood on Rosemary's bedspread with her own experience of being raped by her father and perhaps with her suspicions regarding her husband's attraction to Rosemary, who is a virginal *and* seductive "Daddy's Girl." The fetishization of blood adds to the sexual and racial overtones of the episode. This blood motif recurs in Nicole's own account of her breakdown after the birth of her daughter, Topsy.

This passage describing the birth of Topsy is notable for Nicole's appropriation of the first person narrative voice. The novel momentarily becomes Nicole's story, and her fragmented, stream of consciousness style jaggedly intrudes upon the smooth prose surfaces of the detached, third person narration of the majority of the novel. Nicole proclaims: "You tell me my baby is black—that's farcical, that's very cheap. We went to Africa merely to see Timgad, since my principle interest in life is archeology" (160). The coupling of these two sentences suggests an anxiety over the distinctions between cultural tourism and miscegenation. Nicole angrily protests that her child is *not* black and that she can show a scientifically impartial interest in African culture without crossing the boundaries of race, yet her anxiety implies that cultural crossing and miscegenation are connected. The name Topsy, calling to mind the character from Harriet Beecher Stowe's *Uncle Tom's Cabin*, reinforces the image of Nicole's baby as racially "mixed." The idea that Topsy, a slave character from perhaps the most famous American anti-slavery novel, is Nicole's child illustrates an anxiety over the close ties between "white" and "black" in American culture—ties that have their historical roots in slavery.

Nicole's corrupted innocence deriving directly from within her own socially prominent family, symbolizes the exploitative characteristics of the history of racial interaction in the United States. When Nicole's "crack-up" receives its first direct narrative treatment immediately following the Peterson episode, Nicole equates the bedspread stained with Peterson's blood with her own incestuous rape and with a "domino" she was forced to wear to a masquerade ball (112). The domino image evokes associations with Ku Klux Klansmen's cloaking, hooded robes and with the game in which the playing pieces are white and black. This costume also symbolizes the "cover up" and the masking of the events surrounding Nicole's breakdown. She is not allowed to publicly display the "spreads with red blood on them" (112)—neither the one with her own blood on it nor the one bearing Peterson's blood. She must conceal this secret corruption and present a public image of purity.

Rosemary is also threatened by "tainted" blood. Dick realizes that if he does not properly dispose of Peterson's body then "no power on earth could keep the *smear* off Rosemary" (110, emphasis added). Since Rosemary's cinematic image of innocence is very carefully constructed, it also must be carefully maintained. The "smear" is Peterson's body and his blood – a corruption that threatens to deconstruct the illusion of white female purity. The confusion and chaos pervading this scene appear to stem from the notion that if culture is *learned* rather than inherited through one's *blood* then "mixing" is bound to occur, making the romanticization of all "purity" a hopeless illusion.

The theme of corrupted purity resurfaces as Dick begins a descent into dissipation that clearly parallels Abe's, and figures that represent popular culture, a film actor and a musician, appear in conjunction with the idea of crossing socially constructed boundaries. In a moment when Dick is "frantic with jealousy" (219) over Rosemary's relationship with her film co-star Nicotera, Dick shouts at her, "'He's a spic!'"(219). Shortly afterwards Dick gets drunk in a Roman cabaret and starts a fight with the orchestra leader, who is "a Bahama Negro, conceited and unpleasant" (222). His sexual jealousy over Rosemary becomes indistinguishable from anxieties over social boundary crossing and miscegenation, and the two non-Anglo entertainment industry figures seem to embody similar threats.

These events, Dick's anxieties, and his loss of self-control foreshadow his demise in ways that parallel Abe's downfall. After yet another fight–this time with Italian taxi drivers–Dick is brutally beaten by the Italian police. The brutality of the beating is rendered in vivid detail that evokes a visceral response:

> [H]e was clubbed down, and fists and boots beat on him in a savage tattoo. He felt his nose break like a shingle and his eyes jerk as if they had snapped back on a rubber band into his head. A rib splintered under a stamping heel. Momentarily he lost consciousness, regained it as he was raised to a sitting position and his wrists jerked together with handcuffs. (226)

The description of Dick's experience induces an imaginative correlation with what Abe must have suffered by being beaten to death. Dick survives but continues to sink into debauchery. Although he does not die, Dick's fate, like Abe's, is a kind of nonexistence. He abandons his scientific pursuits and drifts in obscurity somewhere in upstate New York.

Before Dick disappears, a version of "jazz" signals the depths to which Dick has begun to sink. At a party on a yacht that Dick and Nicole attend without invitation, Dick engages in a verbal battle with Lady Caroline Sibly-Biers, a British noblewoman who is the epitome of degradation in the wealthy expatriate set. Dick fairs badly in the argument, and Nicole is angry with him for "having become fuddled, for having untipped the barbs of his irony, for having come off humiliated" (270). The novel implies that the dispute is ridiculous because Lady Caroline is not a worthy adversary.

One of the symbolic indications of Lady Caroline's absurdity is her affiliation with novelty or "nut" jazz. She has written the words to a song played by a young man from Scotland, a member of "The Ragtime College Jazzes of Edinboro." The British lyricist and the Scottish orchestra imply a removal of the music from its American context, and the inanity of the lyrics indicates Lady Caroline and the orchestra's ridiculous rendition of "jazz." Fitzgerald satirizes this kind of novelty jazz with these lyrics:

> *There was a young lady from hell,*
> *Who jumped at the sound of a bell,*
> *Because she was bad–bad–bad,*
> *She jumped at the sound of a bell,*
> *From hell (BOOMBOOM)*
> *From hell (TOOTTOOT)*
> *There was a young lady from hell–.* (269, original italics)

Although Lady Caroline is a wealthy woman who possesses the title of an aristocrat, she attempts to assert an "outsider" status by styling herself as "bad–bad–bad." The depiction of her foray into "jazz" ridicules her self-definition and the inane lyrics she composes to express it. Dick's association with these characters implicates him in their dissipation and signals the demise of his once noble aspirations.

Fitzgerald's musical references often imply that American culture is terribly flawed, terribly far from its ideals and its "roaring" twenties appearance of gaiety and prosperity. This anxiety is coupled with the sense that the music embodies a kind of social "mixing," which Fitzgerald's fiction depicts as accompanied by dangerous repercussions. As he defines American identity through popular music, Fitzgerald negotiates the tensions inherent in the construction of racial boundaries and the class structures that are dependent upon them. In *Tender Is the Night*, which is perhaps Fitzgerald's most anxious representation of popular music, the characterization of Nicole, Abe, and Dick link the music with insanity, alcoholism, and debauchery and violence.

CONCLUSION

Simon Frith, who studies the cultural implications of popular music, asserts that "what makes music special for identity–is that it defines a space without boundaries" (276). Frith argues that music accomplishes this feat because it "is the cultural form best able to cross borders–sounds carry across fences and walls and oceans, across classes, races, and nations…" (276). As Fitzgerald worked to define American identity in his fiction, he struggled with this special relationship of music to identities that were shaped by cultural forces that crossed physical boundaries and flouted socially constructed ones. An analysis of Fitzgerald's musical references clarifies what "jazz" implies within

Fitzgerald's particular cultural and historical context. In Fitzgerald's writing, jazz-influenced popular music symbolizes a threat to the notion of a cultural hierarchy of value and reflects the amalgamated, interracial character of American culture. Fitzgerald's representation of this music reveals more general social trends in the early twentieth century as popular music began to expose an ideology of whiteness, an ideology that struggled to assert that "American" universally equated to "white." Fitzgerald's writing documents and explores some of the anxieties that arose in relation to the controversial modern music.

CHAPTER THREE

Musical Range
Langston Hughes's *The Ways of White Folks*

These short stories, most of which were first published in various periodicals in the early thirties and then as the collection *The Ways of White Folks* in 1933, are connected through their portrayal of characters crossing social boundaries and the various consequences of the resulting cultural intersections. The title of the collection is a reminder that "white" is a specific racial category, too, rather than a term synonymous with universal. The stories explore the prevalent early twentieth-century conception of race as a set of immutable biological characteristics as this idea confronts the notion that race is a social construction supporting a hierarchical system of power and privilege. In these stories, music often symbolically intercedes in the conflict that arises from these two perspectives on the meaning of race. References to music appear in many of the stories, and these allusions frequently symbolize the improvisational energy of the whole of African American vernacular culture as it comes into contact with "the ways of white folks."

   Music serves as a central trope in three of the stories and is used to explore the ramifications of an American intersection where the ways of white folks cross paths with the lives and the cultural capital of black folks. The white folks—particularly characters who view themselves as liberal and unprejudiced—are frequently depicted in these stories as blindly clinging to racial stereotypes that make them unable to recognize either nuances of black culture or the individuality of black people. In three of the stories, Hughes uses music as a trope that dismantles the idea of race as a biological determinant of identity. In this sense, these three stories, "Home," "Rejuvenation through Joy," and "The Blues I'm Playing," resemble James Weldon Johnson's *The*

Autobiography of an Ex-Coloured Man in their treatment of music as a form of expression through which social boundaries are crossed and racial categories are deconstructed. Hughes, however, is more wary of the idea that music (or any of the arts) can effectively eradicate social injustices predicated upon categories of race and class.

In these three stories, Hughes offers a portrait of a segregated society that allots African American people second-class status while attempting to own and/or to discredit the talents of African American artists and the value of their creations. The early twentieth-century debate over the implications of jazz enters into this portrayal of social conflict as Hughes employs musical tropes to reveal the ways that public debates over aesthetic value can frequently be a cloaked method for debating about race. These ideas are developed through Hughes's subtle use of irony, tragedy, and even humor—a full emotional, intellectual, and artistic range that mirrors his representation of the range encompassed by the music itself. The figure of music in each of these stories provides Hughes with powerful and rich symbolism to explore complex relationships among characters situated at all points along the spectrum of the early twentieth-century American color line.

"HOME"

In "Home," the protagonist, Roy Williams, is a successful violinist who returns to his hometown in Missouri after an extensive European tour. Roy has "been away for seven or eight years, wandering the world" (33) until he becomes seriously ill. Believing that he will die, he comes home to see his mother. The irony of the story's title is that Roy finds no "home" and no sense of peace and belonging; his life ends not as a result of his illness but rather as a result of a vicious attack carried out by a white mob. His artistic talent, his race, his sophistication, and his appearance all contribute to his outsider status in his provincial hometown. Like James Weldon Johnson's ex-coloured man, Roy can find no "home" in which he can express the various components of his identity. He does not fit into the narrowly defined social categories. Music enables him to cross social boundaries, but it also, indirectly, leads to his brutal death.

Initially, music seems to be Roy's salvation. A racist society denies him any advancement, but music becomes a means to acquire the education he desires, even if the opportunity begins within the exploitative context of a minstrel show:

> There was no higher school for Negroes in Hopkinsville. For him there had been only a minstrel show to run away with for further education. Then that chance with the jazz band going to Berlin. And his violin for a mistress all the time—with the best teachers his earnings could pay for abroad. Jazz at night

and the classics in the morning. Hard work and hard practice, until his violin sang like nobody's business. Music, real music! (46)

Until Roy gets sick, music offers everything he needs—the chance to travel, relief from loneliness, education, and an expression of his talent and commitment as an artist. He masters the classical and jazz idioms, defying any limitations that might be artificially placed upon him.

Roy finds an escape from racism in Europe but encounters a class system equally full of injustices. The disparity between rich and poor in Vienna literally sickens him and affects his music until "the glittering curtains of Roy's jazz were lined with death" (34). The image of the "glittering curtains" suggests that the music presents a surface gaiety that conceals despair. Roy's distress arises because "so many people were hungry, and yet some still had money to buy champagne and caviar and women in the night-clubs where Roy's orchestra played" (34). He discovers that the situation is even worse in Berlin where the cabaret patrons "laughed and danced every night and didn't give a damn about the children sleeping in doorways outside, or the men who built houses of packing boxes, or the women who walked the streets to pick up trade" (35). The story condemns capitalism on an international scale. The setting is the 1930s, and when Roy returns to Harlem he sees his old friends, "musicians and actors," who are "hungry and out of work" (35). Roy longs to return to his hometown with resigned despair, thinking that life is "[r]otten everywhere" (35). At this point in the narrative, it begins to appear that although music is still an essential component of Roy's life, even music does not offer a cure for the injustices and the suffering of the world.

When he arrives in his hometown, his bags covered with tags and stickers documenting his travels, his urbane manner, and his stylishly elegant clothes make him an object of scorn in the eyes of the poor whites loafing at the train station. He senses their hostility, and "[f]or the first time in half a dozen years he felt his color. He was home" (37). This description, juxtaposed with the images of desperate poverty abroad and in the States, emphasizes the idea that violent reinforcement of the color line is a distinctively American way to keep classes of people divided and consequently weak. Roy is "home" in a place where he can never be at home.

Music, however, cannot be contained within the artificial boundaries of black and white. Roy gives a concert soon after he arrives home, and the music resonates across the color line:

> What little house anywhere was ever big enough to hold Brahms and Beethoven, Bach and César Franck? Certainly not Sister Sarah Williams's house in Hopkinsville. When Roy played, ill as he was, the notes went bursting out the windows and the colored folks and white folks in the street heard them. (39)

This imagery suggests that although music does not eradicate prejudice and injustice, it does burst out across boundaries in a way that cannot be contained according to the narrow thinking of racial categories, thus highlighting the absurdity of such categories and the limitations they place upon individuals.

Roy refuses to have his individual range constrained by racism or the aesthetic hierarchy of value for different genres of music. He had dreamed of playing Brahms at concerts at Carnegie Hall or the Salle Gaveau. He had imagined "a thousand people loook[ing] up at [him] like they do at Roland Hayes singing the Crucifixion" (40). After he gets sick, however, he comes home bearing "the broken heart of a dream come true not true" (40) and expresses his sadness through his performance of Massenet's *Meditation from Thaïs*. The dream reference here is significant in relation to Hughes's poetry, which is filled with allusions to dreams—most notably to dreams "deferred."[1] Roy is another Hughes character whose dreams are thwarted but who continues to express the full range of his emotions by asserting his individual voice, in Roy's case through his music.[2] More than merely personal accomplishment, Roy's achievements serve as inspiration for others.

Many townspeople attend Roy's concert, and he senses the pride of his family and the black community as he performs at Shiloh Church where the whites pay fifty cents to sit in the front rows. The name of the church emphasizes that the history of slavery and the Civil War reverberates in the race relations of the twentieth century. As he performs, Roy's attention gravitates toward a stranger in the audience, "a scrawny white woman in a cheap coat and red hat staring up at [him] from the first row" (42). He wonders, "What is it you want the music to give you? What do you want from me?" (42). These questions seem to highlight the issue of black cultural performance in a white dominated society. The audience and performer dynamic is complicated by an imbalance of power, symbolized in this case by the whites having the front row seats. The questions also indicate, however, that Roy senses some kind of connection with this listener that goes beyond the constraints of racial categories. As the events leading up to his illness reveal, Roy also wants something from the music that perhaps it cannot give. He wants music to eradicate injustice and suffering, and this woman in the front row, whose loneliness and shabbiness are juxtaposed with Roy's loneliness and elegance, perhaps wants the same.

Roy discovers in this woman what he perceives to be a different sensibility and an unusual knowledge. The woman is Miss Reese, the high school music teacher. Her outsider status in the town is reinforced by her "old maid" designation, her unkempt appearance, and her position waiting to speak with Roy "at the edge of the crowd" (42). She shakes Roy's hand (a defiance of protocol in terms of race and gender) and discusses music with him. Roy responds favorably, the implication being that he overlooks her physical unattractiveness because he appreciates her knowledge of music: "Roy looked into her thin, freckled face and was glad she knew what it was all about. He was glad she liked music" (43). He tells his mother that Miss Reese "understands music" (43), a high compliment from such a dedicated musician.

What Miss Reese fails to understand, however, is the reality of the racism that permeates her and Roy's world and leads to his violent death. Like Roy before his illness, she believes that music can eradicate the strict boundaries of the color line. Through her appreciation of Roy's talent and her overt, public praise of him, she becomes unwittingly complicit in his murder. She invites him to the high school to play for her senior class in music appreciation. She wants Roy to demonstrate the beauty of Bach's and Mozart's music, an "appreciation" that she and Roy share, but her students apparently do not. She sends him "a nice note on clean white paper," (43) which foreshadows the disastrous consequences of her "innocence," her blindness to the power of segregation in a racist society. Even though Roy feels very ill when he performs at the high school and consequently does not play his best, Miss Reese praises him:

> But Miss Reese was more than kind to him. She accompanied him at the piano. And when he had finished, she turned to the assembled class of white kids sprawled in their seats and said, "This is art, my dear young people, this is true art!" (44).

This reference to "true art" calls to mind the assertions of the Harlem Renaissance's "talented tenth," who argued that the grandeur of art could help to promote social justice–a claim with which Hughes took issue. He also argued against the idea that black vernacular art forms had to be "lifted up" to attain the greatness of "higher" art forms. The events of "Home" reveal that rather than fostering social equality, the recognition of Roy's musical talent–talent that, interestingly, seems to be particularly strong in the "white" sphere of classical music–sparks hatred and jealousy rather than equanimity. Instead of cultivating music appreciation, Miss Reese's students:

> went home that afternoon and told their parents that a dressed-up nigger had come to school with a violin and played a lot of funny pieces nobody but Miss Reese liked. They went on to say that Miss Reese had grinned all over herself and cried "Wonderful!" And had even bowed to the nigger when he went out! (44)

This description of the students' response clearly defines the possibility that "true art" may be incapable of instilling a true sense of social justice and equality.

Roy remains conspicuous in his small town. His talent and his appearance set him apart. Sick and unable to sleep at night, he dons his accustomed European evening dress and walks the streets, evoking animosity from his prejudiced white neighbors, but, like Miss Reese, Roy seems oblivious to dangerous reality of the world in which he lives. As he walks at night: "He saw only dreams and memories, and heard only music. Some of the people stopped to stare and grin at the flare of the European coat on his slender brown body. Spats and a cane on a young nigger in Hopkinsville, Missouri! What's the big idea, heh?" (46). More than his appearance, however, Roy's interaction with Miss Reese incites a crowd of young white men to violence.

Roy encounters Miss Reese one night and stops to chat about music, and "they smiled at each other, the sick young colored man and the aging music teacher in the light of the main street" (47). This public recognition of the passion that these two people share (even though it is passion for art rather than for each other) is too close to miscegenation for a racist society to accept. Their interaction provokes the stereotypical charge levied against black men by white lynch mobs. In the midst of his conversation about music with Miss Reese, Roy is attacked: "The movies had just let out and the crowd, passing by and seeing, objected to a Negro talking to a white woman–insulting a White Woman–attacking a WHITE woman–RAPING A WHITE WOMAN" (47-48). The changing capitalization of the words indicates the mob's mentality as Miss Reese and Roy are transmuted in their imaginations from individuals to the embodiment of racial stereotypes.

Through characterization and the symbolism of music the entire story has set up the tragedy of the climactic moment. The connection shared by Roy and Miss Reese through music leads to brutality rather than justice. Roy's last thought is to wonder "why Miss Reese had stopped to ask him about Sarasate. He would never get home to his mother now" (48).[3] Ultimately, the pleasure he had found in their mutual appreciation for music becomes confusion over why she has contributed to his demise, preventing him from finding a place of peace and belonging–epitomized by the idea of "home" and his mother.

The final sounds that Roy hears are imaginatively transformed from horror to harmony. As he slips into unconsciousness the mob becomes music as "the roar of their voices and the scuff of their feet were split by the moonlight into a thousand notes like a Beethoven sonata" (49). In the last image of the story, Roy's body transforms into his own instrument and becomes like an Aeolian harp: "And when the white folks left his brown body, stark naked, strung from a tree at the edge of town, it hung there all night, like a violin for the wind to play" (49).

Through the trope of music (both classical and jazz without generic boundaries), this story cautions that aesthetic appreciation does not necessarily ensure social justice–even for the relatively privileged class of artists.

Although her intentions are not malevolent, Miss Reese, who is isolated as a social outsider herself, compromises Roy's safety simply by behaving as if the color line and the oppressive enforcement of segregation in the 1930s did not exist. "Home" suggests that while music can erode social boundaries (as the rapport between Miss Reese and Roy illustrates) color blindness is not a viable solution to a pervasive racial hierarchy. It is significant, too, that for all their shared understanding, these two characters are identified by first name "Roy" and surname "Miss Reese" throughout the story—a detail that emphasizes the social distance between them.

Throughout Hughes's writing—poetry, fiction, and nonfiction—music serves as a central trope for the vitality and improvisational energy of African American culture. Most often Hughes alludes to jazz and blues. Therefore, it is particularly notable that in "Home" Hughes creates a protagonist who is classically trained and whose cultural boundary crossing leads to his murder. Roy is a very different character from the type of street smart, tough, working class hero often portrayed by Hughes. Roy is characterized as sick and fragile, a sensitive, somewhat isolated young man with an artistic sensibility. His connection with Miss Reese, another frail loner, is portrayed as sincere and impossible. In their attempts to focus on music to the exclusion of all else, they fail to see a social reality in which art cannot eradicate social injustice. Roy must pay for Miss Reese's good intentioned carelessness in transgressing the rules of the color line. In a sense, Roy is killed by music's capacity *and* its failure to transcend the boundaries of race and class. Facing these facts in Vienna and Berlin leads to his illness and forgetting them in Hopkinsville with Miss Reese unleashes the violence of the mob. The final image of Roy's body as a violin played by the wind indicates that the transcendence Roy dreams of achieving through music could not be sustained in this world. Roy finds no "home" in this story because music, although it comes close to providing him with a true sanctuary, cannot save him in the end.

"REJUVENATION THROUGH JOY"

"Rejuvenation through Joy" is a comical story that has wonderful resonance in the early twenty-first century culture of self-help—a culture defined by wealthy, famous gurus of spirituality. The bestseller list indicates the marketability of books promising spiritual redemption in an age of materialism. Hughes's protagonist in "Rejuvenation through Joy," the irresistibly handsome Mr. Eugene Lesche, markets the same type of redemption that has now found a mass audience. Lesche, however, sells his services to a coterie of cultured aristocrats. In Hughes's story, rejuvenation appears to be a luxury of the wealthy. The charming Lesche has tried an array of moneymaking schemes, but the one that brings him the greatest notoriety and monetary success involves curing the malaise of rich whites with jazz, blues, and dancing. Here the connection between the "primitive" and the "modern" are sold to wealthy whites as a remedy for their ennui. When they attend Lesche's "colony," they are "reborn" through the "primal" joy and rhythms of jazz to become "New Ones" (92). The story emerges as a funny and poignant critique of white misinterpretation and misappropriation of the New Negro movement, and music is Hughes's central trope for this critique of the faddish "Jazz Age."

The music retains its original identity but is also transformed when it is "colonized" under Lesche's supervision. The story turns on its head the early twentieth-century debate over jazz. It is not the music—emerging from a distinctively African American cultural context—that threatens to corrupt white "civilization" with its "jungle" rhythms. Conversely, in this narrative, white appropriation or colonization of the music for sheer pleasure narrows the emotional range of the music by solely focusing on joy and willfully disregarding other elements such as anger, sadness, frustration, and jealousy that are encompassed and articulated by the music.[4] The story depicts the consequences of a misinterpretation of the music—misreading that occurs because of blind adherence to racial stereotypes. Although Lesche and his followers attempt to sublimate the music's emotional range, it breaks out and ultimately wreaks havoc in the joy-saturated colony.

At the beginning of the story, Lesche is portrayed as a scam artist and a celebrity in the making. His good looks and charisma make him an object of desire for women and an object of envious emulation for men. He conducts lectures in the ballroom of "the big hotel facing Central Park at 59th Street, New York" (69) and creates a sensation among the Manhattan elite. The narrator informs us that Lesche learned many of his performance tricks driving horses at the Roman Chariot races in the circus, but his ignominious past is not shared with his high-class admirers, who are deceived by tales of "research" trips to Africa and phony academic credentials.

In his final lecture on "Negroes and Joy" (73), Lesche repackages for his urbane audience the slavery-era "happy darkie" stereotype as a philosophical system to rejuvenate dead souls in the modern age. For contemporary enlightenment, Lesche urges his audience to seek "Cab Calloway, Brick Top's, and Bill Robinson" (73). One can live fully, he claims, by "living to the true rhythm of our own age, to music as modern as today, yet old as life, music that the primitive Negroes brought with their drums from Africa to America—that music, my friends, known to the vulgar as jazz, but which is so much *more* than jazz that we know not how to appreciate it; that music which is the Joy of Life" (73). Through his description of Lesche's lecture, Hughes satirizes racial stereotypes and engages with the public debate over jazz and the implications of its rhythms. The terms Hughes uses to accomplish this are particularly interesting. Lesche *defines* jazz (a historically vague designation for an array of musical styles in the early twentieth century). He sets jazz apart from "vulgar" definitions, probably alluding to the sexual connotations of the word and calling to mind some questions about his own character since Lesche sounds close to lecherous or "lech," and the harmony of his colony is ultimately disrupted by his sexual transgressions with the colonists. He defines the music as pure joy to the exclusion of any other emotional, intellectual, or aesthetic components. He also authorizes and promises to deliver the *authentic* source of the music, "the famous Happy Lane (a *primitif de luxe*), direct from the Moon Club in Harlem, with the finest Negro jazz band in America" (73). Lesche assures his audience that he will provide them with deliverance through jazz at his new "Westchester colony" (73). Here the idea of "the colony" is rich with connotations in its evocation of the idea of colonization. In this enterprise, Harlem is imported to Westchester for the colonists' entertainment and "rejuvenation." Like the colonization of African American music more generally, a cultural production created and performed within a specifically African American cultural context is transplanted for white consumption. Instead of the colonists' making "exotic" forays into Harlem for entertainment at the numerous 1920s cabarets, Harlem is exported to the wealthy within the safe confines of white Westchester.

Only the wealthy few can afford to attend the Colony of Joy, although the richest among them can pay the price without even flinching:

> These last were mostly old residents of Park Avenue or the better section of Germantown, ladies who had already tried everything looking toward happiness—now they wanted to try Joy, especially since it involved so new and novel a course as Lesche proposed—including the gaiety of Harlem Negroes, of which most of them knew nothing except through the rather remote chatter of the younger set who had probably been to the Cotton Club. (74)

As this passage indicates, Lesche's clients are total strangers to black culture. They are, in fact, at several levels of remove, since even the jazz they might have heard about through "remote chatter" concerns music from the Cotton Club, a Harlem club that admitted whites only and marketed "exotic" entertainment to a white audience. These details emphasize the idea that Lesche can sell them any definition of jazz because they are not only an uninformed audience but also an audience indoctrinated in and acceptant of the prevailing racial stereotypes. In other words, Lesche effortlessly sells them their own stereotypes at a high price through the music. He sells them their own idea that black equals primitive and that this equation is biologically determined but can (paradoxically) be culturally learned and appropriated for their own use by whites. Significantly, this contradictory feat is accomplished through African Americans' performance of music and dance: "Happy Lane's African band, two tap dancers, and a real blues singer were contracted to spread joy, and act as the primordial pulse beat of the house. In other words, they were to furnish the primitive" (76). The focus is on the African component of African American cultural and artistic identity in order to emphasize the "primordial." In this sense, the story parodies the white modernist fascination with a superficial understanding of African culture–particularly as it manifests itself through residual traces in African American culture, which is not seen as "American" at all.

Lesche's history is an interesting component of the story's portrayal of the relationship of jazz to race and class. Lesche, like F. Scott Fitzgerald's James Gatz/Gatsby, is a self-made American man with a sketchy past. His origins are working class, and he acquires his wealth by any means necessary. Unlike Gatsby, however, Lesche does not have the power of a great, illusory love to redeem his quest for success. After launching his career with a job in the circus in California, Lesche finds "a softer job posing for the members of a modernistic art colony who were modeling and painting away under a most expensive teacher at a nearby resort, saving their souls through art" (76). Lesche basically prostitutes himself to wealthy women, and when this work ends, he finds employment as an extra in the movies. Later, he and his friend Sol Blum create a profitable operation selling swimming lessons to wealthy ladies, and then Lesche and Blum get the idea for a colony. The details of Lesche's inauspicious (and even nefarious) past help to develop a significant aspect of the story's portrayal of the colonization of jazz. He knows from past experience that profit can be derived easily from wealthy patrons willing to pay for a version of what they want reality to be. High society ladies paid him well for "love" under the guise of swimming lessons and modeling. The movies also paid him to play a minor role. Lesche's history confirms the idea that make-believe sells. The notion that jazz will sell to wealthy whites as the "primitive" essence of Africa and primordial man fits perfectly with Hughes's construction of Lesche's character. Lesche is depicted as an opportunist who taps the right market at precisely the right moment:

> How did it happen that nobody before had ever offered them Rejuventation through Joy? Why, that was what they had been looking for all these years! And who would have thought that it might come through the amusing and delightful rhythms of Negroes? (90)

The stereotype of the "happy" music compromises the music itself and those who follow it in search of joy. The devotees are transformed through rhythm and abandon their old selves to become "*New Man, New Woman, New One, forgetting the past*" (92). In an ironic allusion to the New Negro movement, Hughes reveals how jealousy destroys the devotees to rhythm who seek only joy but discover other emotions. Joy to the exclusion of other emotions becomes as potentially volatile as anger:

> Spring that year was all too sudden and full of implications. The very earth seemed to moan with excess of joy. Life was just too much to bear alone. It needed to be shared, its beauty given to others, taken in return. Its eternal newness united. (94)

Perhaps in reference to the New Negro movement, bursting with creative energy and destined for divisive factions within and pressure from without, Hughes's story suggests that fixating all of this energy on one objective (here focused on the attainment of joy through Lesche's guidance) can be dangerous. The implication is that following the leader in any movement can be fraught with difficulties and that a search for unadulterated joy is likely to lead to excess.

The blues singer and dancer, Tulane Lucas, sets off the climactic action of the story by shooting "the Earth Drummer," her lover who has been slipping off to the city every night after work and staying out until morning. Tulane's display of violent jealousy triggers an outburst by Mrs. Duveen Althouse, who expresses similar feelings for Lesche when she exclaims: "'How right to shoot the one you love! ... How primitive, how just!'" (97).

Ultimately, jealousy supersedes joy in the story, and it seems significant that jealousy arises over questions of exclusivity and ownership–issues that attended the early twentieth-century jazz controversy. In the early twentieth century as African American musical forms became increasingly popular in mainstream American culture, artistic ownership was particularly difficult to enforce and defend because the recording industry was just emerging and the music was largely improvisational rather than written (and copyrighted) in the form of scores. The story brings this point to light by incorporating the issue of jealousy into a narrative of white appropriation of black culture–more specifically, appropriation based on stereotypes and superficial understanding.

As part of the jazz controversy, the racial stereotypes associated with a vehement reaction for *and* against the music often relied on a biological conception of racial identity. The notion that African Americans had innate "rhythm" was presented on both sides of the debate in similarly damaging ways that implied either that this was a virtue or a vice but in either case it was accepted as some kind of scientifically valid, genetic fact.[5] The story takes up this idea by suggesting that the stereotype is a form of cultural jealousy and an excuse for white misbehavior. The white colonists' believe that Negroes are primitive and that whites can achieve this primitive state by experiencing and embracing the rhythmic components of jazz. This belief becomes justification for them to defy their customary codes of social conduct.[6] Accepting the racial stereotype enables them to define themselves in relation to it. The stereotype reassures them that they are not innately primitive but that giving themselves license to behave in a "primitive" manner will liberate them. They are jealous of black culture because they believe that Negroes have a more direct connection to the primitive but believe that they, too, can tap into "primordial" energy by becoming consumers of black culture. In this sense, the story's portrayal of jealousy that destroys joy mirrors some aspects of the jazz controversy itself. The paradoxical argument that jazz was simultaneously a cultural expression with widespread influence on the mainstream and a biological component of racial identity is depicted in the story in terms of the relationship between joy and jealousy.

Questions about biology and culture or what is genetic and what is social highlight the ambiguity of racial categories and, therefore, the absurdity of racial stereotypes. The story's last line brings this idea into focus: "As a final touch, one of the tabloids claimed to have discovered that the great Lesche was a Negro–passing for white!" (98). The reference to the tabloids throughout the narrative heightens the story's connection to the public debate over jazz, and the last line explicitly addresses how this debate was couched in terms of race. The possibility that Lesche is "passing" for white and flouting the boundaries of the color line reinforces the story's satire of the idea that "primitive African rhythms" are based on race-as-biology rather than jazz being a matter of cultural production and aesthetic preferences. The "truth" of the tabloid's assertion about Lesche's racial identity is irrelevant. All that matters is that, as in James Weldon Johnson's *The Autobiography of an Ex-Coloured Man*, race can be a facet of identity that is assumed or discarded at will. If racial identity can be a choice, then race is simply equivalent to nothing more than skin tone and is not an immutable and wholly definitive feature of one's existence. Lesche's experiment with jazz illustrates how the music can cross social boundaries, even when its white devotees staunchly maintain their prejudices. Lesch understands the music's capacity to cross and uses it for his own financial gain, and ultimately he is identified as "passing" or crossing the color line just as the music has.

In this way, the story illustrates how important the factor of race was in the jazz debate–even when the rhetoric of that debate was cloaked in terms of standards of aesthetic value. By addressing this issue through its treatment of music, the story critiques the prevalent American thinking of the early twentieth century that required individuals to be definitively classified according to racial categories–a lingering manifestation of the thinking behind the acceptance of the "one drop rule." The exposure of Lesche as a charlatan who does not even clearly fit into a designated racial category symbolizes the exposure of "biological" categories of race as social constructions that preserve an established system of power. Lesche's portrayal as a purveyor of jazz to a wealthy white audience places him right in the midst of the controversy surrounding the music and enables Hughes to humorously address the serious implications of the racially charged reactions to the aesthetics of early jazz and blues.

"THE BLUES I'M PLAYING"

"The Blues I'm Playing" immediately follows "Rejuvenation through Joy" in the collection, and it addresses and extends certain ideas about music taken up by the story that precedes it. Through the central trope of music, the story addresses the issue of ownership and autonomy as it pertains to African American music in particular and artistic productions more generally. This story was written only a few years after Hughes's difficult break with Charlotte Mason, the wealthy white widow who had been his patron. Mason also gave financial support to Alain Locke and Zora Neale Hurston, and the representation of Mrs. Dora Ellsworth in "The Blues I'm Playing" raises complex issues surrounding the white patronage of Negro artists during the Harlem Renaissance. Hughes sums up his relationship with Mason in his 1940 autobiography, *The Big Sea*:

> She wanted me to be primitive and know and feel the intuitions of the primitive. But, unfortunately, I did not feel the rhythms of the primitive surging through me, and so I could not live and write as though I did. I was only an American Negro—who had loved the surface of Africa and the rhythms of Africa—but I was not Africa. I was Chicago and Kansas City and Broadway and Harlem. (325)

This passage uses the image of rhythm—a concept central to African American musical traditions and to Hughes's own writing—to describe a misunderstanding between a young black artist and a wealthy white patron. The patron's acceptance of the racial stereotype that black equals primitive and the corollary notion that race is a biological inheritance rather than a cultural construction compels her to demand from Hughes a diminishment of the range of his artistic expression. As in "Rejuvenation through Joy" an obsession with the idea of the primitive, which is closely allied with "rhythm" as it is expressed musically, leads to misunderstanding and a willful disregard of the range and diversity within African American culture.

It is particularly interesting that blues, rather than jazz, is the centerpiece of this story. It is also worth noting that the story's protagonist is a woman and that the conflict over the music is enacted between two female characters. The blues are intertwined in the jazz debate since in the 20s, artists such as Bessie Smith were enjoying major popular success including the sale of millions of records, known at the time as "race records." The blues, however, also have a history that is distinct from jazz because they are often thought to be more closely connected to African aesthetic traditions. Hughes's comments regarding Mason in his autobiography and "The Blues I'm Playing" both indicate that, although the residual cultural traces of Africa in blues (and African American culture more generally) are significant, they have been transformed consciously to create something new, American, and absolutely modern. In this sense, one of the important uses of music in Hughes's writing is to symbolize the impact of African American culture on modernizing the American mainstream.[7]

Like Roy Williams in "Home," Oceola Jones, a pianist, excels in the European classical and the African American blues/jazz traditions. This range of knowledge and talent contributes to her exceptional musicianship, but it is precisely this range that her patron, Mrs. Dora Ellsworth, wants to constrain so that Oceola's style will mesh with Ellsworth's own aesthetic preference for classical only. Oceola resists, however, because she knows that to give in to Mrs. Ellsworth would be to reduce her the range and to homogenize the diverse elements of her identity. In this story, as in "Home" and "Rejuvenation through Joy," musical styles are closely allied with a more general conception of range–emotional, intellectual, and aesthetic or artistic range–all of which are diminished by racial stereotypes and whites' misunderstanding of black culture. In each of these three stories, although the white characters are fascinated with black culture, they fail to interpret effectively enough to understand it, and they fail to interpret effectively because they rely on racial stereotypes passed off as aesthetic value judgements.

In "The Blues I'm Playing," Oceola Jones embraces the full intellectual, emotional, and artistic range of life as essential to living to the fullest. She works hard, devotes herself to her music, and loves Pete Williams without hierarchically ranking any of these activities. Oceola has never had a patron until she meets Mrs. Ellsworth, and "[j]ust to be give things for *art's sake* seemed suspicious to Oceola" (103). She perceives art as another integral facet of the full range of existence, not to be overshadowed or diminished by the other aspects of life, but neither to be given complete ascendancy.

The story clearly indicates that Mrs. Ellsworth sees things differently. She lives a rather stunted and narrow life, despite her wealth and apparent sophistication, and she closes off herself to the range of experience that Oceola demands. One of the strengths of the story is Hughes's avoidance of caricature in his portrayal of Mrs. Ellsworth through the use of details that offer subtle clues about her motives for wanting to control Oceola. As a widow with no children, Mrs. Ellsworth seems quite alone and focuses all of her energy on her love of art and her interest in young artists. Unfortunately, these two passions become intertwined and confused in her patronage: "She was very rich, and it gave her pleasure to share her richness with beauty. Except that she was sometimes confused as to where beauty lay–in the youngsters or in what they made, in the creators or the creation" (99). This significant detail about Mrs.

Ellsworth's character is provided early in the story and establishes the idea that her abilities as a critic are limited. Consequently, at the end of the story, when she attempts to control Oceola's life under the pretense of guiding her "art," the fallacy of Mrs. Ellsworth's role as a patron of the arts is clearly revealed. Rather than supporting the arts, she places herself in a maternal role in relation to the artists. According to the terms by which this "mothering" is offered to Oceola, in order to accept Mrs. Ellsworth's support, Oceola would have to become a "white" daughter who wholly renounces her connections to African American culture. In this sense, if she gives in to Mrs. Ellsworth's offers of material remuneration in exchange for total control, Oceola would have to deny her own identity.

The jazz controversy comes into play in this story through the arguments over aesthetic value between Oceola and Mrs. Ellsworth that are really arguments over Oceola's right to embrace the African American components of her cultural identity. Mrs. Ellsworth is fascinated by Oceola's "blackness," but she also seems to want to make her culturally "white." The role of the music critic is interesting in relation to this debate, just as various music critics played a significant part in the larger public debate over jazz. In "The Blues I'm Playing," Hughes has the music critic, named Ormond Hunter, introduce Oceola to Mrs. Ellsworth. The name Hunter implies his predatory role, and Ormond calls to mind the malevolent art collector from Henry James's *Portrait of a Lady*. Like Mrs. Ellsworth, Ormond believes that Oceola should reside in a "a more artistic atmosphere" (108) for the sake of art.

Mrs. Ellsworth convinces Oceola to move downtown from Harlem to Greenwich Village and gives Oceola money so she no longer has to work, but she cannot convince Oceola to abandon jazz:

> ...she still loved to play for Harlem house parties–for nothing–now that she no longer needed the money, out of sheer love of jazz. This rather disturbed Mrs. Ellsworth, who still believed in art of the old school, portraits that really and truly looked like people, poems about nature, music that had soul in it, not syncopation. And she felt the dignity of art...She wished she could lift Oceola up bodily and take her away from all that, for art's sake...Mrs. Ellsworth really began to hate jazz–especially on a grand piano. (110-111)

Clearly, Mrs. Ellsworth's objections to jazz are rooted in ethnocentrism rather than the objective assessment of artistic merit, and her critique of the music mirrors the public debate over the merits and the dangers of jazz. Interestingly, she especially hates jazz on a grand piano and wonders if it is "in keeping with genius" for Oceola to play jazz for "a studio full of white and colored people every Saturday night" (110). These details imply that, as in the public jazz controversy, the idea of racial "mixing" associated with the music was particularly troubling to many critics of jazz.[8] The grand piano–a symbol of European high culture–producing the sounds of African American culture for a mixed audience evokes Mrs. Ellsworth's greatest ire.

Oceola's attitude toward debates over the aesthetic value of various styles of music is expressed in the following passage:

> Why did they [international students whom she meets in Paris] or anybody argue so much about life or art? Oceola merely lived–and loved it. Only the Marxian students seemed sound to her for they, at least, wanted people to have enough to eat. That was important, Oceola thought, remembering, as she did, her own sometimes hungry years. But the rest of the controversies, as far as she could fathom, were based on air. (112)

Unlike Mrs. Ellsworth, Oceola has a pragmatic attitude toward music and its place in life. Extending an idea explored in "Home," Oceola also gives her opinion on the idea that art can combat social injustice: "And as for the cultured Negroes who were always saying art would break down color lines, art could save the race and prevent lynchings! 'Bunk!' said Oceola" (113). Oceola is purely unpretentious and unashamed in everything she does, and these characteristics make her one of Hughes's consummate folk heroes. These qualities extend to her music: "In her playing of Negro folk music, Oceola never doctored it up, or filled it full of classical runs, or fancy falsities. In the blues she made the bass notes throb like tom-toms, the trebles cry like little flutes, so deep in the earth and so high in the sky that they understood everything" (113). This passage highlights the cultural specificity and the universality of Oceola's approach to music; she achieves the universal through the specific. She also derives equal pleasure from her performance of classical and blues (113-114) and does not feel compelled to hierarchically rank the two styles. In this sense, "The Blues I'm Playing" can be interpreted as a commentary on and an enactment of Hughes's own artistic theories, which also finds clear expression in his famous essay "The Negro Artist and the Racial Mountain."

In the final section of the story, Oceola unsuccessfully attempts to teach an unreceptive Mrs. Ellsworth about the music. Oceola performs the connection between jazz and blues–illustrating the range of African American musical traditions as she explores the range of the keyboard:

> And her fingers began to wander slowly up and down the keyboard, flowing into the soft and lazy syncopation of a Negro blues, a blues that deepened and grew into rollicking jazz, then into an earth-throbbing rhythm that shook the lilies in the Persian vases of Mrs. Ellsworth's music room….the flood of wild syncopation filled the house, then sank into the slow and singing blues with which it had begun. (122)

Physically, the music is moving–it "wander[s]," and "rollick[s]," and makes the earth throb and the lilies shake–and it even escapes the confines of the "music room" to fill the entire house with the "flood" of its rhythms. Who could resist it? It not only moves itself but also moves physical objects in its midst. Mrs. Ellsworth cannot hear its implications, but Oceola tries to explain:

> 'This is mine ... Listen! ... How sad and gay it is. Blue and happy–laughing and crying ... How white like you and black like me. ... How much like a man. ... And how like a woman...'. (122)

Above all else, Oceola attempts through both performance and explanation to help Mrs. Ellsworth understand the range of the music and the way that it can accommodate contradictions without reducing them to binary oppositions. Categories of emotion, race, and gender are blurred in the music and seem to exist on a continuum rather than as dichotomies. Although Mrs. Ellsworth ultimately fails to comprehend Oceola's music lesson, Oceola is triumphant in her refusal to renounce her aesthetic priorities which are inseparable from her desire to live according the full range of her own identity. The story implies that a struggle over ownership and artistic authority is not just a debate over artistic value, it is, more importantly, a struggle to define oneself in one's own terms.

CONCLUSION

In "Home," "Rejuvenation through Joy," and "The Blues I'm Playing," Hughes uses musical tropes to explore the range of African American vernacular culture and to comment upon the idea of aesthetic categories of value. Music is not presented as a cure to all social evil. On the contrary, the events of "Home" clearly indicate that seeing music (or artistic achievement more generally) as a panacea has potentially deadly consequences. In each of the stories, music appears to have the capacity to cross social boundaries and to highlight the social construction of racial categories, but it does not necessarily eradicate injustice and inequality. In these stories, Hughes is realistic about the limitations of music in evoking social change, but he is nonetheless aware of the music's tremendous power, and the stories–especially "The Blues I'm Playing"–convey that passion for the music and its power to move audiences. Hughes vividly describes the effect of music in his 1940 autobiography *The Big Sea*:

> Like the waves of the sea coming one after another, always one after another, like the earth moving around the sun, night, day–night, day–night, day–forever, so is the undertow of black music with its rhythm that never betrays you, its strength like the beat of the human heart, its humor, and its rooted power. (209)

Here music is both culturally specific ("black music") and universal; it resembles a force of nature in its timelessness. Hughes uses the same metaphor for music and for writing, as the title of the book and its last sentences indicate: "Literature is a big sea full of many fish. I let down my nets and pulled. I'm still pulling" (335). The imagery of sea and waves indicates the inextricable connection that Hughes perceived between literature and music.[9] This connection informed almost all of his writing, and an analysis of the musical tropes in the stories from *The Ways of White Folks* reveals that music enabled Hughes to explore the idea of range–musical range as an artistic expression of human range.

CHAPTER FOUR

"Only in the head of a musician"
The Powers of Music in Toni Morrison's *Jazz*

Toni Morrison emerges from a literary tradition that is inexhaustibly rich in its manipulations of musical sources, and yet, even within this tradition, Morrison stands out as a writer whose provocative explorations of the powers of music record its finest nuances and reveal the complex contradictions that it contains. A passage from Morrison's first novel, *The Bluest Eye*, contains hints of the intertwined musical tropes in Morrison's most intricate and expansive approach to music, her novel *Jazz*. In this passage from *The Bluest Eye*, Morrison's narrator describes the capacity of music to order the fragmentation and randomness of personal and collective experience. The narrator suggests that the music offers an alternative approach to one's individual past and to history by providing a kind of coherence that still allows for contradictions and unresolved conflict. Within this coherence, order or form is not based upon binary logic but instead demands space for improvisational unpredictability and the diverse voices that comprise the group. According to the narrator's assessment, music can express experience in its fullest range, and "*only* in the head of a musician" (125, emphasis added) can Cholly Breedlove's life and the sources of his motives adequately obtain their form and substance.

Just before the narrator renders the haunting scene involving Cholly's rape of his daughter Pecola, we are told that words are not enough to achieve a complete understanding of a human life and that music orders personal memory and collective history in a different way than narrative does:

> The pieces of Cholly's life could become coherent only in the head of a musician. Only those who talk their talk through the gold of curved metal,

or in the touch of black-and-white rectangles and taut skins and strings echoing from wooden corridors, could give true form to his life. Only they would know how to connect the heart of a red watermelon to the asafetida bag to the muscadine to the flashlight on his behind to the fists of money to the lemonade in a Mason jar to a man called Blue and come up with what all of that meant in joy, in pain, in anger, in love, and give it its final and pervading ache of freedom. Only a musician would sense, know, without even knowing that he knew, that Cholly was free. Dangerously free. (125)

The suggestion that any treatment of one of her characters is best left to the "head of a musician" is a surprising statement from an apparently omniscient narrator of a novel. A closer look at this passage, however, reveals how Morrison, even in her early writing, taps into musical thinking in order to bring this perspective to her writing. In *Jazz*, she thoroughly infuses her narrator's voice with the improvisational, risky aspects of the music.[1] Written words may never be able to "talk their talk" the same way music does, but Morrison can utilize some of music's alternative approaches to the task of giving form to chaos—a task that plagues a writer as well as a musician.

One of the most striking aspects of this passage is its use of physical descriptions, rather than customary names, for musical instruments that characteristically comprise a jazz ensemble. The horns (saxophones, trumpet, trombone), piano, drums, bass (or guitar or even banjo in early jazz) all appear here as physical, tangible entities rather than as referential names. These instruments tell stories, or "talk their talk," as jazz is often described in storytelling terms.[2] The passage also suggests that the musicians to which it refers understand freedom in complex terms, just as jazz, its social implications and cultural context, and its improvisational essence are often associated with freedom. As composer and pianist Edward "Duke" Ellington representatively describes it by signifying on the First Amendment of the Constitution, the essence of jazz is freedom. According to Ellington:

> Just as the classic form represents strict adherence to a structural standard, just as romantic music represents a rebellion against fixed forms in favor of more personal utterance, so jazz continues the pattern of barrier-breaking and emerges as the freest musical expression we have yet seen. To me, then, jazz means simply the freedom of musical speech! And it is precisely because of this freedom that so many varied forms of jazz exist ... not one of these forms represents jazz by itself ... Jazz means simply the freedom to have many forms. (256-57)

Just as the instruments' conventional names are absent from *The Bluest Eye* passage, however, so is the word "jazz," even though Morrison's representation of the music and musicians clearly evokes the jazz tradition. Morrison establishes jazz in this passage as a form of expression that is at once abstract and absolutely tangible. Similarly, in his definition of the music, Ellington blurs binary distinctions between freedom and form by suggesting that the two can be complimentary when the nature of the musical expression is open enough to allow for multiplicity.

Morrison's *Jazz* attributes a range of impressive powers to the music that furnishes the novel's title, and this chapter will explore the implications of the musical tropes in *Jazz*. The word "jazz" appears nowhere in the novel except in its title, and the representation of music throughout the narrative suggests that Morrison explores not just the "jazz" of the 1920s that pervades the novel's setting but also synecdochically alludes to the whole history of African American music.[3] *Jazz* explores five central powers of the music, all of which are alluded to in the previously discussed passage from *The Bluest Eye*. Each section of this chapter will explore one of the five musical powers in *Jazz*.

Section one considers the relationship between music and an alternative approach to historical inquiry and documentation. Section two examines the representation of music as a mode of expression that gives form to chaos without resorting to binary simplifications of contradictions. Here the music embodies an alternative way of knowing and framing a response to the world one inhabits. Section three provides a brief overview of representations of music in Harlem Renaissance writing and considers how *Jazz* builds upon this foundation and participates in the terms of its debate about the implications of the music and the ways that the music defines modernism. Section four analyzes the ways that music mediates between silence and expression in the novel and manipulates its listeners' in both positive and negative ways. Section five considers how the four previous portrayals of the powers of the music are combined to express, near the end of the novel, the capacity of the music to engender individual and communal healing.

HISTORY, MUSIC, AND THE "SILENT PARADE"

On a sweltering day in July of 1917, thousands of Harlem residents marched down Fifth Avenue in what was described as New York's "Silent Parade." Dressed in the formal fashions of the day, these men and women marched in protest of the East St. Louis riot. On July 2, 1917, in East St. Louis, white mobs had attacked black residents, beating and killing people and burning over $300,000 worth of property. Events leading up to these attacks clearly prophesied their occurrence, and black civic leaders had appealed to the mayor to intercede in order to prevent escalating violence against black citizens. All of the warning signs went unheeded, however, and St. Louis's black community received no legal protection from white attacks until National Guard militia companies finally arrived on the evening of July 2, 1917.[4]

Shortly after these events, Harlem's civic leagues and churches organized their city's silent parade. As a photograph of the parade shows, two men near the front of the group carried a huge banner on which words from the Declaration of Independence were printed: "We hold these truths to be self-evident, that all men are created equal...." Underneath these well-known promises of American freedom, celebrated every 4th of July, was a message to disregard these fundamental and inalienable American civil liberties, if one were of African descent.[5] At the same moment, African American soldiers were preparing to go to Europe to fight for their country and for the cause of democracy as the United States entered World War I. The silent parade dramatized the absurdity of denying people their full rights of citizenship at home while requiring them to make the ultimate sacrifice for their nation in warfare.[6] In addition to the banner, some marchers carried protest signs, but no one sang or shouted slogans or protest chants. The muffled drums provided the only sound as thousands of black New Yorkers marched, and thousands of white New Yorkers observed them from the sidewalks and from the windows of the buildings above the street.

Sociologist Elliott Rudwick, in his book length study of the East St. Louis riot, describes the silent parade by focusing on its overarching political agenda and its public demands for justice. According to Rudwick:

> The N.A.A.C.P. and other Negro organizations tried to exert pressure on [President Woodrow] Wilson by sponsoring a "Silent Parade" in New York and other cities. The marchers sought to use the East St. Louis riot to arouse the public conscience and gain support for federal legislation or a Constitutional amendment outlawing lynching and other forms of mob violence. On New York's Fifth Avenue, thousands marched to the beat of muffled drums draped with black handkerchiefs, petitioning for action on their grievances. *The placards and banners told their story:* "We Are Maligned As Lazy And Murdered When We Work"; "We Have Fought For The Liberty Of White Americans In 6 Wars, Our Reward Is East St. Louis"; "Pray For The Lady Macbeths Of East St. Louis." (134-35, emphasis added)

Morrison's *Jazz* develops the story of the East St. Louis riot and the silent parade down Fifth Avenue that followed its violent events. The novel clearly implies that the "placards and banners" did *not* adequately tell the community's story, and that the task of telling the story viscerally and complexly enough demands an artist's voice and vision, not in place of, but in addition to sociologists' and historians' research and analysis. Through vivid characterization, symbolic language, and an innovative narrative voice and structure, Morrison presents history in *Jazz* with a kind of human immediacy that makes it clear how powerfully the past always shapes the world we inhabit in the present. The entire tradition of African American music frequently serves as her model for the representation of the individual's relationship to history and community, as the novel's depiction of the "Silent Parade" illustrates.

In *Jazz*, history often finds individualized and communal resonance through musical expression. Alice Manfred attends the "Silent Parade" with her niece Dorcas, who was orphaned and left in her aunt's care after her parents were murdered in the East St. Louis riot. Morrison's narrator offers this account of the parade, which portrays the unifying, expressive power of the drums:

> In typical summer weather, sticky and bright, Alice Manfred stood for three hours on Fifth Avenue marveling at the cold black faces and listening to drums saying what the graceful women and marching men could not. What was possible to say was already in print on a banner that repeated a couple of promises from the Declaration of Independence and waved over the head of its bearer. *But what was meant came from the drums.* It was July in 1917 and the beautiful faces were cold and quiet; moving slowly into the space the drums were building for them. (53, emphasis added)

In this passage, as oppposed to Rudwick's sociological reading of the event, the drums assume the central importance, and the words of the banner fade to the background. While Rudwick asserts that "the placards and banners told [the marchers'] story," in Morrison's portrait of the parade, the drums tell the story. The drums express something that neither an academic analysis nor a banner can articulate. The novel suggests that one of the "spaces" that the drums have built is the space for a novelist such as Morrison to enter and seek powerful language that can tell "what was *meant*."[7]

The image of the drums in *Jazz* calls to mind Eric Sundquist's analysis of the fluidity of generic boundaries in African cultural traditions and the relationship of this fluidity to African American aesthetic priorities. According to Sundquist:

> The establishment of an African American cultural poetics had to demonstrate the continued presence in America of an African culture where speech and song more closely approached each other on the continuum of cultural sound, where the vocalized "talk" of drums and rhythmic instruments was paramount and where *nommo*, the power of the word in its oral dimension, governed human interaction to a far greater degree than in the Western tradition. (385)

Morrison's use of musical tropes to communicate unofficial narratives in a print medium contributes to the continued development of this African American cultural poetics. In *Jazz*, the drums and the whole tradition of African American music become metaphors that mediate between silence and a written, novelistic (i.e., artistic) rendition of historical events.

The "Silent Parade" in New York and the violent attacks on African American residents in East St. Louis that preceded it provide crucial aspects of the historical and cultural context for the music in *Jazz*, which is set in 1926. Morrison's writing uncovers silences and gaps in the official history of events and uses these spaces to create the stories that have remained officially unrecorded or inadequately written. The silence of the parade–broken only by the sound of the drums building spaces–symbolizes Morrison's literary approach to music.

Robert Cataliotti observes in his study of the vital role of music in African American fiction, "As with almost every aspect of black culture in America, the African American literary tradition, from its inception, has felt the influence of the culture's music" (ix). In his highly influential book, *The Signifying Monkey*, Henry Louis Gates, Jr. offers a paradigm for tropological revision in African American literature that places African American musical practice and its improvisational and participatory (i.e., "call and response") aesthetics at the center of the literary tradition.[8] Gates writes:

> Improvisation, of course, so fundamental to the very idea of jazz, is "nothing more" than repetition and revision. In this sort of revision, again where meaning is fixed, it is the realignment of the signifier that is the signal trait of expressive genius. The more mundane the fixed text ("April in Paris" by Charlie Parker, "My Favorite Things" by John Coltrane), the more dramatic is the Signifyin(g) revision. It is this principle of repetition and difference, this practice of intertextuality, which has been so crucial to the black vernacular forms of Signifyin(g), jazz–and even its antecedents, the blues, the spirituals, and ragtime–and which is the source of my trope for black intertextuality in the Afro-American formal literary tradition. (63-64)

As Gates, Cataliotti, and other critics and theorists have clearly demonstrated, music has been central to the African American literary tradition from the beginning.[9] Particular musical aesthetics and specific uses of music remain central to that tradition's distinctiveness.[10] Toni Morrison's use of music is certainly grounded in African American literary and musical traditions, and according to Gates's explanation of signification, in order to achieve "expressive genius" her work must disrupt fixed meanings by employing "repetition and difference." Morrison's literary use of music is, in itself, "repetition" because it draws on the established importance of music in African American fiction. Her exploration of the music, particularly, but not exclusively, in *Jazz* signals "difference" because she extends some themes and recreates others in her use of the music.

In her study of Morrison's approach to historical documentation in *Jazz*, Nancy Peterson examines the ways that Morrison uses the mode of fiction to reconstruct African American history in an improvisational style that is similar to that employed by jazz musicians. Peterson argues that jazz, as an improvisational musical form based on the blues and "as a genre [that] revisits its own past melody to claim what is useful and make possible further development" is "the model for [Morrison's] historical reconstructive project" (210). An extended analysis of specific musical tropes in *Jazz* reveals the ways that music in the novel acts as a particularly expressive carrier of individual experience and cultural history that has redemptive powers on individual and communal levels.

The nonlinear form of *Jazz* begins with what appears to be the end of the characters' stories, but as we move around freely in the narrative's depiction of time, the "Silent Parade" becomes one of the many events that shapes the implications of the characters' stories and alters our responses to them. Dorcas, who as an eighteen-year-old becomes Joe Trace's mistress, as a nine-year-old comes to live with her Aunt Alice Manfred in Harlem ("the City"), and they attend the "Silent Parade." The austere drums of the parade get mixed up in Alice's mind with the "lowdown" music that she thinks she despises and that she tries to keep from Dorcas. The shifting, nonlinear narrative structure illustrates the relationship between the drums and the *other* music. As these connections are revealed, the novel suggests that both forms of the music–the "austere" and the "lowdown"–are necessary components of a coherent whole. Together they express the complexity and contradictions of African American history and enable individuals to cultivate knowledge of the past without becoming mired in it or immobilized by it.[11]

The music provides a particularly effective model for an approach to history in part because it bridges the space between binary oppositions. As Frederick Garber observes in his study of representations of jazz in films:

> jazz privileges the solo performance in its radical momentariness, making it, by definition, anti-historical; but jazz is not solely immediate because it also owns a richly textured intertextual life, a life that, by any definition, finds itself at every point immersed in history. Much of what happens in jazz, much of its excitement, emerges out of the interplay of these contradictory elements, their tensions and countering struggles, the productivity of their quarrels. (92)

According to Garber's description, in jazz neither history nor the present is privileged in a hierarchical fashion. In this sense, the aesthetic priorities of jazz have something in common with T. S. Eliot's perspective on the modernist artist's relationship to history as it is articulated in his essay "Tradition and the Individual Talent." Although the material specificities of the artists' experiences differ dramatically, Ralph Ellison observes an aspect of the modernist approach to historical revision shared by Eliot and jazz innovator Louis Armstrong. Ellison writes, "Consider that at least as early as T. S. Eliot's creation of a new aesthetic for poetry through the artful juxtaposition of earlier styles, Louis Armstrong, way down the river in New Orleans, was working out a similar technique for jazz" (225). The aesthetics of the music are inseparable from the concept of historical revision. A significant difference, however, is that while Eliot promoted art for a cultural elite, Armstrong generated music "by the people, for the people." As trumpeter and Jazz at Lincoln Center director Wynton Marsalis describes it, "Louis Armstrong's trumpet speaks to the possibilities available to the individual in a democracy" (qtd. in Peretti, 1). Taken together, the aesthetics and social implications of the music offer a functional model for individual and communal approaches to the struggles and triumphs of daily life. This difference is part of the distinctiveness of the music that Morrison portrays in her writing. The music, as *Jazz* suggests, embodies and creates modernism as it is *lived*.[12]

Jazz revisits the temporal setting of modernism and revises its implications. The nonlinear structure of the novel parallels the music's approach to historical revision. The narrator reveals the whole "plot" in the first few pages.[13] Joe Trace falls for eighteen-year-old Dorcas with "one of those deepdown, spooky loves" (3) that leads him to shoot her. At Dorcas's funeral, Joe's wife Violet cuts her rival's dead face, gets thrown out of the church, and then runs home. At home Violet opens the window and releases all of the pet birds that she and Joe have nurtured, leaving them to "freeze or fly" (3). Later, Joe mopes in despondency and despair while Violet attempts to find out everything she can about Dorcas. Then Violet sees Dorcas's friend Felice coming toward their apartment "with an Okeh record under her arm and carrying some stewmeat wrapped in butcher paper" (6), and, according to the narrator, the cycle inevitably will begin again. What surprises the narrator in the end is that it doesn't.

We abruptly enter the world of these characters, and then we are taken back into their pasts in order to make sense of all of the information the narrator offers in the beginning. The beginning of *Jazz* suggests that nothing makes sense without a knowledge of the past and how it shapes our individual and collective experiences in the present. Even then, knowledge of the past does not allow one to predict the future, as the narrator learns when her prophecies prove wrong. The improvisational aspects of life–mirrored and influenced by the same qualities in the music–make facile determinism (history repeats itself) and ahistorical randomness ("History is over, you all, and everything's ahead at last" (*Jazz*, 7)) equally impossible. The narrative structure of *Jazz* illustrates that the past and present are inextricably intertwined in a way that still opens improvisational spaces for individual free will. The stories of Joe, Violet, and Dorcas are confusing and unfathomable without knowledge of the stories that comprise their past experiences. The same holds true for the music that is so central to the novel. The music, divorced from its cultural and historical context, cannot be properly and effectively interpreted. In the end, however, the narrator realizes that we must still leave space for "something rogue"(228)–the unexpected, the improvisational–to make sense of the complexly overlapping stories.

MUSIC DISRUPTS BINARY OPPOSITIONS

The "Silent Parade" figures prominently in the story Jazz tells about music that expresses "a complicated anger" (59) because the "meaning" of the parade's drums and the emotions they express over the events in East St. Louis are inseparable from the other kinds of music that pervade Harlem in 1926. Despite the summer heat, Alice bolts her windows against the music played by "the men in shirtsleeves [who] propped themselves in window frames, or clustered on rooftops, in alleyways, on stoops and in the apartments of relatives playing the lowdown stuff that signaled Imminent Demise" (56). Even so, Alice realizes that "the lowdown music (and in Illinois it was worse than here) had something to do with the silent black men and women marching down Fifth Avenue..." (57). Alice imagines that the music is responsible for all of the chaos she witnesses in the world, including the violence in East St. Louis. She thinks: "It was the music. The dirty, get-on-down music the women sang and the men played and both danced to, close and shameless or apart and wild ... It made you do unwise disorderly things. Just hearing it was like violating the law" (38). The music symbolizes a kind of rebellion that frightens the staid Alice. It not only expresses an uninhibited sensuality; it also mocks "the law" in general. The music defies artificial constraints that Alice believes give order to existence.

The drums of the march, however, shore up Alice against the obstacles she must face. She wants the drums to connect every fragmented thought and fear in her mind and save her from the abyss of meaninglessness. She seeks something to close the gap between theory and practice—between politics and personal experience. At the parade, she reads the "explanatory leaflets ... [that] the Colored Boy Scouts pass[ed] out ... to whitemen in straw hats who needed to know what the freezing faces already knew" (58). Then she looks at Dorcas, the child she will have to raise in this world. At that moment, the drums seem to offer the solace of fellowship: "Then suddenly, like a rope cast for rescue, the drums spanned the distance, gathering them all up and connecting them: Alice, Dorcas, her sister and brother-in-law, the Boy Scouts and the frozen black faces, the watchers on the pavements and those in the windows above" (58). Alice is satisfied at that moment with her interpretation of the drums and the "rescue" that they offer, but this sturdy "rope" begins to seem unreliable "when the men sat on the windowsills fingering horns, and the women wondered 'how long.' The rope broke then, disturbing her peace, making her aware of flesh and something so free she could smell its bloodsmell..." (58).

The "lowdown" music expresses the grittier, more physical side of life with all of its attendant pains and pleasures. Alice tries to dichotomize these two sides of life, but the music will not allow for binary oppositions. The conservative press and preachers who condemn the "lowdown stuff" assure Alice that it is terrible but ultimately transitory and marginal. The narrator informs us that Alice "knew from the sermons and editorials that it wasn't real music—just colored folks' stuff; harmful, certainly; embarrassing, of course; but not real, not serious" (59). Here the novel directly enters the 1920's jazz controversy and the critical debate over the "meaning" of the Harlem Renaissance. *Jazz* offers an alternative approach to these histories by highlighting the ambiguous spaces in the African American community between "bourgeois conservatives" or the "Old Guard" and the "New Negroes." Joe would be classified chronologically with the older generation, but when he narrates his own story, he tells of all the times he has changed and the choices he has made and proclaims, "You could say I've been a new Negro all of my life" (129). Alice, too, is part of both the new and the old. She understands what lies beneath the surface of the music, even if her ingrained attitudes about propriety lead her to dismiss the music's implications. Just as she secretly admires the "ready-for-bed-in-the-street" (55) fashions of the young women who confidently stroll along Seventh Avenue, her private feelings about the music are ambivalent.

Alice may shut her windows to keep the music out, but not because she is a foolish, prudish woman who succumbs to "white" standards of value. She fears something in the music that "faked happiness, faked welcome" (59). She astutely hears "a complicated anger in it; something that disguised itself as flourish and roaring seduction" (59). "Trombone Blues," the only direct musical allusion in the entire novel (21), is a perfect example of this music. It is an early (1925) Duke Ellington recording with his band the Washingtonians. The instrumental piece is played at a frenzied tempo marked by the tinny banjo sound of early jazz, with none of the earthy assurance of the blues that the title implies.[14]

Alice is afraid to confront the anger that both she and the music seem to conceal. This raucous and "happy" music "made her hold her hand in the pocket of her apron to keep from smashing it through the glass pane to snatch the world in her fist and squeeze the life out of it for doing what it did and did and did to her and everybody else she knew or cared about" (59). The racist violence against the black community in East St. Louis was certainly not an isolated incident in the early twentieth century, but a prevalent phenomenon predicated upon the lingering historical consequences of slavery. Alice hears anger about these injustices including the threat of retaliatory violence in the "lowdown" music; therefore, "It was impossible to keep the Fifth Avenue drums separate from the belt-buckle tunes vibrating from pianos and spinning on every Victrola. Impossible" (59).

As it turns out, it was also impossible for Alice to keep her niece Dorcas away from the "belt-buckle tunes." Dorcas, a generation younger and of a different, more reckless disposition than her aunt, wants the "lowdown" music to define her existence. She feels "tickled and happy knowing that there was no place to be where somewhere, close by, somebody was not licking his licorice stick, tickling the ivories, blowing off his horn while a knowing woman sang ain't nobody going to keep me down you got the right key baby but the wrong keyhole you got to bring it and put it right here, or else" (60). The pervasiveness of the music and its assertive, provocative blues lyrics comfort Dorcas, who thinks of playing the instruments in the metaphorical terms that emphasize the sensual pleasures of both producing and consuming the music. As teenagers sneaking out to a party, the music *leads* Dorcas and her friend Felice: "The two girlfriends climb the stairs, led straight to the right place more by the stride piano pouring over the door saddle than their recollection of the apartment number" (64).

While Alice resists the insistence of the music, Dorcas completely and joyously surrenders to it: "The drums [Dorcas] heard at the parade were only the first part, the first word of a command. For her the drums were not an all-embracing rope of fellowship, discipline and transcendence" (60). For Alice, the drums sound universal, while in the "lowdown" music there is something angry that distinctively speaks to the experience of being black in a segregated and violently racist society. Deep down, Alice knows the two cannot be separated–that the universal arises from the particular and that the public and the private overlap–but she tries to repress this knowledge as she strictly disciplines and diligently works "to privatize her niece" (67). The young and inexperienced Dorcas, however, just hears the sensual lure of the "lowdown stuff." Dorcas cannot resist " a City seeping music that begged and challenged every day. 'Come,' it said. 'Come and do wrong'" (67).

The characters not only grapple with the actual music that surrounds them, but also with the cultural associations with the music that arise from inside and outside of the community. In the 1920s, class and racial biases often shaped these associations. At this time, the term "jazz" characterized not only many types of music–all of which were considered diametrically opposed to "serious" (i.e., European-derived classical) music–but also any activity considered decadent and "new." In an interview, Morrison mentions that, in America, the term "jazz" is "always associated with something vulgar, which is part of its anarchy" (Carabi, 41). Alan Merriam observes in his anthropological study of music:

> The degree to which jazz served as a symbol of culturally defined evil in the United States, and in other countries as well, may seem incredible to us today, but it was a real fact in the 1920's and 1930's. It is an extremely clear illustration of how music, and in this case not individual sounds but an entire

body of sound, can be used symbolically on the level of affective ascribed cultural meaning. The very fact that views of this sort concerning jazz are not nearly so prevalent today illustrates as well how symbolism on the cultural level can be transferred to and from a particular music style over time. (244)

Merriam, whose study was published in 1964, cites rock 'n' roll as an example of contemporary music that is the object of cultural "fears and hostilities" (244), but now one could make a substantial case for this sociological process at work in relation to rap music.[15] Morrison has commented that the word jazz "has implications of sex, violence, and chaos all of which I wanted in the book" (Carabi, 41). Through her representation of the music in *Jazz*, Morrison suggests that the history of the music exemplifies the way that the past is always an active agent in shaping our present lives. The characters in *Jazz* must grapple with what the music means and what to make of the implications it carries with it.

The novel suggests that the public music of the drums on parade is bound up with the private music that is produced by, for, and within the community. Alice is troubled by the music's refusal to dichotomize public and private. Dorcas, however, seems to hear only the "greedy, reckless words" (60) of the music; she hears the "flourish and roaring seduction" (59), rather than the "complicated anger"(59). The novel suggests that selecting one component over the other–the earthy over the spiritual or the sensuality over the anger– detracts from the music's wholeness and its refusal to dichotomize or hierarchically rank its elements. Naïve and youthful, Dorcas wants only its decadent sensuality, while Alice, frightened of explosive anger and retaliatory violence, wants only its promise of fellowship and spiritual transcendence, but the novel implies that they are both mistaken in their impulse to compartmentalize its full range. Perhaps their failure to fully hear the music accounts for its capacity to control them in convulsive, rather than nourishing, ways. This inability to hear (an interpretational error) may also account for the narrator's assertion that Alice "had chosen surrender and made Dorcas her own prisoner of war" (77).

Alice remains convinced that "lowdown" music leads people down the path to destruction and that it dominates their wills. She wonders to herself, "And where there was violence wasn't there also vice? Gambling. Cursing. A terrible and nasty closeness. Red dresses. Yellow shoes. And, of course, race music to urge them on" (79). Of course, the kind of "vice" that Alice describes here does not account for the events in East St. Louis or countless other acts of legally sanctioned violence against African Americans within the historical context of the novel's setting. In its portrayal of Alice's response to the music, the novel suggests that she deliberately mixes up issues of cause and effect in order to defend herself against what she chooses not to admit. She learns the consequences of refusing to confront the truth after her niece is killed. Ironically, Violet / "Violent," who (like the truth) Alice does not want to admit into her home, leads her to a deeper understanding of her own violent anger. Alice gradually becomes aware that when "Violet came to visit (and Alice never knew when that might be) something opened up" (83). Through their surprising friendship, Alice and Violet both move toward confronting their own intense anger, in part through the laughter that they discover is "[m]ore complicated, more serious than tears" (113). Through their brutally honest conversations, they move away from the binary oppositions that have limited their perceptions of themselves, others, the world.

Like Alice, the narrator also moves from limited perceptions to a more expansive way of knowing as the narrative progress. The narrator's shifting perceptions of the implications of the music mark her changes in understanding. At first, she attributes to the music a deterministic power to control even its most casual listeners' actions. She employs a musically related metaphor for the "inevitable" course of Joe's actions in his affair with Dorcas. The narrator proclaims, "Take my word for it, he is bound to the track. It pulls him like a needle through the groove of a Bluebird record. Round and round about the town. That's the way the City spins you" (120). The assertion "take my word for it" engenders doubt when it arises from a self-proclaimed "unreliable" (160) narrative voice. By the end of the novel, we discover that the narrator's predictions have proven wrong, and Joe is not "bound to the track." For most of the novel, however, the narrator attributes the same kind of manipulative and potentially destructive power to the music that Alice hears in it.

The narrator perpetuates this view of music when depicting Dorcas's behavior with Acton, the stylish young man who takes Joe's place as her lover. At the party where Dorcas dances with Acton, "the music bends, falls to its knees to embrace them all, encourage them to live a little, why don't you? Since this is the it you've been looking for?" (188). While they dance, Dorcas and Acton "agree on everything above the waist and below: muscle, tendon, bone joint and marrow cooperate. And if the dancers hesitate, have a moment of doubt, the music will solve and dissolve any question" (188). These sentences render the power of the music through sound as well as verbal imagery. The sentences sway and pause almost imperceptibly like the dancers, as if the feel of the music drives the words themselves.

For example, the placement of the near rhyme of "cooperate" and "hesitate" sets a forward moving rhythm for the two sentences, which is interrupted by the dependent clause "have a moment of doubt" that is also a repetition of "hesitate." Then the rhythm is gently pushed forward again by the round sound of "solve and dissolve," as well as by the words' sensual, surrendering implications. This example represents the novel's tendency not so much to verbally construct the music and its effect on its listeners but to subtly produce those effects for its own readers, who must be "listeners" too. The novel, especially on a first reading, can produce frustration if we approach it seeking resolution and certainties. We are confronted with a narrator who purports to be omniscient in the first sentence of the novel ("Sth, I *know*..."), but who, in the last paragraph, turns out to be malleable ("'make me, remake me'"). If we allow the texture of the language to "solve and dissolve" our desires for definitive answers that are rendered in binary terms, then we allow the music of the text to manipulate us in a positive way, and we can hear more of the range of its implications. If we approach *Jazz* and its narrator on these terms, then we agree to think like the musicians to whom the narrator refers in the previously discussed passage from *The Bluest Eye*.

Musical metaphors often appear in the novel to guide us away from a quest for absolutism dependent upon a dichotomized perspective. Dorcas's final sensations are predominantly musical ones, suggesting that music has ultimately defined her existence. As Dorcas lies bleeding from the gunshot wound that Joe inflicted upon her she thinks, "Somebody they have been waiting for is playing the piano. A woman is singing too. The music is faint but I know the words by heart" (193). She also sees a wooden bowl full of oranges on a table by the doorway, and this strikingly simple visual image is bound up with the sound of the song she *knows*: "So clear the dark bowl the pile of oranges. Just oranges. Bright. Listen. I don't know who is that woman singing but I know the words by heart" (193). Dorcas has become the "knowing woman" (60) who sings. We cannot really pass judgement on Dorcas on her deathbed; she is both/and, neither/nor victim and perpetrator of the crime.[16] Joe shot her, but Felice later asserts that Dorcas *chose* to die, "Dorcas let herself die" (204). The musical image that closes Dorcas's life indicates that she will keep all unreliable words and answers close to her heart and refuse to reveal them.

Dorcas, the little girl who "went to two funerals in five days, and never said a word" (57) after her parents were murdered, will, as a young woman, never say a word to disclose the identity of the man who shot her. Dorcas's "by heart" knowledge of the music suggests that she has access to a deeper way of knowing on the edge of death than she could ever approach during her life. It is as if all the fragmented pieces of her life at that moment coalesce in the music she knows in an intimate, self-sustaining way, or "by heart." She sees the oranges, the wooden bowl, and the table–the material simplicity of the world. She finally comprehends the significance of her relationship with Joe in images that suggest earthy physicality and emotional transcendence of her pain and loneliness. Dorcas tells her friend, "The world rocked from a stick beneath my hand, Felice. There in that room with the ice sign in the window" (193). All of these sensations are embodied for Dorcas in the music she knows "by heart"–music she has internalized for better and for worse.

HISTORY, MUSIC, AND THE HARLEM RENAISSANCE

In order to understand the tremendous powers attributed to the music in *Jazz*, it is useful to consider Morrison's representation of the music in relation to both fictional and nonfictional portraits of the music provided by Harlem Renaissance writers who explored the implications of jazz during the actual historical period in which Morrison's novel is set. An analysis of this earlier writing offers insights into Morrison's portrayal of the importance of African American music in defining modernism. A brief look at these works may help to clarify the approach to music *Jazz*. While it is far beyond the scope of this chapter to offer an overview of the Harlem Renaissance, several literary examples from this period illustrate how African American music was represented as a globally influential artistic form, a culturally distinctive and unifying creative achievement, and a uniquely powerful register and agent of social change. In every instance, the music is, for some listener(s), an absolutely irresistible force.

Langston Hughes's novel *Not Without Laughter* (1930) depicts the power of the music over its listeners in his chapter titled "Dance," where Benbow's band plays to the dancers' delight. The narrator ponders the life force—which includes death—embodied in the music: "The earth rolls relentlessly, and the sun blazes for ever on the earth, breeding, breeding. But why do you insist like the earth, music? Rolling and breeding, earth and sun for ever, relentlessly. But why do you insist like the sun? Like the lips of women? Like the bodies of men, relentlessly?" (101). This musical insistence acts as a physical, universal force emerging from a particular cultural context. In the novel, music and dancing epitomize material success and spiritual transcendence for the protagonist, Sandy, and he wants the achievement of both, rather than either/or. At the end of the novel, Sandy hears the physicality of Harriet's stellar blues performance and the spirituality of "the deep volume of sound roll[ing] through the open door" (299) of a side street Chicago church, and these sounds overlap in his mind. He grasps a line of continuity that runs through the whole tradition of African American music–the secular and the sacred– and this continuity sustains him in his personal quest because it is "vibrant and steady like a stream of living faith" (299).[17]

In Claude McKay's *Home to Harlem* (1928) the music holds an equally powerful sway over the characters. Jake cannot resist "the contagious fever of Harlem" (15), of which music is an essential part, because "all night long [there are] ragtime and 'blues' playing somewhere, ... singing somewhere, dancing somewhere! (15, ellipsis in original). In Hughes's and McKay's novels the music is clearly portrayed as a "primitive" force, and its very life force is attributed to this primitivism. In *Not Without Laughter*, Harriet, who becomes the "Princess of the Blues"–calling to mind Bessie Smith, "the Empress of the

Blues"–is described in her stage regalia as "barbaric, yet beautiful as a jungle princess" (293). In *Home to Harlem* the narrator describes blues, "Humming in harmony, barbaric harmony, joy-drunk, chasing out the shadow of the moment before" (54), and a jazz pianist plays "in a sort of savage ecstatic dream" (92) that musically evokes a "barbaric beauty" (94). These images of primitivism are reworked in *Jazz*, so that, just as the previous literary examples deconstruct the dichotomy between secular and sacred, *Jazz* blurs the binary distinction between "primitivism" and "civilization."

The cultural associations of primitivism with forms of vernacular expression–associations which prevailed in the 1920s particularly in relation to "race" music but also in conjunction with "hillbilly" music–are stripped down in *Jazz* and exposed as social constructions rather than inherent, "natural" characteristics.[18] The tensions and the inextricable connections between the "lowdown" music and the parade drums in *Jazz* exemplify how cultural associations shape individual and collective responses to the music. Dorcas feels irresistibly attracted to the "lowdown" music as a seductive force. Alice disdains the "lowdown" but hopes the parade drums will help her make sense of chaos and senseless violence. For Violet, the music represents and even motivates her husband's affair with the youthful Dorcas. Violet imagines Joe and Dorcas at a club called the Indigo where they listen to the music and one of Dorcas's hands holds "her glass shaped like a flower" while the other is "under the table drumming out the rhythm on the inside of his thigh, his thigh, his thigh, thigh, thigh..." (95). In Violet's imagination, the music embodies the passion shared by her husband and another woman who is young enough to be her daughter.

Joe knows that the music can manipulate a person's mind. When he follows Dorcas's trail, he goes immediately to the beauty shop where he hears guitar playing performed by "the blind twins" (131)–who are not really twins and one of whom is not really blind. The nature of their street music captures his attention because it is not their usual gospel style but a secular blues expression instead, which Joe refers to as "something sooty" (131). The churchwomen are captivated by the music, even though it deviates from the only music they publicly deem acceptable, gospel. Joe observes that "the women selling fish dinners [from Salem Baptist church] frowned and talked about their mother bad, but they never said a word to the twins and I knew they were having a good time listening because one of the loudest ones could hardly suck her teeth for patting her foot" (131). Joe does not disapprove of the music (or pretend to like the churchwomen) on moral grounds, but it conjures doubt in his mind, and he imagines Dorcas's infidelity. He decides that the music must be the source of his doubts: "I dismissed the evil in my thoughts because I wasn't sure the sooty music the blind twins were playing wasn't the cause. It can do that to you, a certain kind of guitar playing. Not like the clarinets, but close" (132).

Although each of the characters hears something different in the music, each of them attributes to the music tremendously influential powers to shape thought and behavior. This attitude, which ascribed such force to the music, was central to the jazz controversy in the 1920s. Whether commentators expressed negative or positive cultural associations with the music, they shared the belief that the music was irresistibly powerful.[19] As historian Lawrence Levine demonstrates in his study of the music, as jazz gained international recognition and popularity in the 1920s, it disrupted established notions about the meaning of "culture" in America. Levine writes:

> In their refusal to be governed by categorical orthodoxies that prevailed, in their unwillingness to make absolute distinctions between the vernacular and classical traditions, in their insistence that they were just attempting to play *music* and just wanted to be accepted as musicians, in their determination to utilize the *entire* Western tradition, as well as other cultural traditions, jazz musicians were revolutionizing not only music but also the concept of culture. (187)

According to Levine's account of the music, jazz epitomizes an alternative way of understanding "culture" as it is learned, reconfigured, and practiced in daily life. Perhaps this tendency of the music to redefine the meaning of "culture" is what made it seem so powerful in the 1920s.

Zora Neale Hurston, a Harlem Renaissance writer who studied with anthropologist Franz Boas, was very interested in the meaning of "culture." Her writing often explores the distinctively American cultural tensions between consent and descent, particularly as these tensions are negotiated in African American musical forms.[20] Like Hughes and McKay, Hurston sometimes depicts the music as a culturally specific kind of force of nature. In her novel, *Their Eyes Were Watching God* (1937), Hurston explores ways of knowing that are beyond verbalization and beyond human reason. The narrator of her novel describes Janie, the protagonist's, way of understanding in these terms, "there is a depth of thought untouched by words, and deeper still a gulf of formless feelings untouched by thought" (23). Music, in Hurston's novel, seems to tap into this alternative way of knowing. Close to the natural order of the world, music becomes metaphorically associated with Janie's emerging, adolescent awareness of her own sexuality. An irresistible power

> had called her to come gaze on a mystery. From barren brown stems to glistening leaf-buds; from the leaf-buds to snowy virginity of bloom. It stirred her tremendously. How? Why? It was like a flute song forgotten in another existence and remembered again. This singing she heard that had nothing to do with her ears. (10)

Here musical metaphors contain the eternal mysteries of life highlighted by a young woman's sexual awakening and the implied physicality central to that awakening.

Hurston's representation of Janie's emerging sexuality has interesting parallels with Morrison's portrayal of Dorcas. Musical metaphors, as we have seen, accentuate sensuality for Dorcas, and through their dancing, Dorcas and Acton ritualistically and publicly express their mutual desire. Joe, the betrayed older lover, discovers Dorcas and Acton dancing at a party, not secluded in private lovemaking. Joe shoots Dorcas while she dances, and her dying thoughts are of a song. The way music defines Dorcas's entire existence conveys its power. Hurston and Morrison both seem interested in the music as a transcendent *and* a material force.

Hurston's nonfiction directly explores a kind of physical power associated with the music. In her essay, "Characteristics of Negro Expression," Hurston disparages weak white imitations of the traditional blues emerging from the context of "the Jook." Performers who attempt to "purify" or "refine" the blues of the Jook only accomplish a diminishing "bleaching" of it. According to Hurston, "The Negro theater, as built up by the Negro, is based on Jook situations ... [and] Negro shows, before being tampered with did not specialize in octoroon chorus girls" (307). Hurston explains how a singer's expertise was initially determined based on a Jook frame of reference:

> The girl who could hoist a Jook song from her belly and lam it against the front door of the theater was the lead, even if she were as black as the hinges of hell. The question was "Can she jook?" She must have a good belly wobble, and her hips must, to quote a popular work song, "Shake like jelly all over and be so broad, Lawd, Lawd, and be so broad." ... [T]he bleached chorus is the result of a white demand and not the Negro's. (307)

According to Hurston's account, the commercialized "bleaching" of the music to cater to the demands of white audiences results in stripping from the music the physical power imparted to it by the singer who was strong, confident, and "as black as the hinges of hell."

Hurston's writing is invested in uncovering what is culturally distinctive about the music. In her essay "How It Feels to Be Colored Me," Hurston asserts, "At certain times I have no race, I am *me*" (154). When she goes to hear jazz with her white friend at The New World Caberet, however, she feels that "[her] color comes" (154). The music evokes a powerful and even a violent physical response at the same time that it suggests drowsy intoxication: "It constricts the thorax and splits the heart with its tempo and narcotic harmonies" (154). The music is described in primitive, animalistic terms that suggest "jungle" associations with an imagined Africa. Hurston's narrative persona responds jubilantly and seemingly uncontrollably to these associations, while her white friend, with his European derived sensibility, remains entirely detached and constrained. Hurston writes:

> This orchestra grows rambunctious, rears on its hind legs and attacks the tonal veil with primitive fury, rending it, clawing it until it breaks through to the jungle beyond. I follow those heathen–follow them exultingly. I dance wildly inside myself; I yell within, I whoop; I shake my assegai above my head ... I want to slaughter something–give pain, give death to what, I do not know. But the piece ends. The men of the orchestra wipe their lips and rest their fingers. I creep back slowly to the veneer we call civilization with the last tone and find the white friend sitting motionless in his seat, smoking calmly.
>
> "Good music they have here," he remarks...
>
> Music. The great globs of purple and red emotion have not touched him. He has only heard what I felt. He is far away and I see him but dimly across the ocean and the continent that have fallen between us. He is so pale with his whiteness then and I am so colored. (154)

Hurston's strikingly vivid description of her response to the music suggests that it expresses a vital aspect of her own sense of being "colored." She embraces what she hears as primitivism in the music as a crucial aspect of her identity that seems to be an African inheritance. At the same time, however, she can "have no race," or she can be "the eternal feminine with its string of beads" (155), or she can be "merely a fragment of the great Soul that surges within the boundaries" (155).

Ultimately, Hurston suggests that identity is bewilderingly overdetermined and that she feels like "a brown bag of miscellany propped against a wall" (155). In this guise she finds herself:

> Against a wall in company with other bags, white red and yellow. Pour out the contents, and there is discovered a jumble of small things priceless and worthless. A first-water diamond, and empty spool, bit of broken glass, lengths of string, a key to a door long since crumbled away, a rusty knife-blade, old shoes saved for a road that never was and never will be, a nail bent under the weight of things too heavy for any nail, a dried flower or two still a little fragrant. (155)

These strikingly ordinary and extraordinary images powerfully convey the fragmentation of identity, but in the music, Hurston imaginatively holds on to something tangible that juggles form and formlessness. The "primitivism" that she attributes to the music may be a conscious embrace of residual cultural practices transmitted from African ancestors that make African American culture distinctive and that provide Hurston with an artistically productive, personally and socially empowering sense of difference.

This passage from Hurston's essay calls to mind the passage from *The Bluest*

Eye that began this chapter. In Morrison's novel, "The pieces of Cholly's life could become coherent only in the head of a musician" because only a musician "would know how to connect the heart of a red watermelon to the asafetida bag to the muscadine to the flashlight on his behind to the fists of money to the lemonade in a Mason jar to a man called Blue…" (125). This passage has arresting similarities to (and differences from) Hurston's portrayal of the fragmented and overdetermined nature of identity.

In both passages, music offers a means to merge disparate, fractured experiences into a complete self. For Hurston, however, this complete self, as it is achieved through the music, is necessarily a "primitive" self. While in Morrison's imagery, the music provides access to a self that is "[d]angerously free" (125). This complete self is free to be primitive, civilized, or anything else in the entire range of human thought and action. In Cholly's case, this dangerous freedom includes the violation of one of the most widely held social taboos, incest. Morrison uses the music to convey the idea that for all people "freedom" is not a carefree, happy state of being but instead is a bewilderingly complex concept. Her writing suggests that the music does contain primitivism because it contains the full range of human experience and expression, and "primitivism" is always part of that range no matter how "civilized" a society might claim to be.

Like Hurston, other Renaissance commentators on the music also heard "primitivism" in it, but, unlike Hurston, they expected that "lower" element to be stripped away eventually in order to create new forms. J. A. Rogers wrote the official treatise on jazz for Alain Locke's epoch defining anthology, *The New Negro* (1925). In his essay, "Jazz at Home," Rogers describes jazz as having an "epidemic contagiousness" (216) that makes it appeal universally, adding that it has cultural specificity too because, "Like the measles … somebody had to have it first: that was the Negro" (216). Here Rogers takes up the metaphors of disease and epidemic that were popular with 1920's jazz opponents in the press and in the pulpit and turns these to his own rhetorical advantage.[21] No one, according to Rogers, can resist the music, and it will change the whole social order because, "The true spirit of jazz is a joyous revolt from convention, custom, authority, boredom, even sorrow…" (217). Unlike Hurston, Rogers believes that the commercialization of jazz increases its global influence in a fashion that outweighs the detriment that might be ascribed to diminishment or "bleaching," but he too wants to make sure that the music's cultural origins are acknowledged and respected. Since "Broadway studies Harlem," Rogers writes, "it is difficult to say whether jazz [in its popular forms] is more characteristic of the Negro or of contemporary America … Jazz proper, however, is in idiom–rhythmic, musical and pantomimic– thoroughly American Negro; it is his spiritual picture on that lighter comedy side, just as the spirituals are the picture on the tragedy side" (219-20).

The whole African American musical tradition, as Rogers sees it, conflates the sacred and secular, the culturally specific and the universally appealing, the physical and the sublime. The music's power lies in its capacity to express such a vast range without oversimplifying or hierarchically ranking the components that make up this range. Rogers was one of the many voices of his generation who found in some jazz "vulgarities and crudities of the lowly origin" (221) and who described the "jazz spirit ... [as] primitive" (223). The very qualities that Hurston admired as the life force of the music some of the staunchest supporters of jazz such as Rogers and Alain Locke wanted "to lift and divert into nobler channels" (Rogers, 224).[22] Rogers, however, also proclaimed that "jazz with its mocking disregard for formality is a leveller that makes for democracy" (223)–certainly a powerful claim to make for any art form. The history of the music reveals that Rogers's accolades were not exaggerated, since the music has proven to be not just a register but also, to some degree, an agent of social change. As Andre Millard points out in his study of the American recording industry, "The single most important cultural accomplishment of the industry of recorded sound in the twentieth century was to make the music of black Americans the popular music of the world" (96). While this does not ensure social justice, it can contribute to the impetus for social change.

James Weldon Johnson, whose literary use of music is examined in the first chapter of this book, also argued for the global significance of African American music and prophesied the music's role in the growth of American democracy. In his writing, Johnson often used musical metaphors to communicate the simultaneous distinctiveness and universality of African American culture. Johnson found in the trombone a metaphor for the intonations of the traditional Negro folk preacher. Explaining his choice of the title, *God's Trombones*, in his introduction to that work, Johnson writes that "a trombone [is] the instrument possessing above all others the power to express the wide and varied range of the human voice–and with greater amplitude" (7). Johnson clearly links the sacred and secular traditions in African American music and suggests the power of the music to move its listeners spiritually and in more earthly ways. In each case, the music's sway over its listeners has to do with a dynamic combination of the ethereal or abstract with the material or tangible. The music refuses the oversimplification inherent in the construction of binary oppositions.

Even though Harlem Renaissance intellectuals discussed the music in different terms, they had some key points in common with each other and with Morrison's later portrait of the 1920s music. All of the writers considered in this brief survey understood the music as a powerful social force that helped to unify the diverse members of the African American community. These writers agreed upon the music as an expression of a distinctive artistic sensibility arising from a specific cultural context.

Several decades later, this artistic approach would come to be known as "the Black aesthetic."[23] Perhaps a central difference between the two groups of Renaissance writers who have been discussed here was that Hurston, McKay, and Hughes thought that this Black aesthetic would develop while retaining and expressing close ties to its folk origins, and Rogers, Locke, and Johnson believed that those ties would be transformed through some kind of "higher" forms of art. These disagreements critically represented divergent attitudes toward the issue of social class as it complicated the issue of racial identity. Historical knowledge of the music provides insight into this debate, both in its past and its present forms, because, as Kathy Ogren observes in her study of the 1920s jazz controversy, "the class tensions which intensified between middle- and working-class blacks after migration ... helped make jazz controversial among blacks as well as whites" (115).

Morrison's depiction of the Harlem Renaissance, or the Jazz Age, or, specifically, 1926 intervenes in this jazz-infused debate by channeling the terms of its argument through, not culturally elite artists and intellectuals, but through more "ordinary" characters. Joe Trace works at a downtown hotel and sells Cleopatra cosmetics on the side; his wife Violet cuts and styles women's hair in their homes or in her own kitchen; Alice Manfred leads a quiet existence at home while her niece Dorcas desperately tries to squeeze a little excitement out of life. These characters represent regular people defining their own lives within a monumental historical context–the 1920s in Harlem. Since Morrison's narrator creates the context for this setting in relation to the stories of these characters, we are offered alternative perspectives on a self-consciously epoch-making moment.

In a letter to Langston Hughes, painter Aaron Douglas delineates the task at hand for "New Negro" artists such as himself and Hughes in a way that is representative of the Renaissance artists' self-conscious sense of their own central role in carving out a historically monumental epoch:

> Your problem Langston, my problem, no our problem is to conceive, develop, establish an art era. Not white art painted black ... No, let's bare our arms and plunge them deep through laughter, through pain, through sorrow, through hope, through disappointment, into the very depths of the souls of our people and drag forth material crude, rough, neglected. Then let's sing it, dance it, write it, paint it. Let's do the impossible. Let's create something transcendentally material, mystically objective. Earthy. Spiritually earthy. Dynamic. (qtd in Powell, 192).

Douglas powerfully articulates the impulse to create art in a variety of media that refuses to be constrained by binary oppositions—including those delineated by "race" and "class"—that everywhere threatened to choke the artistic impulses of all the Renaissance artists. Douglas's call for the "impossible"—for the creation of the "spiritually earthy"—is taken up in *Jazz*, which applies these aesthetic criteria to the portrayal of characters who lived in the "art era" but who did not *monumentally* create it.

Morrison builds upon the foundation of the Renaissance writers' approach to music while revising this approach to encompass the tensions in the music in pluralistic, rather than binary terms. A passage from the work of another writer who was particularly interested in the implications of jazz may help to illustrate the tension between chaos and coherence or freedom and form that energizes the improvisational aesthetics of jazz and that serves as a model for Morrison's approach to the music. In his short story "Sonny's Blues," James Baldwin offers a striking literary portrait of the implications of improvisational jazz performance. Baldwin's narrator observes:

> All I know about music is that not many people ever really hear it. And even then, on the rare occasions when something opens within and the music enters, what we mainly hear, or hear corroborated, are personal, private, vanishing evocations. But the man who creates the music is hearing something else, is dealing with the roar rising from the void and imposing order on it as it hits the air. What is evoked in him, then, is of another order, more terrible because it has no words, and triumphant, too, for that same reason. And his triumph, when he triumphs, is ours. (861)[24]

This is the other "order," the coherence without oversimplification, which Morrison's writing seems to seek in its approach to history, including the history of the music as it was recorded by the Harlem Renaissance artists.

Morrison's version of "historical fiction" puts the reader in touch with history in a participatory role—a role that is central to African American cultural traditions, and which, not surprisingly, figures prominently in the aesthetics of the music. The reader cannot passively observe the narrative portrayal of historical events but must actively engage in the construction of their human complexity and the range of their implications. Morrison's use of a musical, improvisational model for an approach to history allows her to render historical events in a way that evokes a visceral response from her readers and that makes history a vital component of our present, lived experiences. History in *Jazz* appears not as a static force but as "something rogue" (*Jazz*, 228) that is as unpredictably wandering—and at the same time as rooted in the past—as the improvisational essence of the music that inspires the novel's title.

MUSIC MEDIATES BETWEEN SILENCE AND EXPRESSION

Jazz confronts three central silences: the silence of history/stories that have not been adequately documented in a print medium, the silence that is an unavoidable attribute of the printed page, and the silence of emotions that feel too complicated and too fragmented to find adequate verbal expression. Musical tropes most often serve as Morrison's mediator between these silences and the written narrative.

In *Jazz*, as the novel's title indicates, when the narrative approaches these silences, particular musical tropes most often intercede in the effort to give new linguistic form to the previously unwritten. The manipulation of jazz/blues aesthetics and tropes contributes to the quality of Morrison's prose that is frequently described as its "lyricism." In Morrison's case, this lyricism might be defined as a kind of language that sings.[25] If we apply Sundquist's previously discussed definition of a culturally distinctive poetics that carries residual forms of the African cultural practice "where speech and song more closely approached each other on the continuum of cultural sound…" (385), Morrison's lyricism can be understood as the transmutation of residual cultural practices into an emergent form that builds upon the African American tradition of the "talking book."[26]

The concept of lyricism also calls to mind Ralph Ellison's classic definition of the blues. According to Ellison: "The blues is an impulse to keep the painful details and episodes of a brutal experience alive in one's aching consciousness, to finger its jagged grain, and to transcend it, not by the consolation of philosophy but by squeezing from it a near-tragic, near-comic lyricism. As a form, the blues is an autobiographical chronicle of personal catastrophe expressed lyrically" (78-79). Morrison's language expresses the kind of blues lyricism Ellison describes, and her portrayal of jazz always includes blues as an essential aspect of the music's foundation. A blues undertone runs throughout *Jazz*.

In contemplation of Joe's feelings and his desperate hunt for Dorcas, the narrator "sings": "Blues man. Black and bluesman. Blacktherefore blue man. Everybody knows your name. Where-did-she-go-and-why man. So-lonesome-I-could-die man. Everybody knows your name" (119). This narrative "song" evokes associations with Louis Armstrong's "What Did I Do to Be so Black and Blue," which in the course of its history has been both musical and literary. In its most famous literary manifestation, Armstrong's song introduces and concludes Ralph Ellison's *Invisible Man*. The solid blues foundation of Armstrong's early jazz appeals to Ellison's narrator, and the invisible man listens intently "as Louis bends that military instrument into a beam of lyrical sound" (*Invisible Man*, 8). The beauty of Armstrong's music, which makes "poetry out of being invisible" (8), lies in its manipulation of standard time. The invisible man observes:

> Invisibility, let me explain, gives one a slightly different sense of time, you're never quite on the beat. Sometimes you're ahead and sometimes behind. Instead of the swift and imperceptible flowing of time, you are aware of its

nodes, those points where time stands still or from which it leaps ahead. And you slip into the breaks and look around. That's what you hear vaguely in Louis' music. (8)

In this passage, the invisible man explores the implications of Armstrong's improvisation on time signatures, melody, and rhythms, as they are conventionally composed in European derived music.

Morrison also places Armstrong at one of her own narrative beginnings. A reference to Armstrong begins her critical work, *Playing in the Dark*. Here, too, Armstrong symbolizes a different sense of time because his playing provides "the illusion of permanence…Unbearable equilibrium and duration; nerve-wracking balance and permanence" (vii-viii). The permanence is illusory because, as improvisational music, it is based upon change and unpredictability, but the music is simultaneously grounded in the musical, cultural traditions out of which it emerges. As the invisible man's description of the music suggests, an awareness of permanence can only exist in the exploration of the "nodes" of time where what is eternal *seems* to stop or leap forward. The listener/writer under consideration in Morrison's analysis, however, cannot "slip into the breaks and look around" (Ellison, 8). Marie Cardinal, the subject of Morrison's analysis, is paralyzed by what Morrison calls the "cultural associations of jazz" (viii). According to Morrison, Cardinal's terror prevents her from responding to the music on its own terms.

Cardinal misinterprets the music because she hears it out of context and projects herself into the music, erasing Armstrong's active role in its production and substituting a set of associations with which she is personally familiar. Analyzing Cardinal's work, Morrison writes, "encouraged me to reflect on the consequences of jazz—its visceral, emotional, and intellectual impact on the listener" (viii). Much of this reflection on "the consequences of jazz" must have informed *Jazz*, which explores the music's "cultural associations" and its aesthetic priorities. Placing the music at the center of her novel helps Morrison craft her lyrical language to draw from her audience a "jazz response," which is by definition participatory. The influence of the music also contributes to her nonlinear narrative structure that embodies a different sense of time. Both of these stylistic devices work to remake the form novel into "a sympathetic, singing instrument."[27] In its use of music, *Jazz* engages aspects of the African American literary tradition in which literature and music are inseparably intertwined entities that, in the 1920s, began to have a profound impact on the definition of "modernity," not just in the United States, but in Europe as well.

Some critics align these stylistic aspects of Morrison's writing–the nonlinear structure, the use of multiple narrative voices, and the participatory role of the reader–with the literary innovations of "high" modernism. Parallels are most often drawn between Morrison's writing and that of Virginia Woolf and

William Faulkner, particularly since Morrison wrote her master's thesis on these two authors.[28] Undoubtedly Morrison's writerly imagination must be engaged by a whole range of authors she has encountered, especially the two authors who provided the subject matter for an intensive academic analysis. To focus more heavily on these literary modernist influences, however, rather than on her self-proclaimed cultural resources, dichotomizes form and content, a binary distinction that Morrison's writing works to dissolve. This interpretive approach also results in the same kind of willful misreading that Morrison describes in her analysis of Cardinal's response to Armstrong's music.

This kind of misinterpretation involves a projection onto the music (or the literature) of the aesthetic framework with which the interpreter is most familiar. In his study of Songhay culture in the Republic of Niger, anthropologist Paul Stoller observes a similar phenomenon in his own response to the concept of sound, which is experienced differently by the Songhay people than by a westerner like Stoller. In this context, Stoller learns, "Words, then are seen as a kind of energy by many peoples of the world, and energy which should be apprehended in and of itself rather than only as a representation of something" (562). While Morrison's cultural context is certainly not as far removed from Woolf's or Faulkner's as Stoller's is from the Songhay people, some similarities in these situations can be observed. African American culture is both a crucial part of the white American "mainstream" and a distinctive element in relation to the mainstream.

Ralph Ellison has demonstrated some of the ways that African American culture has shaped American culture as a whole. Ellison argues that African American cultural practices are a significant part of the very foundation of the American character:

> The master artisans of the South were slaves, and white Americans have been walking Negro walks, talking Negro flavored talk (and prizing it when spoken by Southern belles), dancing Negro dances and singing Negro melodies far too long to talk of a "mainstream" of American culture to which they're alien. (256)

Eric Sundquist employs a similar theoretical approach in his expansive study *To Wake the Nations* in order "to trace the expressive heritage of a biracial culture" (9). In his historically-minded anthropological study, *Black Legacy: America's Hidden Heritage*, William Piersen demonstrates his claim that the "creation of American culture cannot be understood by adopting a single ethnic perspective. Whatever American culture is, it is a blending, a blending in which the Afro is an essential part" (xv).[29]

These arguments for the interracial character of American culture are not incompatible with but are predicated upon the idea of African American cultural difference. Critics who attempt to place Morrison's work *primarily* in the context of modernist writers such as Woolf and Faulkner are not hearing the difference, in the same way that Stoller initially brought only his Western understanding of the meaning of sound to his experience with Songhay culture. The nuances of cultural difference, as Franz Boas demonstrated about eighty years ago, can be *learned*, as Stoller's essay also reveals. Critics who intensively study African American literary and musical history will uncover different cultural resources at the foundation of Morrison's writing than those who interpret her work without knowledge of this context. Research, rather than identity politics, is at the heart of the matter of interpretation. Through research one might also discover Faulkner's native Southern language was saturated with the style and rhythms of black speech, so if one hears Faulkner in Morrison, the "origins" of that sound may be more complex than a direct line from emerging from Morrison's graduate studies.

Morrison's writing reveals and draws upon the distinctiveness African American cultural practices. Her novels (perhaps especially *Jazz* because of its historical setting) do engage with "high" modernism, but with a difference that has to do with form as well as content. Often in Morrison's writing jazz and blues provide artistically inspirational models for formalistic innovation. While this chapter focuses on the tropological uses of the music in *Jazz*, several critics have explored the ways that Morrison utilizes jazz aesthetics in her writing.[30] Eusebio Rodrigues offers an impressively detailed close reading of the *sound* of the language in *Jazz* and examines the ways that the novel's structure parallels jazz performance. He concludes that because of the sound of the language and the rhythms of the prose in the novel, readers are invited to "set aside Cartesian logic in order to enter a magic world that cries out for deeper modes of knowledge" (734). From Rodigues's analysis, one can conclude that the music serves as a model for the dissolution of binary oppositions in *Jazz*. The novel suggests that the music expresses another way of comprehending the great mysteries of life–a strategy for knowing that the narrator finally concludes is "something rogue" (228) because it is wandering and unpredictable or improvisational.

One critic in particular, however, objects to the entire notion of "jazz aesthetics" in literature, and he analyzes both Morrison's writing and the commentators whom he derisively calls her "jazz critics." Alan Munton seems most invested establishing that neither jazz nor Morrison's relationship to it should be explicated in terms of an "Africentric" (251) perspective. Munton argues that Morrison is "an ideologically radical practitioner who performs conservatively within the received narrative strategies of the novel" (251). In this statement, Munton implies that Morrison has a clear and militant political agenda (content), but, formalistically, her writing is not strikingly innovative.

Again, this perspective reinforces the form/content divide. He asserts that there is no cultural difference expressed through her writing style, especially in relation to jazz, because music and fiction are absolutely and unequivocally separate entities.

The central problem with Munton's analysis is that he seems to consider Morrison's writing in a vacuum, as if there were no long-standing historical tradition for the centrality of African American music in the literature emerging from or participating in that cultural context. He also diminishes the significance of the blues foundations of *Jazz* (and jazz), to which the novel alludes–particularly in its references to the Okeh recording label.[31]

Okeh was one of several independent record labels in the 1920s, and its parent company was General Phonograph. In 1920, Okeh released what is considered by most jazz/blues historians to be the first big hit blues recording, Mamie Smith's "Crazy Blues." Smith quickly rose to star status, and her success became a source of communal pride for many. In her study of the "blues queens" of the 1920s, Daphne Duval Harrison writes:

> In less than a year [after Okeh's release of "Crazy Blues"], the race market was jumping with 'discovery after discovery' of blues singers ... Meanwhile, Mamie Smith was propelled into the limelight by the rave reviews appearing in the black press. She was pointed to with pride as the first artist of the race to record popular songs. Her entry in the market was a boon to music publishing companies as well as to music stores in every town and city. (46-47)

Rick Kennedy, in his study of jazz and the recording industry, also notes the huge success of Smith's recordings and their impact on the music industry:

> A key milestone in jazz recording was the birth of "race records" in 1921, sparked by the Harlem blues singer Mamie Smith's hits on Okeh records. Perry Bradford, a southern black entrepreneur and composer, could not interest Victor and Columbia in his songs, but he attracted Okeh with Mamie Smith as his vocalist. Okeh's second disc by Smith in late 1920, Bradford's 'Crazy Blues' and 'It's Right for You,' sold more than a million copies by early 1921. (50)

In 1926, Louis Armstrong and his Hot Five group gathered at the Okeh studio in Chicago to record a session that became momentous in the history of jazz. With this second Hot Five session, Armstrong biographer Laurence Bergreen observes, "the group, especially its *de facto* leader, Louis Armstrong, instantly became names to be reckoned with not only among those who purchased race records [i.e., a predominantly African American market], but in mainstream [i.e., white] popular culture" (275). This history of Okeh and its stars lies behind the reference to the label in *Jazz*. The allusion evokes important artistic voices shaping modernism in the 1920s and reminds us that some prominent, epoch-defining voices of the era were neither white nor literary.

Munton correctly argues that jazz has been internationally influential and that it has utilized and fused other cultural styles of music (including European, African, Indian, Latin, etc.) to create, expand, and transform its own idiom.[32] This type of generic boundary crossing, however, does not divorce the music from its specific cultural and historical context. When the "jazz critics" who Munton condemns argue that this musical tradition has shaped African American literature, including Morrison's writing, they do not claim that novels and music are the *same* thing.

Instead, Morrison's critics often observe that the music and the fiction may derive from the same cultural context and that one form may serve as artistic inspiration for the other. The process is still reliant upon the artist's skill and vision in deciding how one form can be translated into another. Just as, in the visual arts, Romare Bearden's collages are inspired in a large part by the improvisational and amalgamative aesthetics of jazz music, so Morrison's writing can utilize African American musical traditions as a model for her use of language and for her approach to history. This does not mean that Bearden refused to study European artists; it means that knowledge of jazz aesthetics adds to an appreciation of his work because he drew heavily from those musical traditions. Bearden himself explains it this way:

> In the twenties, Benny Goodman used to come up to Harlem a lot. He was teaching himself about jazz the only way he could, and he had to become a little black to learn it. By the same token, when I started copying and learning from those pictures by Vermeer and Delacroix and the rest, in a sense I was joining the white world. It's all a little more complicated that some people try to make out. (qtd in Tomkins, 237)

Richard Hardack seems to have a firm grasp of the complexity of these issues, and he examines the ways that *Jazz*, particularly through its use of music, reconfigures the Du Boisian trope of double-consciousness. Hardack argues that the novel first accepts the idea of double-consciousness and then, twisting this concept at the end, leaves its burden to be shared by the narrator and her readers, while Felice, Violet, and Joe are portrayed as taking a path to healing and wholeness. In the end, Hardack observes, "the music itself [is] the one thing rendered inviolate in the whole book" (466) because, "It is only the music–half Nature, half City–which ultimately transcends double-consciousness…" (457). Hardack's analysis can be applied to the ways the novel negotiates the boundaries between other dichotomies as well. For example, musical tropes often mediate between oral and written modes of expression in the novel, refuting the dichotomy that implies an absolute distinction between sound and silence.

From the first *sound* of the novel, the narrative voice takes on the qualities of the music that are inseparable from the tone and style of oral storytelling.

In a confidential, gossipy tone initiated by what sounds like the soft scratch of a wire brush on a snare drum ("Sth, I know that woman") the narrative begins by blurring the generic boundaries between oral storytelling, music, and the novel. This mixed media experience, engendered by a unique narrative voice, proposes formalistic innovations in the novel that have significant social implications. The narrator, although first presenting herself as confidently authoritative, eventually reveals herself to be somewhat uncertain and willing to revise her previous assertions. As readers, we must follow her lead.

MUSIC ENGENDERS HEALING

The narrator, despite her self-proclaimed elusive, superhuman expansiveness, is still somehow among the living. She is, therefore, limited in her perceptions, and she admits this near the end of the novel, employing a musically related metaphor to explain her mistaken impression of the meaning of the past:

> I was sure one would kill the other. I waited for it so I could describe it. I was so sure it would happen. That the past was an abused record with no choice but to repeat itself at the crack and no power on earth could lift the arm that held the needle. I was so sure, and they danced and walked all over me. Busy they were, busy being original, complicated, changeable–human, I guess you'd say, while I was the predictable one.... (220)

At this point, the narrator observes that the concept of improvisation can be applied to an understanding of the complexity and contradictions of the past. This improvisational approach to the past, of course, does not imply that one can randomly recreate historical events according to personal whim and ideological inclination.

According to Nancy Peterson, in her study of Morrison's approach to history, "Morrison's emphasis on the mutual and collective construction of the story is not an invitation to radical historical relativism, but an insistence on a necessary, collective support for counternarratives in order for them to become something other than marginalized or alternative or muted perspectives" (216-17). Peterson concludes that Morrison's historical reconstruction project suggests that "(black) history books have no life, no meaning, unless they engage readers and compel them to 'make' and 'remake' the story in order to locate something useful for living today and tomorrow" (216). Peterson's observation calls to mind musicologist John Miller Chernoff's seminal study of African music in which he explores "perhaps the fundamental aesthetic in Africa: without participation there is no meaning" (23).

Chernoff's description suggests the presence of the residual cultural practices that Morrison expresses in her writing most frequently through musical metaphors, perhaps because in African American musical traditions she finds the strongest traces of an African cultural inheritance. In *Jazz*, the narrator's account of the music in "the City" on a beautiful spring day describes the music as a cultural inheritance that is expressed through the metaphor of trees (rootedness) that provides the young musicians' source of strength and inspiration:

> You would have thought everything had been forgiven the way they played. The clarinets had trouble because the brass was cut so fine, not lowdown the way they love to do it, but high and fine ... On the rooftops ... I could hear the men playing out their maple-sugar hearts, tapping it from four-hundred-year-old trees and letting it run down the trunk, wasting it because they didn't have a bucket to hold it and didn't want one either ... That's the way the men on brass sounded that day. Sure of themselves, sure they were holy, standing up there on the rooftops, facing each other at first, but when it was clear that they had beat the clarinets out, they turned their backs on them, lifted those horns straight up and joined the light just as pure and steady and kind of kind. (196-97)

This rooftop music is not only "high and fine" it is also healing. When Violet and Joe, in the process of their own emotional recovery, get a new bird to replace those that Violet left "to freeze or fly" (3), the bird turns out to be sick with "[h]ardly any peck to it" (224). Violet determines that food, shelter, and companionship have not provided a cure, so she and Joe agree that "nothing was left to love and need but music" (224). After they expose the bird to the City's rooftop music, it revitalizes, and "From then on the bird was a pleasure to itself and to them" (224).

Felice also brings healing music to Violet and Joe's apartment. She buys Okeh records, alluding to historical associations that imply a kind of communal pride that promotes healing. When they hear music, the Traces are revitalized like their bird, and they dance. Felice says:

> Somebody in the house across the alley put a record on and the music floated in to us through the open window. Mr. Trace moved his head to the rhythm and is wife snapped her fingers in time. She did a little step in front of him and he smiled. By and by they were dancing. Funny, like old people do.... (214)

Violet no longer tries to perform "the dance steps the dead girl used to do" (5)–steps that made her look like "an old street pigeon pecking the crust of a sardine sandwich the cats left behind" (6). Now she joins Joe in a dance that symbolizes their "whispering, old-time love" (228) and that suits both of them.

At the end of the novel, the narrative itself heals the damage of large historical omissions, evasions, and lies in part by telling the story of the music pulsing within and animating monumental modernism. The narrator offers a picture of Gatsby's "jazz age" world of parties. We imagine these characters from F. Scott Fitzgerald's world, "In the T-strap shoes of Long Island debutantes, the sparkling fringes of daring short skirts that swish and glide to music that intoxicates them even more than champagne" (227). The narrator tells us that the lure of black culture sends them on voyeuristic tourist trips uptown to Harlem clubs, and that this culture is embodied by the music they love. They "sway on unlit porches while the Victrola plays in the parlor. The click of dark and snapping fingers drives them to Roseland, to Bunny's; boardwalks by the sea. Into places their fathers have warned them about and their mothers shudder to think of. Both the warning and the shuddering come from the snapping fingers, the clicking" (227).

This "clicking" is the sound of the life force of African American people in the City, and it evokes the rhythms of the culture as it is lived daily and as it shapes the lives of the Long Island debutantes and their beaus. The clicking informs "the graceful slouch of the men slipping their hands into the pockets of their tuxedo trousers. Their teeth are bright; their hair is smooth and parted in the middle" (227). Here is a brief catalogue of conventional images from the "jazz age" that *Jazz* offers us. This portrait highlights the life-giving, style-defining energy ("snapping," "clicking") of the jazz age that arises from African American cultural practices and their influence on white America.

The novel not only redefines the implications of jazz in the "jazz age;" it also uses the aesthetic priorities of the music to engage with Virginia Woolf's representative portrait of modernist alienation and suffering in her essay "Old Mrs. Grey." Here is Woolf in the last two sentences of "Old Mrs. Grey":

> So we—humanity—insist that the body shall still cling to the wire. We put out the eyes and the ears; but we pinion it there, with a bottle of medicine, a cup of tea, a dying fire, like a rook on a barn door; but a rook that still lives, even with a nail through it. (19)

The narrator of *Jazz* repeats this striking image from Woolf's essay with a *difference* that has implications for form as well as content. Pinioned flesh used to inform Morrison's narrator's understanding of the world until she "figured in" (228) what lies beneath the surface of the music, which epitomizes a completely different approach to life. The narrator explains:

> I started out believing that life was made just so the world would have some way to think about itself, but that it had gone awry with humans because flesh, pinioned by misery, hangs on to it with pleasure ... I don't believe that anymore. Something is missing there. Something rogue. Something else you have to figure in before you can figure it out. (228)

The word "pinion" is distinctive in its resonance. As a noun, a pinion is the end segment of a bird's wing or the flight feather that is sometimes metonymically used to represent the whole wing. As a verb, pinion implies cutting off or disabling a bird's wings so that it cannot fly, but it can also mean binding a person's arms so that they cannot be used. It carries the implications of shackling a person or immobilizing something in one spot. "Pinion" extends the bird imagery in both Woolf's and Morrison's writing, but it works differently in *Jazz* in conjunction with the bird imagery found throughout the novel.[33]

Domesticated parrots, city pigeons, and wild redwings figure prominently in *Jazz*, but even the parrot that says "'I love you'" (3) has the option to "freeze or fly" (3). No bird is pinioned in *Jazz*. With her birds, Morrison signifies on Woolf's rook, a kind of crow and a word that has metaphorical associations with cheating and swindling. In her redwing imagery, Morrison refers to a kind of North American blackbird that has migratory significance and that is the novel's symbol for the character who may be Joe's mother, Wild.[34] Morrison makes the redwings a symbol for movement and freedom that is not without its attendant sacrifices and complications. In the process, she subtly dismantles historically negative associations with blackness by expanding the symbolic significance of the blackbird. In this sense, she counters a kind of stereotypical symbolism exemplified by the word "rook," which is attended by sinister connotations that are metaphorically linked to its blackness.

The title of Morrison's novel indicates that the "something rogue" that is left out of the image of human life as a pinioned rook is symbolized by the music. The "rogue" quality implies movement and wandering, similar to Houston Baker's description of this characteristic of the blues. Baker writes: "Like signification itself, blues are always nomadically wandering. Like the freight-hopping hobo, they are ever on the move, ceaselessly summing novel experience" (8). In *Jazz*, the music serves as a trope for the ways that black culture has shaped the implications of modernity, infusing modern existence with "something rogue" that combats static and "universal" modernist visions of alienation and despair and that disrupts the impulse to impose any *absolute* order—mythical or otherwise—on chaos.

This is the attraction of the blues as Ralph Ellison describes it: "[T]hey at once express both the agony of life and the possibility of conquering it through sheer toughness of spirit. They fall short of tragedy only in that they provide no solution, offer no scapegoat but the self" (94). Here Ellison's use of the phrase "fall short" has a sardonic tone. He suggests that the strength of the blues resides in the music's refusal to oversimplify the contradictions of lived experience. Houston Baker makes a related claim for the music: "As a driving force, the blues matrix thus avoids simple dualities. It perpetually achieves its effects as a fluid and multivalent network" (9). Both Baker's and Ellison's accounts of the music correspond to blues/jazz representations in *Jazz* of the music as a form of expression that refutes the binary opposition of pleasure and pain and improvisationally refuses to be pinioned.

Morrison's narrative exploration of the powers of the music in *Jazz* moves toward artistically completing modernism—not by providing closure but by opening up its historical implications to attune our ears to its cultural resonance. *Jazz* provides a narrative of the age as it was lived, responding to the stories of the age as it was monumentally created. The novel suggests that spaces exist for all the voices, narratives, and counternarratives, but if we willfully shut out any of them, then we consciously limit the range of our understanding and diminish our access to varied ways of knowing. In *Jazz*, Morrison offers her readers the opportunity to participate in the roguish reconstruction of the meanings of the jazz age—as long as we agree to think like the musicians whose wandering spirits always seek new possibilities rather than absolute answers.

Conclusion

An analysis of the twentieth-century jazz controversy demonstrates how debates over aesthetic value can be another way of arguing about issues such as race and class. The capacity of music to cross social barriers has history of threatening those who have a vested interest in maintaining an established cultural hierarchy. The early twentieth-century debate over jazz illustrates this phenomenon. Despite vehement protest by some members of the cultural elite, however, the widespread appeal of jazz could not be arrested. According to historian Lawrence Levine:

> That this music which was characterized as vulgar at best and as harmful trash at worst by the Guardians of Culture and that for a long time was appreciated largely by those on the margins of American society; that this form of music which seemed so firmly ensconced on the American cultural periphery should become the most widely identifiable and emulated symbol of American culture throughout the world by the mid-20th century is one of the more arresting paradoxes of American history. ("Jazz and American Culture," 440)

The four writers included in this study–James Weldon Johnson, F. Scott Fitzgerald, Langston Hughes, and Toni Morrison–express a profound understanding of the music's potential (well before the mid-twentieth century) to define and reflect American culture. Their writing helps to reveal the implications of the music and its impact as an artistic innovation and a social force.

Analyzing fiction that engages with the jazz controversy can help uncover what is really at stake when we argue about issues of aesthetic value, and considering these novels and short stories in relation to the public debate over jazz unravels the implications of their use of musical tropes.[1] Throughout the twentieth century, jazz (in its various forms) has been an essential component of American culture, and these writers, clearly aware of the cultural significance of the music, have used it to create narratives that express the timbre and the rhythms of American life. In this sense, each of these writers is engaged in some manner with what Robert O'Meally describes as the "jazz factor":

> *The jazz factor:* this subtle set of threads seems to sparkle within virtually every aspect of modern American living ... [jazz] is a massive, irresistibly influential, politically charged part of our culture. The predominance of the jazz factor may make it the master trope of this American century: the definitive sound of America in our time. The sound of the American twentieth century is the jazz line. (xi)[2]

Johnson, Fitzgerald, Hughes, and Morrison have all recognized that there was something about jazz that defined American culture in the twentieth century. Of course, their interpretations of how jazz shaped and expressed American identity varied significantly.

The narratives in this study suggest that popular music, including various forms of jazz, can metaphorically occupy what might be imagined as a kind of border space, a space in which the binary absolutism of boundaries is continually negotiated. Gloria Anzaldúa writes out of the context of the border between the U. S. and Mexico, and she calls this place "a border culture." Her definition of border culture illuminates the character of cultural boundaries. In the place she describes, the border fails to maintain separatism, and identities, held apart by force, defiantly merge like the Spanish and English in her own writing. She observes that:

> Borders are set up define the places that are safe and unsafe, to distinguish *us* from *them*. A border is a dividing line, a narrow strip along a steep edge. A borderland is a vague and undetermined place created by the emotional residue of an unnatural boundary. It is in a constant state of transition. The prohibited and forbidden are its inhabitants. (3)

Anzaldúa offers an alternative perspective regarding borders—a strategy for dismantling them that she calls "The Mestiza Way" (82).[3] Following this way, the Mestiza:

> reinterprets history and, using new symbols, she shapes new myths ... She is willing to share, to make herself vulnerable to foreign ways of seeing and feeling. She surrenders all notions of safety, of the familiar. Deconstruct, construct. (82)

This kind of radical revision draws the reader into her project and demands a critical sensibility that can meet the challenges she poses. Cultural theorist Homi Bhabha describes the kind of interpretive accountability that is required.

Conclusion

He warns that "the critic must attempt to fully realize, to take responsibility for, the unspoken, unrepresented pasts that haunt the historical present" (12). Bhabha's observation suggests the ways that cultural difference should be recognized and understood without the oversimplification of binary oppositions. Binary logic fails to grasp the complex contradictions that writing such as Anzaldúa's–with its "border culture" sensibility–contains. Bhabha points out that crossing cultural borders requires us to rethink conventional assumptions in order to reach a clearer understanding. He writes that

> borderline engagements of cultural difference may as often be consensual as conflictual; they may confound our definitions of tradition and modernity; realign customary boundaries between the private and the public, high and low; and challenge normative expectations of development and progress" (2).

This study has considered the ways that certain novels and short stories use musical tropes to explore what Bhabha calls "borderline engagements of cultural difference." In these narratives' representations of styles of early jazz, they examine consent and conflict. They question the way modernity is and has been defined. They consider how the public and the private interact, and they probe the distinctions between high and low. They wonder what the future may hold and challenge us, as readers, to do the same. The music in these novels serves as an integral aspect of their characters' lives. It contributes to the characters' self-definitions; it situates them in relation to history and their personal memories.

The music in these novels makes boundaries difficult to distinguish. It suggests a kind of "border culture" in which its listeners may discover surprising connections and may feel unexpected sympathetic resonance. In her novel *Corregidora*, Gayl Jones's heroine Ursa, who is a blues singer, turns to the blues and experiences unanticipated realizations that link her to other people and to her past but that also save her from being mired in their stories and their remembered lives:

> I started humming the part about taking my rocking chair down by the river and rocking my blues away. What she said about the voice being better because it tells what you've been through. Consequences. It seems as if you're not singing the past, you're humming it ... [W]e're all consequences of something. Stained with another's past as well as our own. (45)

Ursa comes to understand that the contradictions of her own past and her family's history–the hate and love, the abuse and tenderness, the domination and submission–can be contained in the music, which gives voice to reverberating consequences. The irreconcilable oppositions that comprise the stories of the past also make up her own experience of the present and demand an alternative mode of expression to prevent stagnation or paralysis. She believes she can "*explain it, in blues, without words, the explanation somewhere behind the words*" (66).

The music is an enemy of the boundaries that rely on binary logic to sustain their exclusionary and prohibitive force. The authors in this study examine that quality in the styles of music that they represent. They explore the ways that various styles of jazz can negotiate boundaries and give expression to the complexities of "border cultures," which we may recognize as the predominant style of contemporary culture that is sometimes masked by the illusion of cultural purity. Purity is an illusion, and a frightening one at that, because as Homi Bhabha observes:

> The very concepts of homogenous national cultures, the consensual or contiguous transmission of historical traditions, or "organic" ethnic communities—*as the grounds for cultural comparativism*—are in a profound process of redefinition. The hideous extremity of Serbian nationalism proves that the very idea of a pure, "ethnically cleansed" national identity can only be achieved through the death, literal and figurative, of the complex interweavings of history, and the culturally contingent borderlines of modern nationhood. (5)

In this sense "the border culture," in addition to its historical and cultural specificity, can also symbolize the heterogeneous character of contemporary culture that can only be eradicated through systematic and deliberate annihilation of its diverse elements. The narratives in this study, as they confront popular music loosely grouped under the headings of ragtime or jazz, also confront the dynamics of border culture that the music embodies. Through musical tropes, they offer us insight into the shifting and continually transformational negotiation of boundaries in our own border cultures. They reveal that when sound crosses social barriers—as jazz and ragtime did in early twentieth-century America—questions about the way the social hierarchy is constructed inevitably arise.

By the 1930s the controversy over jazz had begun to settle down, but it would be followed by other heated, public debates over music (particularly rock 'n' roll and rap) and these debates were (and are) often couched in terms similar to those used in the jazz controversy. In her study of early twentieth-century reactions to jazz, Kathy Ogren writes, "The jazz controversy signified the attempts of Americans to analyze the difficult and contested routes they had followed in the past, and their willingness to chart a more flexible, 'modern' future" (165). In this sense, jazz was highly significant in modernizing America, and the controversy it engendered encapsulated the aspects of American culture that would continue to be contested throughout the twentieth century.

The musical tropes in the fiction included in this study suggest the nuances of the jazz debate and the role of the music in making America modern. Early jazz was an indicator and an agent of social change, and the narratives in this study respond to its role in the modern processes of cultural amalgamation.

Perhaps it is the improvisational energy central to the jazz tradition that makes it so expressive of modernity. Novelist and cultural theorist Albert Murray notes that this type of improvisation "is something that not only conditions people to cope with disjuncture and change but also provides them with a basic survival technique that is commensurate with and suitable to the rootlessness and the discontinuity so characteristic of human existence in the contemporary world..." ("Improvisation...," 113).

The music embodies, as Toni Morrison describes it in *Jazz*, "something rogue" (228). It is difficult to contain or define. It resists the delineation of boundaries and crosses barriers. Early jazz critics often referred to the music in terms of contagion and disease. From their perspective, the music was a threat that entered and contaminated the minds and bodies of all listeners. Such metaphors indicate the perceived power of the music, and the representation of the jazz controversy in American fiction reveals that this was not simply a debate over aesthetic value but rather an argument over national identity and who has the authority to define it.

Notes

INTRODUCTION

1. Both Hamm and Levine extensively cite contemporary newspaper and journal articles as primary sources of evidence for their assertions.

2. Two studies that have influenced my project in their examination of issues pertaining to cultural "mixing" in modernist literature are Michael North's *The Dialect of Modernism: Race, Language, and Twentieth-Century Literature* and George Hutchinson's *The Harlem Renaissance in Black and White*. North and Hutchinson do not focus on the role of music in modernist cultural mixing, so I hope that my project compliments their critical approach by addressing music.

CHAPTER ONE: "A SYMPATHETIC, SINGING INSTRUMENT"

1. My reading of the novel follows William Andrews's assertion that "the importance of the *Autobiography* to African American literary history becomes much clearer when its original publication date is reckoned with" (xv), rather than situating the novel solely in the historical context of its 1927 reissuing under Johnson's name. The relationship of ragtime to jazz history, which is a significant aspect of the historical context of the novel, will be explored in more depth in the first and third sections of this chapter.

2. 1896 was the year that the first ragtime songs were published as sheet music and the year that the Supreme Court upheld the constitutionality of segregation based on race in the *Plessy v. Ferguson* case. The crowning irony of this case, illustrating the artificiality of American racial categories, is that Homer Plessy, who was of both African and European descent, looked so "white" that the railroad officials had to be alerted to the fact that a "black" man was sitting in the first class car, so that he would be arrested.

3. In his introduction to a recent edition of *The Autobiography*, William Andrews

points out that Johnson first published the novel anonymously because he intended it to be taken as a "true" account (xvi-xvii).

4. In one of his essays Ralph Ellison observes that "The master artisans of the South were slaves, and white Americans have been walking Negro walks, talking Negro flavored talk (and prizing it when spoken by Southern belles), dancing Negro dances and singing Negro melodies far too long to talk of a 'mainstream' of American culture to which they're alien" (256). Johnson's writing is part of the foundation for the documentation of this "mainstream" cultural influence.

5. Blesh and Janis's study, *They All Played Ragtime*, was the first book length consideration of ragtime, and with its 1950 publication, it became part of the foundation for the interpretations of the music that followed. Edward Berlin's *Ragtime: A Musical and Cultural History* (1980) is the first book length study that analyzes the music by situating it within its cultural and historical context. Berlin's writing on ragtime offers the most comprehensive perspective on the music.

6. Preface to *The Book of American Negro Poetry*, xix.

7. Preface to *The Book of American Negro Poetry*, vii.

8. In his studies of labor history, historian David Roediger interrogates "whiteness" as a social and political construct. Roediger argues in his collection of essays, *Towards the Abolition of Whiteness*, that while African American culture and community has been built upon positive defining features, whiteness has been built entirely upon what it is *not*. Roediger writes, "Whiteness describes, from Little Big Horn to Simi Valley, not a culture but precisely the absence of culture. It is the empty and therefore terrifying attempt to build an identity based on what one isn't and on whom one can hold back" (13). Toni Morrison brings a similar argument to the field of literary criticism in her *Playing in the Dark: Whiteness and the Literary Imagination*. Here Morrison explores how projected images of African American identity, or "American Africanism" (6) helped Americans from divergent ethnic backgrounds define themselves as "American" and "white" by defining themselves, first and foremost, as "not black." Morrison argues that "the process of organizing American coherence through a distancing Africanism became the operative mode of a new cultural hegemony" (8). For a thorough account of the recent history of critical studies on the ideology of whiteness, see Shelley Fisher Fishkin's essay "Interrogating 'Whiteness,' Complicating 'Blackness': Remapping American Culture." These sources provide the background from which I draw the phrase "the ideology of whiteness."

9. Examples include not only fairly recent works directly focusing on African American culture such as Ishmael Reed's *Mumbo Jumbo*, Michael Ondaatje's *Coming Through Slaughter*, and Toni Morrison's *Jazz*, but also other novels that use popular music as an integral trope such as Thomas Pynchon's *The Crying of Lot 49*, Maxine Hong Kingston's *Tripmaster Monkey: His Fakebook* and Bobbie Ann Mason's *In Country*.

10. Charles Chesnutt brought African American vernacular culture into the novel with his troping of the cakewalk. W.E.B. Du Bois anthologized the spirituals in 1903. Johnson, in part, followed their lead with his thematization of African American secular music, which at the time of his novel's first publication had already begun to establish itself as America's popular music.

11. In the preface, Johnson's statement appears in this form: "Ragtime music was

originated by colored piano players in the questionable resorts of St. Louis, Memphis, and other Mississippi River towns. These men did not know any more about the theory of music than they did about the theory of the universe. They were guided by their natural musical instinct and talent, but above all by the Negro's extraordinary sense of rhythm" (x).

12. The assertion is the same in the novel. Referring to ragtime and the cakewalk, the narrator claims, "These are lower forms of art, but they give evidence of a power that will someday be applied to higher forms" (87).

13. For a detailed account of their arguments see the introduction to this book.

14. Berlin, in his *Ragtime*, offers the fullest account of the debate. Neil Leonard, in his *Jazz and the White Americans*, and Kathy Ogren, in her *Jazz Revolution*, focus on the debate over 1920's jazz, and they both briefly discuss the earlier ragtime controversy. Leonard's essay, "The Reactions to Ragtime," in Hasse's anthology of essays on the music also offers important insights into this topic.

15. Berlin documents the rage for "ragged classics" (*Ragtime*, 68-69).

16. Historian David Roediger asserts as part of his work on the ideology of whiteness that "the central political implication arising from the insight that race is socially constructed is the specific need to attack *whiteness* as a destructive ideology, rather than to attack the concept of race abstractly" (3).

17. The circumscription of identity arising from rigid American racial categories must have been especially striking to Johnson at the time of the book's composition, since he wrote much of it in 1906 while serving as a U.S. consul in Venezuela, a country noted for the fluidity of it racial categories. Neil Brooks offers an interesting "postmodern reading" of the novel that does not seem at all anachronistic. Brooks argues that traditional readings of narrative irony in the novel do not account for the full complexity of the implications of "passing." He observes that "the narrative disallows all constructions that seek to map a stable center of self or other that the narrator might use as a guide in self-definition" (17-18). Brooks concludes, "The tragedy is that society has chosen arbitrary categorizations, constructed a meta-narrative of race that cannot be applied adequately to the personal narratives of its individual members" (23).

18. Nathan Huggins in his *Harlem Renaissance* uses the phrase "cultural elitism" (5) to describe the tendencies of Harlem Renaissance leaders such as Johnson who aspired to a vision of "high" culture that would unite the races. According to Huggins, "Jazz was definitely not the 'high art' that James Weldon Johnson and Alain Locke were hoping for. Thus, these literary men were encumbered by a self-consciousness that crippled art. They were provincials within a provincial America" (198). Both David Levering Lewis's and Huggins's assumptions that the Renaissance failed because of too much white influence have been very influential but have more recently been contested by other scholars. Houston A. Baker, Jr. argues that Renaissance artists created their own kind of counter-modernism through strategies of "the mastery of form" and the "deformation of mastery" (*Modernism and the Harlem Renaissance*). Jon Michael Spencer builds on Baker's work to demonstrate that the Renaissance was a success because it achieved its goals of "vindication" and "mastery of form" through music and musical influence on the other arts (*The New Negroes and Their Music*). George Hutchinson argues that the interracial character of the Harlem Renaissance had more positive

effects than negative ones, and he offers a carefully researched historical approach the movement (*The Harlem Renaissance in Black and White*).

19. Berlin describes this song as " a gentle tale of the courtship of a jungle maid of 'dusky shade' by a 'Zulu from Matabooloo'" with a "chorus [that] features both syncopations and the added syllables of ragtime lyrics" ("Ragtime Songs," 74). According to Berlin, "So entranced was the public by this song that numerous imitations ensued. Songwriters created subcategories of 'jungle' songs…" (ibid). The song also crossed over into "high" modernism; T. S. Eliot parodied it in his poem, "Fragment of Agon." The parody indicates Eliot's fear that "black dialect is a flaw, a kind of speech impediment, a remnant of the inarticulate that clogs his language and stands in the way as he attempts to link his own individual talent with tradition" (North, 78). Eliot's poetic gesture also suggests the tremendous impact of African American music on shaping the language and the style of modernism, even when the anxiety over its influence was contained through the use of parody. As Aldon Nielson points out, T. S. Eliot's ragtime is certainly not Scott Joplin's, but it is not "uninflected English" either (7). As both North and Nielson demonstrate in their studies of modernism, American "high" modernism is not nearly as "white" as some critics have tended to assume in the past.

20. In his historical dictionary of musical theater, *A Century of Musicals in Black and White*, Bernard Peterson cites many examples of what he describes as "white-oriented" musicals, or musicals marketed with white audiences in mind—musicals marketed as "white," despite the creative input of African American musicians. E.g., *Whoop-Dee-Doo* (1903), *The Supper Club* (1901), *Sleeping Beauty and the Beast* (1901-2), *Sally in Our Alley* (1902), and *Mother Goose* (1903). Cole and the Johnson brothers wrote music used in all of these shows, often employing ragtime-influenced rhythms. Thomas Riis, in his history of black musical theater, *Just Before Jazz*, notes that the team was hired by the powerful Klaw-Erlanger production company, and for this company, they "wrote songs for white singers in productions aimed at the average white Broadway theatergoer, rather than an exclusively black or even racially mixed audience, as had been the case with Williams and Walker" (110). After the Cole and Johnson brothers acquired fame and financial security, however, they were able to launch their own theater company, producing all black shows (111).

21. Walter Benn Michaels argues that "culture" cannot be "owned," and, therefore, a cultural practice, such a particular musical style, cannot be "stolen." Michaels asserts, "The idea that whites who learn to sing like blacks are stealing black culture thus depends upon the racialist idea that cultural identity is a function of racial identity" (129). While cultural practices are clearly learned rather than biologically inherited, Michaels's claims do not account for the particular history of African American music in this country. There has been a long history of cultural exchange in the field of American music, but this began with blatant white appropriation of the music of African American innovators *as white*. Even when we agree that racial categories are a social construction, we cannot simply disregard the concept of race as it has shaped national identity. Johnson's project is based on a desire for historical accuracy rather than an advocacy of "purism" or separatism.

22. Jasen and Tichenor assert that "Joplin's formal training at Smith College … allowed him to write down his ideas in details. Whereas the rags before, during, and

after Joplin were simplified by schooled arrangers, Joplin's rags were published the way he conceived them" (85).

23. According to John Edward Hasse, "The piano was a symbol of respectability–of arrival in the middle class. Before the advent of the automobile, the piano represented for many families the biggest single purchase, other than a house" (11). Hasse points out that the piano's percussive capabilities were well suited to ragtime rhythms and that the pianos produced at this time were grands or full uprights (not spinets). Most of the homes were made of solid wood with wooden floors and walls, so all of this provided powerfully resonant acoustics (15). Ragtime basically imbibed its new amateur performers and audiences, and this certainly must have contributed to its popularity.

24. In his *Black Manhattan,* Johnson writes that "the club" is based on an actual professional club run by Ike Hines in the Tenderloin district (the upper Twenties and the lower Thirties west of 6th Avenue), and in the decades just before and after the turn of the century this area was known as "Black Bohemia" (73-75).

25. For a detailed account of the Fair as "the place where a general public became familiar and intoxicated with the music" (2), see Berlin's *Reflections and Research on Ragtime* (1-3).

26. The kind of condescension that surfaces in both Rogers's and Johnson's descriptions of "untrained" musicians will be explored in depth later in this chapter when we turn to an examination of the binary discourse of "high" and "low" culture in the early twentieth century.

27. "Jazz" experienced a similar fate in the twenties, when popular music, fashion, and other commodities were affixed with the label "jazz" in order to increase sales and to define these cultural products and the consumers who purchased them as "modern."

28. In his essay "'Out of Notes': Miles Davis," Robert Walser discusses a Davis solo on the standard "My Funny Valentine." Walser argues that Davis signifies on the traditional range of the trumpet in the European scalar system. Walser points out that Davis's movement from A flat to G "without changing valves ... is difficult, risky, and relatively rare ... Davis must bend the note with his lips without letting it crack down to the next harmonic" (174). Walser continues: "The result is a fuzzy sound, not quite in tune. There is no conceivable situation in classical trumpet playing where such a sound would be desirable. Yet in this solo, it is the audible sign of Davis's effort and risk, articulating a moment of strain that contributes to the affect of his interpretation" (174). This account of the manipulation of standard notes to achieve effects beyond functional tonality is a good example of the kind of innovation in jazz that cannot be easily notated by conventional scoring methods.

29. This phenomenon should not surprise us in the early twenty-first century, since it has repeated itself in various manifestations so many times. In its latest manifestation, we see suburban and urban young people from a divergent array of cultural and ethnic backgrounds listening to hip hop music, dancing, dressing, and talking slang in hip hop styles. We also see these tendencies incorporated into "mainstream"music, fashion, dance, and slang that adults find fashionable. Repeatedly in American society, African American culture is the vanguard of "style."

30. Johnson discusses the constraints of dialect conventions in much of his writing,

including his 1928 article published in the *Philadelphia Tribune*, "Double Audience Makes Road Hard for Negro Writers." In this article, Johnson examines both the "taboos of black America" (411) and the "conventions of white America" (411) that hinder the expressive freedom of "the Aframerican author" (409). In his preface to his *God's Trombones*, Johnson describes conventional literary representations of African American speech as "an instrument with but two complete stops, pathos and humor" (7). Johnson works to establish in print the fullness of the *range* of vernacular speech in his own writing. He uses the trombone as a symbol of this range—again a musical metaphor—because it is "the instrument possessing above all others the power to express the wide and varied range of emotions encompassed by the human voice" (7).

31. This style is best characterized by Sondra Katherine Wilson's description of Johnson as a "mass educator" (4). Wilson performed the very useful service of collecting and editing two volumes of Johnson's *New York Age* editorials and other nonfiction writing.

32. Handy was the first to use the flatted third note of the chromatic scale to indicate the "blue" note in African American music. Abbe Niles, who wrote the introduction to Handy's blues anthology, commented in the revised 1949 edition of the book that, for example, "one could not reproduce on paper what Bessie Smith [the great blues singer] could do with this ["blue"] note; it is necessary to work out conventions" (20). Consequently, Handy devised the flatted third to indicate the sound.

33. Johnson used the term "Aframerican" to indicate the cultural and historical affinities between people of African descent who were citizens of both North and South America. His position as U.S. consul in South America undoubtedly heightened his awareness of African cultural retentions and recreations as a diasporic phenomenon. In *God's Trombones*, Johnson renders the cadences and the subject matter of African American sermons in his own style of poetic verse.

34. Chapter four of this book analyzes several Renaissance writers' approach to 1920's jazz and blues in relation to Toni Morrison's portrait of the era in her novel *Jazz*.

35. For two provocative studies of modernism and vernacular African American speech, see Michael North's *The Dialect of Modernism* and Aldon Nielson's *Writing Between the Lines: Race and Intertextuality*. Nielson argues that "American English, like American music, beats with a black heart" (6). It seems that for many white modernists, black speech, like black music, represented revolutionary rebelliousness and independent self-assertion. Although black speech imitated for white social and aesthetic priorities often amounted to verbal clichés or romanticized primitivism divorced from historical and cultural specificity, this engagement with African American forms of expression reflects the amalgamated (though often distorted) character of American culture.

36. In their study of Kafka as a "minor" writer, or a minority writer voicing ideas and practices oppositional to the dominant culture, Guattari and Deleuze describe the "deterritorialization" of language as the central characteristic of "minor" literature (16). This linguistic practice involves opposing a "purely intensive usage of language to all symbolic or even significant or simply signifying uses of it" (19). "Deterritorialization" relies on making the written text *sound* as well as *mean*.

37. These particular recordings of "Spiritual" appear on *Coltrane: The Complete 1961*

Village Vanguard Recordings. Impluse, IMPD4-232, 1997. On these recordings of "Spiritual," the band includes Eric Dolphy (bass clarinet), McCoy Tyner (piano), Reggie Workman (bass), Elvin Jones (drums), and, on two cuts, also Gavin Bushell (contrabassoon).

38. Quoted by Nat Hentoff in his liner notes to the first Village Vanguard recordings. *Coltrane "Live" at the Village Vanguard.* Impulse AS-10, 1961.

CHAPTER TWO: "A BIG SENSATION"

1. Styles such as "nut" or novelty jazz, "orchestrated" or "sweet" jazz, and "hot" or improvised jazz (usually performed by small combos rather than orchestras) all fell under the general heading "jazz" in the 1920s. "Hot" jazz has been historically documented as the center of the jazz tradition as we know it today, and African American artists almost exclusively created the innovations in this style. Each style can be sampled on the following recordings: *The Riotous, Raucous, Red-Hot 20's!* (featuring novelty jazz such as "Yes, We Have no Bananas!"), any record by the Paul Whiteman Orchestra (featuring orchestrated jazz such as George Gershwin's famous composition "Rhapsody in Blue"), and Louis Armstrong's *Hot Fives* and *Hot Sevens* (featuring improvisation and bringing the soloist to the forefront of jazz performance).

2. For detailed accounts of this phenomenon and numerous examples from the press see Neil Leonard, *Jazz and the White Americans: The Acceptance of a New Art Form* and Kathy Ogren, *The Jazz Revolution: Twenties America and the Meaning of Jazz.*

3. Darrel Mansell, in his article "The *Jazz History of the World* in *The Great Gatsby*," argues that the composition refers to Strauss's *Also Sprach Zarathustra* that was originally scheduled for performance at Carnegie Hall in 1921. This symphonic work was billed as a history of humanity, and Mansell concludes that it became the *Jazz History of the World* because "jazzing" it would make it fitting for Gatsby and his party. The allusion, according to Mansell, alludes to " a major theme of the novel: America's brash energetic and meretricious vulgarization of European culture" (62). In his "*The Great Gatsby*: Grief, Jazz and the Eye-Witness," Mitchell Breitwieser offers an array of possible sources for the reference, including Paul Whiteman's Aeolian Hall Concert, "An Experiment in Modern Music," performed in 1924 (62-63). With *Jazz History*, Breitwieser claims, Fitzgerald is "cluing us" that "this is not black jazz" (62).

4. In the manuscript, "interruptive" is inserted with a carrot symbol. The adjective remains in the galleys.

5. Improvisation is essential to the jazz tradition. Kathy Ogren points out that this element of the music is, to a large extent, what made it so expressive of the modern condition because "improvisational music promises no sure passages; rather it captures the inevitability of mobility and change" (165). Nick's descriptions of *Jazz History* suggest that the music is, at least in part, improvisational because its themes and variations are unpredictable.

6. Information on Whiteman's "Three O'Clock in the Morning" comes from Arnold Shaw's *The Jazz Age: Popular Music in the 1920s.*

7. For a concise history of jazz dance in America see Katrina Hazzard-Gordon, *Jookin': The Rise of Social Dance Formations in African-American Culture* (Philadelphia,

1990), and on jazz and dance traditions see Marshall and Jean Stearns, *Jazz Dance: The Story of American Vernacular Dance* (New York: Schirmer Books, Macmillan, 1968). The participatory aspect of jazz, including its accompanying dances, was a major point of contention in anti-jazz attacks in the media.

8. See Levine's *Highbrow/Lowbrow: The Emergence of Cultural Hierarchy in America*.

9. Lawrence W. Levine. "Jazz and American Culture." *The Unpredictable Past: Explorations in American Cultural History*, 172-188.

10. For a good accounts of the role of jazz and blues in the growth of the recording industry, including historical accounts of the emergence of "race records," see Andre Millard's *America on Record: A History of Recorded Sound* and Rick Kennedy's *Jelly Roll, Bix, and Hoagy: Gennett Studios and the Birth of Recorded Jazz*.

11. In Ellison's *Invisible Man* the protagonist learns from his Liberty Paints job that it takes ten drops of black to make "the purest white that can be found" (202). This is the paint that will cover the National Monument. The episode implies that what is visibly white (optic white) is actually infused with black to make it appear white. In other words, the symbolism indicates that mid-twentieth-century segregated America relied upon its infusion of African American culture to define its apparently "white" identity.

12. As Philip Eberly points out, "jazz" on the radio could mean anything from a sprinkling of jazz effects to "a self-conscious impersonation of Louis Armstrong" (5). Differences in styles were not always delineated along color lines. There were African American bands that played "nut" jazz and white bands that studied the black innovators and learned the art of improvisation. The radio programming in the twenties indicated that "in the minds of its mass audience it was [all] jazz nonetheless" (102). The term "jazz" was used indiscriminately, although audiences certainly must have been aware of stylistic differences.

13. In some ways this intermingling of the dynamics of race and class with musical expression can be traced back to nineteenth-century minstrel show practices. In his historical study of minstrelsy, *Love and Theft*, Eric Lott explores the complex interrelations of race and class that contributed to the popularity of this particularly American form of entertainment. For white audiences, minstrel shows deflected "an acute sense of class insecurity by indulging in feelings of racial superiority" (64). In the minstrel theater, "It was through 'blackness' that class was staged..." (64). Of course, music (appropriated and *defused*) from black cultural practices was central to the minstrel show, just as African American jazz expressions were transmuted and, to some degree, regulated through parody in novelty jazz.

14. In one of her essays, Zora Neale Hurston writes, "Musically speaking, the Jook is the most important place in America" (306). Hurston traces the blues influence of Jook music to urban forms of jazz and musical theater.

15. As far as the music is concerned, this same cultural phenomenon persisted with the emergence of first rock 'n' roll and now rap and hip hop. This does not mean that the music was/is severed from its ties to black audiences, but the way the meanings of the music change as it is popularized for white audiences exemplifies what Tricia Rose describes as "mainstream social constructions of black culture as forbidden narrative, as a symbol of rebellion" (*Black Noise*, 5).

16. An example of the negativity in recent criticism appears in James Lincoln

Collier's history of jazz. Collier dismisses Handy as a "former minstrel bandsman who Europeanized folk blues for a white market" (81).

17. Chapter one of this book examines James Weldon Johnson's response to Handy's blues notation. Johnson's essay praises Handy's documentation work for historical purposes but also recognizes the difficulties of trying to notate the African-influenced music according to the conventional European scalar system.

18. Small notes that African American musicians in the twenties drew their inspiration from every source available to them in order to enrich their art and to make it a statement of individual and collective identity. According to Small, "for black Americans there were not two repertoires but only one. Black American musicians have approached the European Classical tradition, like any other way of musicking, with respect and love but not with subservience, according it no specially privileged status but simply its legitimate place among the material of their musical experience and performance" (263).

19. According to music historians Schafer and Riedel: "Ragtime reached across America in the form of sheet music, piano rolls, and itinerant pianists traveling in show business. Both classical ragtime and its spawn of popular and commercial imitations [e.g., "Alexander's Ragtime Band"] had a wide hearing in the first decade of the century…Ragtime style became, for a generation of musicians and listeners, the basic style for all popular music. It reached by musical and cultural osmosis into all the basic forms of American music…Every kind of popular and folk music absorbed valuable materials from ragtime, from primitive country music forms on through the slickly manufactured musical comedies. The first campaign in the black music revolution of the twentieth century was clearly carried by ragtime" (46).

20. For example, Kathy Ogren demonstrates that Chicago *Defender*'s music columnist, Dave Peyton, exerted his influence in condemning the cabaret music of what he called "the gut bucket orchestra," players who Peyton believed "have no consciousness of what real music is" (qtd. in Ogren, 115). According to Ogren, Peyton's attitudes exemplify "the class tensions which intensified between middle and working-class blacks after migration [from the South to Northern urban centers] and which helped make jazz controversial among blacks as well as whites" (115).

21. This is typical of some early twentieth-century attitudes about the relationship between "race" and "culture," despite anthropologist Franz Boas's demonstration of culture as a set of practices acquired through learning. As Walter Benn Michaels argues, "The modernist concept of culture is racialized because it envisions one's culture as something that is biologically inherited and dependent upon one's race" (141). Michaels's description holds true for many, but not all, factions of modernism.

22. Ralph Ellison. "What America Would Be Like Without Blacks." *Going to the Territory*, p.111. In this essay Ellison notes that this "troubling suspicion" lurks within the American theme of the quest for identity and self-definition. Ellison does not directly mention Fitzgerald here, but I think his argument is applicable to Fitzgerald's fiction.

23. Toni Morrison uses the term "Africanist presence" to describe African American characters who represent "the denotative and connotative blackness that African people have come to signify, as well as the entire range of views, assumptions, read-

ings, and misreadings that accompany Eurocentric learning about these people" (6-7). Fitzgerald's African American characters are sometimes invoked as Africanist presences in conjunction with popular music as a kind of shortcut or stereotype that eludes the contradictions embedded within American history.

24. Cultural theorist Paul Gilroy notes that "the most important lesson music still has to teach us is that its inner secrets and ethnic rules can be taught and learned" (134).

25. The name Van Vleck is so close to Van Vechten that one wonders if it is an allusion to that writer's forays into Harlem nightlife. Perhaps the story suggests that Van Vechten was also seeking a degree in "jazz."

26. Information on the publication dates of the songs comes from Ruth Prigozy's "'Poor Butterfly': F. Scott Fitzgerald and Popular Music" and Kurt Ganzl's *The Encyclopedia of the Musical Theater*.

27. Details on the songs' publication dates and performance venues come from Ruth Prigozy's "'Poor Butterfly': F. Scott Fitzgerald and Popular Music." The dates of these songs and their musical theater venue suggest that they might be described as ragtime-influenced popular music. In his *Early Jazz*, music historian Gunther Schuller asserts that most pre-1923 recordings "were made by society orchestras, novelty bands, or jazz groups who were forced by the companies recording them to play novelty or polite dance music" (64). James Weldon Johnson documents the influence of ragtime and early jazz on musical theater in much of his writing.

28. Abe tells Dick, "'Something tells me I'll have a new score on Broadway long before you've finished your scientific treatise'" (61) but neither character achieves his goal.

29. Robert Forrey "Negroes in the Fiction of F. Scott Fitzgerald." and Bryan R. Washington *The Politics of Exile*. Forrey argues that characters of African descent appear in "clownish and inferior roles" (293) in Fitzgerald's fiction. According to Washington, "Black exiles in *Tender is the Night* are caricatures...When blacks are the focus, the language employed hybridizes the minstrel show..." (64-65).

30. In his *Race Matters* Cornel West points out the inevitable entanglement of issues of race and sex: "Everyone knows [that] it is virtually impossible to talk candidly about race without talking about sex. Yet most social scientists who examine race relations do so with little or no reference to how sexual perceptions influence racial matters" (83-84).

31. In this same essay, written in 1931, Fitzgerald describes the death of one of his former classmates, the circumstances of which are almost exactly the same as his portrayal of Abe's demise. This man was "beaten to death in a speak-easy in New York and crawled home to the Princeton Club to die" (20).

32. Abe's character (as an alcoholic musician) also appeared in earlier drafts of the novel, and he was first called Abe Herkimer, then Abe Grant. In the Melarky Narrator version of the novel Abe is "going back to ~~Washington~~ New York ... to ~~get himself out of the State Department~~ see ~~Otto Kahn~~ about an 'All American' opera" (191). Abe wants to write the musical version of the "great American novel," and as an American musician, he must negotiate social boundaries.

33. In his reading of the Peterson episode, John Callahan asserts: "Diver's own sub-

liminal violations do not allow him to tell Nicole that the rape of America and the murder and enslavement of black people are linked. He will not acknowledge, let alone bear, his share of the guilt" (111). The trivializing narrative tone, however, takes the sting out of the irony and implies that the sublimation may be occurring on an authorial level.

34. The *Oxford English Dictionary* defines the archaic meaning of "exquisite" as overly careful and fastidious. In this sense, "exquisite manners" calls to mind the attributes of a social pretender—a dandy or a fop.

CHAPTER THREE: MUSICAL RANGE

1. It also seems significant that Hughes chose French composer Jules Massenet (1842-1912) for this particular musical allusion. Massenet represents a close relationship between music and literature. For example, his opera *Thaïs* is based on Anatole France's novel by the same title, and his famous opera *Werther* is based upon Goethe's *The Sorrows of Young Werther*. The *Meditation from Thaïs*, which Roy plays, is the renowned violin solo from the opera. The tale told by the opera is particularly relevant to Roy's situation. It is a story of conflict between spiritual and earthly love that parallels Roy's desire to achieve transcendence through music and his inability to do so in the face of the harsh realities of worldly injustice.

2. Larry Scanlon describes this imagery as a particular facet of Hughes's modernism. According to Scanlon: "Modernism's reactionary strain viewed modernity as an irrevocable break, a wasteland dominated by the finality of loss and incoherence. But Hughes understands modernity as a dream deferred, an on-going confrontation with the contradictions of the past rather than a fallen alienation from its certainties" (512).

3. Pablo de Sarasate (1844-1908) was a violin virtuoso from Spain.

4. David Chinitz points out in his essay "'Dance, Little Lady': Poets, Flappers, and the Gendering of Jazz" that "Hughes continually reminds us of his conviction that jazz, like the blues, only 'laughs to keep from crying'; its narcotic effects are temporary stays against the harsher realities of life for the disenfranchised African American" (331).

5. An interesting historical account of the emergence and perpetuation of the stereotype of "black rhythm" is presented in Ronald Radano's essay "Hot Fantasies: American Modernism and the Idea of Black Rhythm."

6. In an essay on *The Ways of White Folks*, Jane Olmsted observes: "It is one thing for Hughes to refer to the rhythm of Black music, 'its strength like the beat of the human heart, its humor and its rooted power,' and quite another for it to be appropriated by White people who would use 'the primitive' as a means of narrowing Black people's humanity to a misunderstood fragment—moreover, doing so for the precise reason that they can then project what they are most uncomfortable about themselves onto African Americans" (77).

7. In his study of Hughes as a modernist poet, Larry Scanlon notes, "In contrast to many of his contemporaries, [Hughes] took modernism to be both a public and a quintessentially popular phenomenon" (511).

8. Radano's study of the notion of rhythm in African American music examines this component of the jazz controversy. Radano concludes, "The vast repetition of refer-

ence to black music as a fever, drug, disease, and intoxicant indicate that the threat of black music related above all to fears of miscegenation…" (474).

9. This imagery also illustrates the centrality of rhythm in Hughes's conception of African American musical and linguistic traditions. As Larry Scanlon asserts, "Rhythm for Hughes is nothing less than an alternate mode of cultural articulation: material, embodied, oral, musical. This mode of articulation shadows language, neither fully distinct from it nor fully subordinate to it" (518).

CHAPTER FOUR: "ONLY IN THE HEAD OF A MUSICIAN"

1. In her study of the jazz controversy in the 1920s, Kathy Ogren observes that the revolutionary, modernistic aspects of the music derive in part from the risks it takes and articulates. She concludes that "improvisational music promises no sure passages; rather it captures the inevitability of mobility and change" (165).

2. A comment made by saxophonist Dexter Gordon exemplifies this tendency: "When Lester [Young] came out he played very melodic … He was always telling a story and Bird [Charlie Parker] did the same thing. That kind of musical philosophy is what I try to do because telling a story is, I think, where it's at" (qtd. in Chambers, 54).

3. Morrison commented in an interview: "Black music's always called something–spiritual, gospel, jazz, boogie-woogie, bop, bebop, rap–but it's never called music, for example, 20th century music, modern music. So it's argued about in another way … I believe the 20's began to be the moment when black culture, rather than American culture, began to alter the whole country and eventually the western world … So that's why I used the term jazz, because it sums all this up. But nobody in the book would call it that" (Carabi, 41).

4. Elliott M. Rudwick's *Race Riot at East St. Louis* provides an account of the riot and events leading up to it. His primary sources are newspaper reports, police records, interviews, and congressional and military hearings. Rudwick discusses the organization of a "Silent Parade" in New York and in other major cities (134-35). In his history of Harlem, *This Was Harlem*, Jervis Anderson also mentions the events in East St. Louis and New York's "Silent Parade" (105-6).

5. This photo is part of the Schomberg Center's collection at the New York Public Library. It is reprinted in Jervis Anderson's *This Was Harlem* (88-89).

6. A political cartoon had run in the *New York Evening Mail*, an image of which marchers had intended to carry until police officials ordered them not to do so. In the cartoon, an African American woman on her knees with arms outstretched appears with two frightened children against a backdrop of East St. Louis in flames. President Woodrow Wilson stands above her holding a paper that reads "the world must be safe for democracy." The caption asks, "Mr. President, why not make America safe for democracy?" (Rudwick 58-61, 247).

7. Morrison places a focus on linguistic innovation at the center of her craft as a novelist. In her critical work, *Playing in the Dark*, she writes, "The kind of work I have always wanted to do requires me to learn how to maneuver ways to free up the language from its sometimes sinister, frequently lazy, almost always predictable employ-

ment of racially informed and determined chains" (xi). This approach can be considered a kind of deterritorialization of language that Deleuze and Guattari describe as the most important characteristic of "minor literature," which voices ideas and engages in artistic practices that are opposed to those of the dominant culture. The deterritorialization of written language involves opposing a "purely intensive usage of language to all symbolic or even significant or simply signifying uses of it" (19). Deterritorialization relies on making the written text *sound* as well as mean. Morrison uses the aesthetic priorities of African American music, including improvisation, call and response, inflected timbre, manipulation of European harmonics, and African derived polyrhythms as her particular model for deterritorialization. One could say that African American music, even in its earliest forms, has itself deterritorialized the functional tonality of European musical traditions imported to the United States, so even though music and language may remain separate entities, the music certainly provides a successful model for the process of deterritorialization. See musicologist John Shepherd for a detailed account of the ways that African American musical practices and aesthetics disrupt functional tonality (*Music as Social Text*, chapter 6, "Functional Tonality: A Basis for Musical Hegemony").

8. Gates defines "tropological revision" as "the manner in which a specific trope is repeated, with differences, between two or more texts" (xxv).

9. Recent critical examples include the following: Craig Hansen Werner's *Playing the Changes: From Afro-Modernism to the Jazz Impulse*, Jon Panish's *The Color of Jazz: Race and Representation in Postwar American Culture*, Houston A. Baker's *Blues, Ideology, and African American Literature: A Vernacular Theory*, Albert Murray's *The Blue Devils of Nada*.

10. Other novels published within the last twenty-five years that participate significantly in this tradition include: Ishmael Reed's *Mumbo Jumbo* (1972), Gayl Jones's *Corregidora* (1975) and *The Healing* (1998), Nathaniel Mackey's *Bedouin Hornbook* (1986), Toni Cade Bambara's *The Salt Eaters* (1980), and Michael Ondaatje's *Coming Through Slaughter* (1976). Born in Sri Lanka and now residing in Canada, the multicultural Ondaatje taps into African American literary traditions with his historically informed and stylistically innovative fictional story of the life of early New Orleans jazz cornetist Buddy Bolden. It is interesting to note that the most formally experimental novels in this group were written by Reed, Mackey, and Ondaatje, all of whom are established poets and representative "postmodernists."

11. The passage in which Violet ponders the connections between herself and "*that* Violet" echoes this representation of the music. She must understand herself as Violet *and* "Violent" in order to achieve coherence. Coherence, according to Morrison's portrayal of it as a concept, is always overdetermined, and the music serves as her central trope for this idea.

12. Houston Baker, in his exploration of the "blues matrix" (3), which serves as his trope for African American culture and extends to represent "the *All* of American culture" (13), describes the democratic appeal of the blues as an expression of modernism. Baker concludes, "The signal expressive achievement of blues, then, lay in their translation of technological innovativeness, unsettling demographic fluidity, and boundless frontier energy into expression which attracted avid interest from the American

masses" (11).

13. The narrative voice of *Jazz* is one of the novel's most intriguing and most frequently analyzed features. Critics have offered various interpretations of who or what the narrative voice is. In an early review, John Leonard called the narrative voice the book itself, citing the narrator's final directive, "Look where your hands are. Now." Eusebio Rodrigues and Craig Werner both interpret the narrator as the thunder goddess from *The Nag Hammadi*, an excerpt from which appears as the novel's epigraph. Paula Gallant Eckard makes a case for jazz music itself as the narrator. The variety of interpretations attests to the complexity and uniqueness of this narrator. Since it is cumbersome to write she/he/it for every pronominal reference to the narrator, I will simply refer to the narrator as she, while noting that, in terms of gender, the binary division of he/she is a reductive way to conceptualize this narrative voice. In an interview, Morrison stated that she "was trying to align [herself] with more interesting and intricate aspects of [her] notion of jazz as a demanding, improvisatory art form, so [she] had to get rid of the conventions, which [she] distrust[s]" (Carabi, 42). Her strategy for accomplishing this involves her construction of a different kind of narrative voice, which she describes as "the voice of a talking book" (Carabi, 42). Houston Baker's description of the expressive form of the blues and the identity of the blues singer has interesting connections with the tone and style of the narrator of *Jazz*. Baker writes: "Rather than a rigidly personalized form, the blues offer a phylogenic recapitulation–a nonlinear, freely associative, nonsequential meditation–a species of experience. What emerges is a filled subject, but an anonymous (nameless) voice issuing from the black (w)hole" (5).

14. *Duke Ellington: Volume I, 1924-1926* (Nanterre - France: Media7 MJCD 8, 1991).

15. Tricia Rose persuasively makes this case in her book on rap and hip hop, *Black Noise*.

16. This scene calls to mind another of Morrison's "knowing" women who sings on her deathbed – Sula. When Sula crawls into the bed to die, "she sang a little wandering tune made up of the words *I have sung all the songs all the songs I have sung all the songs there are* until, touched by her own lullaby, she grew drowsy..." (137). Sula also reminds Nel that the binary distinctions between "good" and "evil" are unreliable, and poses this final question to her estranged best friend: "About who was good. How do you know it was you?" (146).

17. Chapter three examines a similar portrayal of the powers of music in several short stories from Langston Hughes's *The Ways of White Folks*.

18. For an account of "hillbilly music" (154) in the 1920s, see Rick Kennedy's analysis of the role of independent labels in recording history, *Jelly Roll, Bix, and Hoagy: Gennett Studios and the Birth of Recorded Jazz*.

19. For the most comprehensive study of the jazz controversy in the twenties, see Kathy Ogren's *The Jazz Revolution: Twenties America and the Meaning of Jazz*.

20. The terms "consent" and "descent," as I use them here, derive from Werner Sollors's theories in *Beyond Ethnicity: Consent and Descent in American Culture*.

21. Ishmael Reed comically toys with these metaphors of disease and epidemic in his novel *Mumbo Jumbo*, which creates a portrait of the music as a cultural force that he calls "Jes Grew," a term borrowed from James Weldon Johnson's description of early

ragtime music. In his essay, "Hot Fantasies: American Modernism and the Idea of Black Rhythm," Ronald Radano points out that during the jazz controversy, "References to black rhythm's 'infectious' nature in an era of epidemic diseases are particularly revealing, for they focus specifically on fear of material (human) transmission through the immateriality of sound" (462-63).

22. In his 1936 work, *The Negro and His Music*, Alain Locke attributes "authenticity" to folk productions while urging aspiring young artists to make "high" cultural musical statements rooted in a folk idiom. By studying folk traditions, composers could avoid, for example, "the glossed over versions [of the spirituals] characteristic of those arrangers and singers who have not closely studied the primitive Negro folk-ways of singing" (23). He argues for a line a continuity that links all African American musical forms, and he places this music in an international folk tradition that has inspired "high" art: "What Glink and his successors did for Russian music, Liszt and Brahms for Hungarian music, Dvorak and Smetana for Czech music, can and must be done for Negro music" (130).

23. For groundbreaking work in defining this aesthetic see Addison Gayle's anthology, *The Black Aesthetic* (1971). On the subject of African American music, Amiri Baraka's study, *Blues People* (1963), is an important part of this critical tradition. Although when reading this work, one might want to keep in mind Ralph Ellison's observation: "The tremendous burden of sociology which Jones would place upon this body of music is enough to give even the blues the blues" (249). At this point in history, the issue of African American cultural difference and its impact on the "mainstream" is (or should be) central to any attempt to theorize an American literary tradition.

24. Morrison selected the contents for the recently published volume of Baldwin's collected fiction in which "Sonny's Blues" appears.

25. In his study of James Weldon Johnson's prefaces, Brent Edwards traces the etymology of the term "lyric" (582-83). Edwards concludes that Johnson's theorization of the concept of lyricism in writing refutes " a dichotomy between form and content" (598). A similar argument could be made for Morrison's approach to music in *Jazz*.

26. The concepts of residual and emergent cultural practices, as they are used here, derive from Raymond Williams's theories in *Marxism and Literature*. Williams describes a residual cultural practice as one which "has been effectively formed in the past, but it is still active in the cultural process, not only and often not at all as an element of the past, but as an effective element of the present" (122). According to Williams, in emergent cultural practices "new meaning and values, new practices, new relationships and kinds of relationship are continually being created" (123). Williams points out, however, that it is difficult to determine which practices "are substantially alternative or oppositional to [the dominant culture]: emergent in the strict sense, rather than merely novel" (123). Henry Louis Gates, Jr. defines the trope of the Talking Book as that of "double-voiced texts that talk to other texts" (xxv), and he describes this as the "ur-trope" (xxv) of the African American literary tradition.

27. This phrase is part of a statement made by the narrator in James Weldon Johnson's *The Autobiography of an Ex-Coloured Man*, and it is analyzed at length in the first chapter of this book. Johnson's narrator suggests that his familiarity with African-

derived spirituals sung by his mother helped him to transform the piano from "the source of hard or blurred sounds it so generally is" (26-27) into a "sympathetic, singing instrument" (26). One might argue that what African American musical traditions have done for European derived instruments like the piano, trumpet, or saxophone, African American literary traditions have done for the European derived literary form of the novel.

28. Louis Menand's *New Yorker* review of Morrison's most recent novel, *Paradise*, is representative of this critical tendency. Menand mentions that Morrison attributes her "collaborative" (80) or participatory style to the call and response style of black preaching and jazz. He challenges these sources: "But the technique has a literary source: it comes out of the modernist fiction of Woolf, Joyce, Hemingway, and Faulkner. Morrison wrote a master's thesis, at Cornell, on Woolf and Faulkner back in 1955, and her novels reflect their influence ... Her achievement is to have adapted that modernist literary tradition to her own subject matter, which is the experience of African American women, and thereby to have made it new" (80).

29. *Criticism and the Color Line: Desegregating American Literary Studies*, edited by Henry Wonham, provides an excellent overview of these critical trends that examine the interrelatedness of black and white culture in America. Werner Sollors's *Neither Black Nor White Yet Both* offers a fascinating account of interracial themes in American literature. Sollors concludes, "Whether the interracial character is proved white or black, in either case the 'mixed-race' space is cleared in favor of a monoracial occupancy" (6). This trend leads Sollors to wonder, "Is there such a thing as 'amalgophobia' or mixophobia'?" (10).

30. In addition to the two critics discussed in the following paragraph, seven others who have focused on Morrison's use of music, particularly in *Jazz*, should be mentioned. In an article written before *Jazz* was published, Anthony Berret argues that Morrison uses jazz in her writing to express and encourage African American communal awareness. Craig Werner asserts that "Morrison grounds her jazz vision in a gospel impulse" (92), and he situates her writing within a long tradition of musical prominence in African American literature. Cheryl Hall explores the connections between jazz and storytelling in *Beloved*, but her article would benefit from more extensive research on the music itself. Her primary sources are Marshall Stearns (1956) and Winthrop Sargeant (1946), both of whom were knowledgeable commentators on the music, but whose perspectives are a bit outdated. She cites 1920s pop jazz icon Paul Whiteman as an authority on the subject of jazz (95). Paula Eckard Gallant argues that jazz music itself is the narrator of *Jazz*, and that the music is closely associated with the City. She claims that the devices that illustrate this are the use of "jazz terms" (16), "call and response" (17), blank pages that indicate "a pause or break" (18), and most importantly, "signifying" (19). Barbara Williams Lewis also focuses on Morrison's use of jazz devices in *Jazz*, such as the "break" (273, 275), words associated with jazz music (274), and "repetition" or riffs (276-77). Robin Small-McCarthy also analyzes jazz devices that translate into the episodic structure (293), the "polyrhythmic pattern" (294), and the "call and response" (296) style of *Jazz*. Alan Rice argues for "the centrality of jazz music stylistically to [Morrison's] whole corpus of work" (423). He, too, focuses on the use of the "riff" (425), which is a kind of signifying or repetition with a

difference. He also cites the jazz characteristics of "non-linearity and circuitousness" (431), "change and communality" (431), and more generally, "signifyin'" (431). He concludes that jazz is a sign of African American cultural difference in Morrison's work that she uses to remake the literary language in the music's image.

31. In his analysis of the music in *Jazz*, Munton never mentions the Okeh allusions. Felice carries an Okeh record at the beginning and the end of the novel.

32. Munton focuses on the European cultural infusion. He writes, "The exact process by which jazz was formed out of musical practices imported into North America is obscure because insufficiently documented; but there can be no doubt that the mix was broadly European form married to African rhythm" (236). This statement replays an old stereotype.

33. In *Jazz*, the bird imagery also conjures the image of Charlie "Bird" Parker whose bebop innovations post-date the novel's setting by at least twenty years. Bird and flight imagery is central to jazz (musicians' nicknames, song and album titles) and to much of Morrison's writing, especially in *Song of Solomon*, a novel that explores African cultural inheritance and that recreates the myth of the flying African. An entire study could be devoted to images of birds and flight in Morrison's writing.

34. The movement of the novel's red-winged blackbirds also symbolizes the African American "Great Migration," in which Joe and Violet Trace participate, moving from the South to the urban North in the early twentieth century.

CONCLUSION

1. Of course, it almost goes without saying that the fiction included in the study is just a small sample of literature that engages with jazz, but I have tried to demonstrate the principle that approaching literature and music from interdisciplinary perspective can be rewarding in any musical-literary study.

2. From O'Meally's preface to the collection of essays that he edited, *The Jazz Cadence of American Culture* (New York: Columbia University Press, 1998). Signifying on W. E. B. Du Bois's famous proclamation in his preface (or "The Forethought") to *The Souls of Black Folk* (1903) that "[t]he problem of the Twentieth Century is the problem of the color-line," O'Meally brings a jazz awareness to the study of American culture.

3. *Mestiza* and *mestizo* refer to a part of Anzaldúa's ancestry. She explains that this term serves the purpose of affirming Indian and Spanish cultural heritage (63).

Bibliography

Anderson, Jervis. *This Was Harlem: A Cultural Portrait, 1900–1950.* New York: Farrar Straus Giroux, 1982.

Andrews, William L. "Introduction to James Weldon Johnson's *The Autobiography of an Ex-Coloured Man.* New York: Penguin, 1990.

Anzaldúa, Gloria. *Borderlands: La Frontera.* San Francisco: Aunt Lute Books, 1987.

Baker, Houston A., Jr. *Blues, Ideology, and Afro-American Literature: A Vernacular Theory.* Chicago: University of Chicago Press, 1984.

———. *Modernism and the Harlem Renaissance.* Chicago: University of Chicago Press, 1987.

Baldwin, James. "Sonny's Blues." *Early Novels and Stories.* New York: Library of America, 1998.

Bambara, Toni Cade. *The Salt Eaters.* New York: Vintage, 1992; reprint, New York: Random House, 1980.

Baraka, Amiri (LeRoi Jones). *Blues People.* New York: William Morrow, 1963.

Bergreen, Laurence. *Louis Armstrong: An Extravagant Life.* New York: Broadway Books, 1997.

Berlin, Edward A. *Ragtime: A Musical and Cultural History.* Berkeley: University of California Press, 1980.

———. "Ragtime Songs." *Ragtime: Its History, Composers, and Music.* Ed. John Edward Hasse. New York: Schirmer-Macmillan, 1985.

———. *Reflections and Research on Ragtime*. Brooklyn: Institute for Studies in American Music, 1987.

Berman, Ronald. *The Great Gatsby and Modern Times*. Chicago: University of Illinois Press, 1994.

Berrett, Anthony J. "Toni Morrison's Literary Jazz." *CLA Journal*. 32:3 (March 1989): 267–283.

Bhabha, Homi K. *The Location of Culture*. New York: Routledge, 1994.

Blesh, Rudi and Harriet Janis. *They All Played Ragtime*. New York: Alfred A. Knopf, 1950.

Breitwieser, Mitchell. "*The Great Gatsby*: Grief, Jazz, and the Eye-Witness." *Arizona Quarterly*. Autumn 47 (3) 1991: 17–70.

Brooks, Neil. "On Becoming an Ex-Man: Postmodern Irony and the Extinguishing of Certainties in *The Autobiography of an Ex-Coloured Man*. *College Literature*. 1995 October: (22–23), 17–29.

Callahan, John F. *Illusions of a Nation: Myth and History in the Novels of F. Scott Fitzgerald*. Chicago: University of Illinois Press, 1972.

Carabi, Angels. "Toni Morrison Interview." *Belles Lettres*. 10:2 (Spring 1995): 40–43.

Cataliotti, Robert. *The Music in African American Fiction*. New York: Garland, 1995.

Chambers, Leland H. "Improvising and Mythmaking in Eudora Welty's 'Powerhouse.'" *Representing Jazz*, Ed. Krin Gabbard. Durham: Duke University Press, 1995.

Chernoff, John Miller. *African Rhythm and African Sensibility: Aesthetics and Social Action in African Musical Idioms*. Chicago: University of Chicago Press, 1979.

Chinitz, David. "'Dance, Little Lady'": Poets, Flappers, and the Gendering of Jazz." *Modernism, Gender, and Culture: A Cultural Studies Approach*. Ed. Lisa Rado. New York: Garland, 1997.

Collier, James Lincoln. *The Making of Jazz: A Comprehensive History*. New York: Delta, 1978.

Coltrane, John. *Coltrane: The Complete 1961 Village Vanguard Recordings*. Impulse, IMPD4–232, 1997.

Deleuze, Gilles and Felix Guattari. *Kafka: Toward a Minor Literature*. Minneapolis: University of Minnesota Press, 1986.

Eberly, Philip K. *Music in the Air: America's Changing Taste in Music, 1920–1980*. New York: Hastings, 1982.

Eckard, Paula Gallant. "The Interplay of Music, Language, and Narrative in Toni Morrison's *Jazz*." *CLA Journal*. 38:1 (September 1994): 11–19.

Edwards, Brent. "The Seemingly Eclipsed Window of Form: James Weldon Johnson's Prefaces." *The Jazz Cadence of American Culture*. Ed. Robert O'Meally. New York: Columbia University Press, 1998.

Ellington, Duke (Edward). *The Duke Ellington Reader*. Ed. Mark Tucker. New York: Oxford University Press, 1993.

Ellison, Ralph. . *Invisible Man*. New York: Vintage, 1990; reprint, New York: Random House, 1952.

———. *Shadow and Act*. New York: Vintage, 1995; reprint, New York: Random House, 1964.

———. "What America Would Be Like Without Blacks." *Time* 6 April 1970; reprint, *Going to the Territory*. New York: Random House, 1986.

Faulkner, Anne Shaw. "Does Jazz Put the 'Sin' in Syncopation?" *Ladies Home Journal* 38 (August 1921).

Fishkin, Shelley Fisher. "Interrogating 'Whiteness,' Complicating 'Blackness': Remapping American Culture. *Criticism and the Color Line: Desegregating American Literary Studies*. Ed. Henry B. Wonham. New Brunswick, NJ: Rutgers University Press, 1996.

Fitzgerald, F. Scott. *The Crack-Up*. Ed. Edmund Wilson. New York: New Directions, 1945.

———. *F. Scott Fitzgerald: A Life in Letters*. Ed. Matthew J. Bruccoli. New York: Charles Scribner's Sons, 1994.

———. *F. Scott Fitzgerald Manuscripts*. Ed. Matthew J. Bruccoli. New York: Garland Publishing, 1990.

———. *The Great Gatsby*. New York, Charles Scribner's Sons, 1925.

———. *The Great Gatsby: A Facsimile of the Manuscript*. Ed. Matthew J. Bruccoli. Washington, D.C.: Microcard Editions Books, 1973.

———. *The Letters of F. Scott Fitzgerald*. Ed. Andrew Turnbull. New York: Charles Scribner's Sons, 1963.

———. *The Short Stories of F. Scott Fitzgerald*. Ed. Matthew J. Bruccoli. New York: Scribner-Simon & Schuster, 1989.

———. *Tender is the Night*. New York: Charles Scribner's Sons, 1934; reprint, New York: Collier-Macmillan, 1986 (page references are to reprint edition).

Forrey, Robert. "Negroes in the Fiction of F. Scott Fitzgerald." *Phylon* 28 (3) 1972: 293–98.

Frith, Simon. *Performing Rites: On the Value of Popular Music.* Cambridge: Harvard University Press, 1996.

Ganzl, Kurt. *The Encyclopedia of the Musical Theater.* Vol. 1 and 2. New York: Schirmer Books, 1994.

Garber, Frederick. "Fabulating Jazz." *Representing Jazz.* Ed. Krin Gabbard. Durham: Duke University Press, 1995.

Gates, Henry Louis, Jr. *The Signifying Monkey.* New York: Oxford University Press, 1988.

Gayle, Addison, Ed. *The Black Aesthetic.* Garden City, NJ: Doubleday, 1971.

Gilroy, Paul. "Sounds Authentic: Black Music, Ethnicity, and the Challenge of a *Changing* Same." *Black Music Research Journal.* 10 (2) 1990.

Goldberg, Isaac. *Tin Pan Alley: A Chronicle of American Popular Music.* New York: Frederick Unger, 1961. [rpt. 1930]

Hadlock, Richard. *Jazz Masters of the Twenties.* New York: Da Capo, 1988.

Hall, Cheryl. "Beyond the 'Literary Habit': Oral Tradition and Jazz in *Beloved.*" *MELUS.* 19:1 (Spring 1994): 89–95.

Hamm, Charles. *Putting Popular Music in its Place.* Cambridge: Cambridge University Press, 1995.

Handy, W. C. (William Christopher), Ed.. *A Treasury of the Blues.* Intro. Abbe Niles. New York: Charles Boni-Simon and Schuster, 1949. [revised and reprinted: *Blues: An Anthology,* 1926]

Hardack, Richard. "A Music Seeking Its Words: Double-Timing and Double-Consciousness in Toni Morrison's *Jazz.*" *Callaloo.* 18:2 (1995): 451–471.

Harrison, Daphne Duval. *Black Pearls: Blues Queens of the 1920s.* New Brunswick, NJ: Rutgers University Press, 1988.

Hase, John Edward. "Ragtime: From the Top." *Ragtime: Its History, Composers, and Music.* Ed. John Edward Haase. New York: Schirmer-Macmillan, 1985.

Huggins, Nathan Irvin. *Harlem Renaissance.* New York: Oxford University Press, 1971.

Hughes, Langston. *The Big Sea.* New York: Hill and Wang, 1940.

–––. *Not Without Laughter.* New York: Scribner, 1995; reprint, 1930.

–––. *The Ways of White Folks.* New York: Vintage, 1933.

Hurston, Zora Neale. "Characteristics of Negro Expression." *The Jazz Cadence of American Culture.* Ed. Robert O'Meally. New York: Columbia University Press, 1998.

---. "How It Feels to Be Colored Me." *I Love Myself When I am Laughing...And then Again When I am Looking Mean and Impressive*. Ed. Alice Walker; Intro. Mary Helen Washington. Old Westbury, NY: The Feminist Press, 1979; reprint, 1928.

---. *Their Eyes Were Watching God*. New York: Harper & Row, 1990; reprint, 1937.

Hutchinson, George. *The Harlem Renaissance in Black and White*. Cambridge: Harvard University Press, 1995.

Jasen, David A. and Trebor Jay Tichenor. *Rags and Ragtime*. New York: Seabury Press, 1978.

Johnson, James Weldon. *The Autobiography of an Ex-Coloured Man*. Intro. Henry Louis Gates, Jr. New York: Vintage-Random House, 1989. [rpt. New York: Alfred A. Knopf, 1927]

---. *Black Manhattan*. New York: Arno Press, 1968. [rpt. 1930]

---. "Double Audience Makes Road Hard for Negro Writers." *Selected Writings of James Weldon Johnson*, Volume II. Ed. Sondra Kathryn Wilson. New York: Oxford University Press, 1995. [rpt. *Philadelphia Tribune*. November 29, 1928]

---. *God's Trombones*. New York: Penguin, 1990. [rpt. Viking-Penguin, 1927]

---. "Now We Have the Blues." *Selected Writings of James Weldon Johnson*, Volume II. Ed. Sondra Kathryn Wilson. New York: Oxford University Press, 1995. [rpt. *New York Amsterdam News*. July 7, 1926]

---. Preface to *The Book of American Negro Poetry*. ("The Negro's Creative Genius"). *The Book of American Negro Poetry*. Ed. James Weldon Johnson. New York: Harcourt, Brace, and Company, 1922.

---. *The Selected Writings of James Weldon Johnson, Volume I: The New York Age Editorials* (1914–1923). Ed. Sondra Kathryn Wilson. New York: Oxford University Press, 1995.

Jones, Gayl. *Corregidora*. Boston: Beacon Press, 1975.

---. *The Healing*. Boston: Beacon Press, 1998.

---. *Liberating Voices: Oral Tradition in African American Literature*. Cambridge: Harvard University Press, 1991.

Kennedy, Rick. *Jelly Roll, Bix, and Hoagy: Gennett Studios and the Birth of Recorded Jazz*. Bloomington and Indianapolis: Indiana University Press, 1994.

Leonard, Neil. *Jazz and the White Americans: The Acceptance of a New Art Form*. Chicago: University of Chicago Press, 1962.

———. "The Reactions to Ragtime." *Ragtime: Its History, Composers, and Music.* Ed. John Edward Haase. New York: Schirmer-Macmillan, 1985.

Levine, Lawrence W. *Black Culture and Black Consciousness.* New York: Oxford University Press, 1977.

———. *Highbrow/Lowbrow: The Emergence of Cultural Hierarchy in America.* Cambridge: Harvard University Press, 1988.

———. "Jazz and American Culture." *The Unpredictable Past: Explorations in American Cultural History.* New York: Oxford University Press, 1993 172–188.

Lewis, Barbara Williams. "The Function of Jazz in Toni Morrison's *Jazz*." *Toni Morrison's Fiction: Contemporary Criticism.* Ed. David L. Middleton. New York: Garland, 1997.

Locke, Alain. *The Negro and His Music.* New York: Arno Press, 1969; reprint, Washington D.C.: Associates in the Negro Folk Education, 1936.

Lott, Eric. *Love and Theft: Blackface Minstrelsy and the American Working Class.* New York: Oxford University Press, 1993.

Mackey, Nathaniel. *Bedouin Hornbook.* Los Angeles: Sun & Moon Press, 1997; reprint, 1986.

———. "Other: From Noun to Verb." *Jazz Among the Discourses.* Ed. Krin Gabbard. Durham, NC: Duke University Press, 1995.

Mansell, Darrell. "The *Jazz History of the World* in *The Great Gatsby*." *English Language Notes* 25: 2 (December, 1987) 57–62.

McKay, Claude. *Home to Harlem.* Boston: Northeastern University Press, 1987; reprint, New York: Harper and Brothers, 1928.

Menand, Louis. "The War Between Men and Women" (Review of Toni Morrison's *Paradise*). *The New Yorker.* 12 January 1998: 78–82.

Merriam, Alan P. *The Anthropology of Music.* Evanston: Northwestern University Press, 1964.

Michaels, Walter Benn. *Our America: Nativism, Modernism, and Pluralism.* Durham: Duke University Press, 1995.

Millard, Andre. *America On Record: A History of Recorded Sound.* Cambridge: Cambridge University Press, 1995.

Morrison, Toni. *The Bluest Eye.* New York: Washington Square Press, 1970.

———. *Jazz.* New York: Knopf, 1992.

———. *Playing in the Dark: Whiteness and the Literary Imagination.* Cambridge: Harvard University Press, 1992.

———. *Song of Solomon.* New York: Knopf, 1977.

---. *Sula*. New York: Plume-Penguin, 1973.

Murray, Albert. *The Blue Devils of Nada*. New York: Vintage, 1997; reprint, New York: Pantheon, 1996.

---. "Improvisation and the Creative Process." *The Jazz Cadence of American Culture*. Ed. Robert O'Meally. New York: Columbia University Press, 1998.

Munton, Alan. "Misreading Morrison, Mishearing Jazz: A Response to Toni Morrison's Jazz Critics." *Journal of American Studies*. 31:2 (1997): 235-251.

Nielson, Aldon L. *Writing Between the Lines: Race and Intertextuality*. Athens: University of Georgia Press, 1994.

Nisenson, Eric. *Ascension: John Coltrane and His Quest*. New York: St. Martin's, 1993.

North, Michael. *The Dialect of Modernism: Race, Language, and Twentieth-Century Literature*. New York: Oxford University Press, 1994.

Ogren, Kathy. *The Jazz Revolution: Twenties America and the Meaning of Jazz*. New York: Oxford University Press, 1989.

Olmsted, Jane. "Black Moves, White Ways, Every Body's Blues: Orphic Power in Langston Hughes's *The Ways of White Folks*." *Black Orpheus: Music in African American Fiction from the Harlem Renaissance to Toni Morrison*. Ed. Saadi A. Simawe. New York: Garland, 2000.

Ondaatje, Michael. *Coming Through Slaughter*. New York: Vintage, 1996; reprint, New York: W. W. Norton, 1976.

Panish, Jon. *The Color of Jazz: Race and Representation in Postwar American Culture*. Jackson: University of Mississippi, 1997.

Peretti, Burton. *The Creation of Jazz: Music, Race, and Culture in Urban America*. Chicago: University of Illinois Press, 1994.

Peterson, Bernard L., Jr. *A Century of Musicals in Black and White*. Westport, CT: Greenwood Press, 1993.

Peterson, Nancy J. "'Say Make Me, Remake Me': Toni Morrison and the Reconstruction of African-American History." *Toni Morrison: Critical and Theoretical Approaches*. Ed. Nancy J. Peterson. Baltimore: Johns Hopkins University Press, 1997.

Piersen, William D. *Black Legacy: America's Hidden Heritage*. Amherst: University of Massachusetts Press, 1993.

Porter, Lewis. *John Coltrane: His Life and Music*. Ann Arbor: University of Michigan Press, 1998.

Powell, Richard J. "Art History and Black Memory: Toward a 'Blues Aesthetic.'" *The Jazz Cadence of American Culture.* Ed. Robert O'Meally. New York: Columbia University Press, 1998.

Prigozy, Ruth. "'Poor Butterfly': F. Scott Fitzgerald and Popular Music." *Prosepects. 2 (1976) 40–67.*

Radano, Ronald. "Hot Fantasies: American Modernism and the Idea of Black Rhythm." *Music and the Racial Imagination.* Eds. Ronald Radano and Philip V. Bohlman. Chicago: University of Chicago Press, 2000.

Reed, Ishmael. *Mumbo Jumbo.* New York: Macmillan, 1972.

Rice, Alan J. "Jazzing It Up a Storm: The Execution and Meaning of Toni Morrison's Jazzy Prose Style." *Journal of American Studies.* 28:3 (December 1994): 423–432.

Riis, Thomas L. *Just Before Jazz: Black Musical Theater in New York, 1890–1915.* Washington, D. C.: Smithsonian Institution Press, 1989.

Rodrigues, Eusebio L. "Experiencing Jazz." *Modern Fiction Studies.* 39: 3–4 (Fall-Winter 1993): 733–754.

Roediger, David R. *Towards the Abolition of Whiteness: Essays on Race, Politics, Working Class History.* London: Verso, 1994.

Rogers, J. A. "Jazz at Home." *The New Negro: An Interpretation.* Ed. Alain Locke. New York: Albert and Charles Boni, 1925.

Rose, Tricia. *Black Noise: Rap Music and Black Culture in Contemporary America.* Hanover: Wesleyan University Press, 1994.

Roulston, Helen. and Robert. The Winding Road to West Egg: The Artistic Development of F. Scott Fitzgerald. London: Associated University Presses, 1995.

Rudwick, Elliott M. *Race Riot at East St. Louis.* Carbondale: Southern Illinois University Press, 1964.

Scanlon, Larry. "'Death is a Drum'": Rhythm, Modernity, and the Negro Poet Laureate." *Music and the Racial Imagination.* Eds. Ronald Radano and Philip V. Bohlman. Chicago: University of Chicago Press, 2000.

Schafer, William J. and Johannes Riedel. *The Art of Ragtime: Form and Meaning of an Original Black American Art.* Baton Rouge: Louisiana State University Press, 1973.

Schuller, Gunther. *Early Jazz: Its Roots and Musical Development.* New York: Oxford University Press, 1968.

Shaw, Arnold. *The Jazz Age: Popular Music in the 1920s.* New York: Oxford University Press, 1987.

Shepherd, John. *Music as Social Text.* London: Polity Press, 1986.

Sidran, Ben. *Black Talk.* New York: Holt, Rinehart, and Winston, 1971.

Small, Christopher. *Music of the Common Tongue: Survival and Celebration in Afro-American Music.* New York: Riverrun Press, 1987.

Small-McCarthy, Robin. "The Jazz Aesthetic in the Novels of Toni Morrison." *Cultural Studies.* 9:2 (1995): 293–300.

Sollors, Werner. *Beyond Ethnicity: Consent and Descent in American Culture.* New York: Oxford University Press, 1986.

———. *Neither Black Nor White Yet Both.* New York: Oxford University Press, 1997.

Solomon, Maynard. *Beethoven.* New York: Schirmer, 1977.

Southern, Eileen. *The Music of Black Americans* (3rd Edition) New York: W.W. Norton, 1997.

Spencer, Jon Michael. *The New Negroes and Their Music: The Success of the Harlem Renaissance.* Knoxville: University of Tennessee Press, 1997.

Stearns, Marshall W. *The Story of Jazz.* New York: Oxford University Press, 1962. [rpt. 1956]

Stoller, Paul. "Sound in Songhay Cultural Experience." *American Ethnologist.* 11:3 (August 1984): 559–570.

Sundquist, Eric J. *The Hammers of Creation: Folk Culture in Modern African-American Fiction.* Athens: University of Georgia Press, 1992.

———. *To Wake the Nations: Race in the Making of American Literature.* Cambridge: Harvard University Press, 1992.

Tomkins, Calvin. "Profiles: Putting Something Over Something Else." *The Jazz Cadence of American Culture.* Ed. Robert O'Meally. New York: Columbia University Press, 1998.

Walser, Robert. "'Out of Notes': Signification, Interpretation, and the Problem of Miles Davis." *Jazz Among the Discourses.* Ed. Krin Gabbard. Durham, NC: Duke University Press, 1995.

Washington, Bryan R. *The Politics of Exile: Ideology in Henry James, F. Scott Fitzgerald, and James Baldwin.* Boston: Northeastern University Press, 1995.

Waterman, Guy. "Ragtime." *The Art of Jazz: Ragtime to Bebop.* Ed. Martin T. Williams. New York: Da Capo, 1959.

Werner, Craig Hansen. *Playing the Changes: From Afro-Modernism to the Jazz Impulse.* Chicago: University of Illinois Press, 1994.

West, Cornel. *Race Matters.* Boston: Beacon, 1993.

Whiteman, Paul and Mary Margaret McBride. *Jazz*. New York: J.H. Sears and Company, 1926. Williams, Martin. *The Jazz Tradition*. New York: Oxford University Press, 1983. [revised and reprinted from 1970 edition]

Williams, Raymond. *Marxism and Literature*. New York: Oxford University Press, 1977.

Wilson, Sondra Kathryn. "Introduction." *The Selected Writings of James Weldon Johnson*, Volume I. Ed. Sondra Kathryn Wilson. New York: Oxford University Press, 1995.

Wonham, Henry B. *Criticism and the Color Line: Desegregating American Literary Studies*. New Brunswick, NJ: Rutgers University Press, 1996.

Woolf, Virginia. "Old Mrs. Grey." *The Death of the Moth*. New York: Harcourt Brace and Company, 1942.

Index

Adorno, T. W., 10
Anderson, Jervis, 138n.4, 138n.5
Andrews, William, 127nn.1, 3
Anzaldúa, Gloria, 112-23, 143n.3
Armstrong, Louis, 50, 110, 114, 133n.1, 134n.12

Baker, Houston A., Jr., 119, 129n.18, 139n.9, 139-40n.12, 140n.13
Baldwin, James, 109
Bambara, Toni Cade, 139n.10
Baraka, Amiri (LeRoi Jones), 14, 15, 141n.23
"Beale St. Blues," 51, 52
Bearden, Romare, 115
Beethoven, Ludwig van, 20, 21
Bergreen, Laurence, 114
Berlin, Edward A., 14, 19, 21, 23, 26, 27, 28, 128n.5, 130n.19, 131n.25
Berlin, Irving, 52
Berret, Anthony, 142n.30
Bhabha, Homi, 122-23, 124
Blesh, Rudi, 14, 25, 28, 128n.5
Boas, Franz, 57, 103, 113, 135n.21
Bolden, Buddy, 139n.10
Brown, Sterling, 32
Breitwieser, Mitchell, 48, 133n.3
Brooks, Neil, 129n.17
Brooks, Shelton, 52

Bushell, Gavin, 133n.37

Cahill, Marie, 24
Callahan, John, 137n.33
Cardinal, Marie, 111, 112
Castle, Vernon, 30
Cataliotti, Robert, 92
Chernoff, John Miller, 45, 116
Chesnutt, Charles, 128n.10
Chicago World's Fair (World's Columbia Exposition 1893), 26
Chinitz, David, 137n.4
Chopin, Frédéric, 20, 21-22
Cole, Bob, 14, 24-25, 26, 130n.20
  and the Troubadours, 24
Collier, James Lincoln, 134-35n.16
Coltrane, John, 34-36, 132n.37
Coming Through Slaughter, 128n.9, 139n.10
Corregidora, 123, 139n.10
"Crazy Blues," 114
The Crying of Lot 49, 128n.9

Davis, Miles, 131n.28
Dolphy, Eric, 133n.37
Douglas, Aaron, 108-9
Du Bois, W. E. B., 30, 115, 128n.10, 143n.2

155

Eberly, Philip, 134n.12
Eckard, Paula Gallant, 140n.13, 142n.30
Edwards, Brent, 23, 141n.25
Eliot, T. S., 93, 130n.19
Ellington, Edward "Duke," 88, 96
Ellison, Ralph, 5-6, 36, 49, 53, 55, 93, 110, 112, 119, 128n.4, 134n.11, 135n.22, 141n.23

Faulkner, William, 112, 113, 142n.28
Fishkin, Shelley Fisher, 128n.8
Fitzgerald, F. Scott, 4, 7, 8, 9, 68, 78, 117, 121, 122
   "Dice, Brassknuckles, and Guitar," 47, 56-59
      outsiders, 57-58
   "Echoes of the Jazz Age," 43, 47-48
   The Great Gatsby, 9, 37-59, 78, 117
     "Ain't We Got Fun," 47
     Alexander's Ragtime Band," 52
     "Beale St. Blues," 51, 52
     "Darktown Strutter's Ball," 52
     Gatsby and music, 46-47
     improvisation, 38, 41, 42
     Jazz History of the World, 37, 38-44, 48, 50, 51, 133n.3, 133n.5
     "The Love Nest," 47
     outsiders, 55-56
     "nut" jazz, 49
     Queensboro bridge, 54
   Tender Is the Night, 9, 59-67
     "Good-by [sic] Alexander," 60
     "Hindustan," 60
     "I'm Glad I Can Make You Cry," 60
     incest and miscegenation, 59
     music and alcohol, 61-62
     outsiders, 62, 67
     "Poor Butterfly," 61
     racial stereotypes, 62-64
     "So Long Letty," 60
     "Tea for Two," 60
     "There Was a Young Lady from Hell," 49, 67
     "Wait Till the Cows Come Home," 60
     "Why Do They Call Them Babies," 60
Forrey, Robert, 62, 136n.29
Frith, Simon, 5, 6-7, 9-10, 67

Ganzl, Kurt, 136n.26
Garber, Frederick, 93
Gates, Henry Louis, Jr., 92, 141n.26
Gayle, Addison, 141n.23
Gershwin, George, 133n.1
Goldberg, Isaac, 28-29
Goodman, Benny, 115
Gordon, Dexter, 138n.2
Grant, Madison, 39

Hall, Cheryl, 142n.30
Hamm, Charles, 1-2, 18, 44, 45
Handy, W. C. (William Christopher), 23, 31, 51-52, 132n.32, 135n.16, 135n.17
Hardack, Richard, 115
Harlem Renaissance, 32, 73, 89, 96, 101-9, 129n.18
Harris, Joel Chandler, 30
Harrison, Daphne Duval, 114
Hasse, John Edward, 28, 131n.23
Hayes, Roland, 72
Hazzard-Gordon, Katrina, 133n.7
Hentoff, Nat, 133n.38
Home to Harlem, 101-2
Huggins, Nathan, 129n.18
Hughes, Langston, 4, 7, 8, 9, 32, 49-50, 103, 108, 121, 122
   The Big Sea, 81, 85-86
   "The Blues I'm Playing," 8, 69, 81-85

Index

patronage, 81, 82-83
racial stereotypes
  (disguised as aesthetic value judgments), 82, 83-84
  range, 84-85
"Home," 8, 69, 70-75, 82, 84, 85
  art and social justice, 73-75
  dreams, 72
  Europe, 71
  HarlemRenaissance, 73
Not Without Laughter, 49-50, 101
"Rejuvenation through Joy," 8, 69, 75-81, 82, 85
  jealousy, 79
  New Negro movement, 76, 78, 79
  rhythm, 78, 79-80
The Ways of White Folks, 8, 9, 69
Hurston, Zora Neale, 32, 81, 103-4, 108, 134n.14
  "Characteristics of Negro Expression," 104
  "How It Feels to Be Colored Me," 104-6
  There Eyes Were Watching God, 103-4
Hutchinson, George, 127n.2, 129n.18

In Country, 128n.9
Invisible Man, 110-11, 134n.11

James, Henry, 83
Janis, Harriet, 14, 25, 28, 128n.5
"Jazz at Home," 106-7
Johnson, James Weldon, 4, 7, 9, 11-36, 51, 69-70, 80, 107, 108, 121, 122, 136n.27, 141-42n.27
  Along This Way, 29
  The Autobiography of an Ex-Coloured Man, 7, 9, 11-36, 70, 80, 141-42n.27
    cultural identity, 12, 14, 18, 19-20
    documentation, 24, 25, 26-27, 28-29, 30, 31, 32
    ideology of whiteness, 22
    improvisation, 11, 16, 19, 25-27, 35-36
    lynching, 12, 16-17
    race as social construction, 17, 24-25
    ragging the classics, 21
    written language and African American oral traditions, 15-16
  Black Manhattan, 24, 26, 29, 131n.24
  The Book of American Negro Poetry, 18, 19
  The Book of American Negro Spirituals, 35
  "Double Audience Makes Road Hard for Negro Writers," 132n.30
  Dyer Anti-Lynching Bill, 33
  God's Trombones, 15, 29, 31, 36, 107, 132n.30, 132n.33
  "The Japanese Question in California," 33-34
  "Lift Every Voice and Sing," 24
  "Now We Have the Blues," 23, 30
  "Russian Democracy and the Jews," 33
  "Under the Bamboo Tree," 24
  "Under the Dome of the Capitol," 33

Johnson, Rosamond, 14, 24, 29
Jones, Elvin, 133n.37
Jones, Gayl, 32-33, 123, 139n.10
Joplin, Scott, 25, 130n.19, 130n.22

Kafka, Franz, 132n.36

Index

Kennedy, Rick, 114, 134n.10, 140n.18
Kingston, Maxine Hong, 128n.9

Lawrence, Icky, 12
Leonard, John, 140n.13
Leonard, Neil, 19-20, 129n.14, 133n.2
Levine, Lawrence, 2-3, 4, 18, 32, 34, 45-46, 103, 121
Lewis, Barbara Williams, 142n.30
Lewis, David Levering, 129n.18
"Lift Every Voice and Sing," 24
Locke, Alain, 27, 81, 106, 107, 108, 129n.18, 141n.22
Lott, Eric, 134n.13

Mackey, Nathaniel, 139n.10
Mansell, Darrel, 133n.3
Marsalis, Wynton, 94
Marxism and Literature, 141n.26
Mason, Bobbie Ann, 128n.9
Mason, Charlotte, 81
Massenet, Jules Émile Frédéric, 72, 137n.1
McKay, Claude, 32, 49, 50, 101-2, 103, 108
Meditation from Thaïs, 72, 137n.1
Menand, Louis, 142n.28
Mendelssohn, Felix, 21
Merriam, Alan, 97-98
Michaels, Walter Benn, 130n.21, 135n.21
Millard, Andre, 107, 134n.10
Moderwell, Hiram K., 20
Morrison, Toni, 4, 7, 8, 9, 121, 122, 125, 128n.8, 128n.9, 135-36n.23
   The Bluest Eye, 87-88, 89, 100, 105-6
      improvisation, 87-88
   Jazz, 8, 9, 87-120, 125, 128n.9
      birds, 119-20
      East St. Louis Riot (1917), 89, 90, 91, 95, 96, 98
      Harlem Renaissance, 96, 101-9
      improvisation, 94, 109
      narrator, 99, 115-161, 40n.13

"Silent Parade" (New York 1917), 89-95
Playing in the Dark, 111,128n.8, 135-36n.23, 138-39n.7
Sula, 140n.16
Mumbo Jumbo, 128n.9, 139n.10, 140-41n.21
Munton, Alan, 113-14, 115
Murray, Albert, 125, 139n.9

Nielson, Aldon, 23, 130n.19, 132n.35
Niles, Abbe, 132n.32
Nisenson, Eric, 34
North, Michael, 127n.2, 130n.19, 132n.35

Ogren, Kathy, 4, 23, 37, 49, 50, 108, 124, 129n.14, 133n.2, 133n.5, 135n.20, 138n.1, 140n.19
Okeh, 114, 117, 143n.31
"Old Mrs. Grey," 118-19
Olmsted, Jane, 137n.6
O'Meally, Robert, 122
Ondaatje, Michael, 128n.9, 139n.10

Page, Walter, 12
Panish, Jon, 139n.9
Parker, Charlie "Bird," 138n.2, 143n.33
Peretti, Burton, 26, 42, 43
Perry, Edward B., 21
Peterson, Bernard, 130n.20
Peterson, Nancy, 92, 116
Peyton, Dave, 135n.20
Piersen, William, 112
Plato, 1
Plessy, Homer, 127n.2
Porter, Lewis, 35
Portrait of a Lady, 83
Prigozy, Ruth, 44, 136n.26, 136n.27
Pynchon, Thomas, 128n.9

Radano, Ronald, 137n.5, 137-38n.8, 141n.21
Reed, Ishmael, 128n.9, 139n.10, 140-41n.21

Index

Rice, Alan, 142-43n.30
Riedel, Johannes, 25, 135n.19
Riis, Thomas, 130n.20
Rodrigues, Eusebio, 113, 140n.13
Roediger, David, 128n.8, 129n.16
Rogers, J. A., 26, 27, 106-7, 108, 131n.26
Rose, Tricia, 29-30, 134n.15, 140n.15
Ross, Andrew, 6
Rudwick, Elliot, 90, 138n.4

Sarasate, Pablo de, 74, 137n.3
Sargeant, Winthrop, 142n.30
Scanlon, Larry, 137n.2, 137n.7, 138n.9
Schafer, William J., 25, 135n.19
Schuller, Gunther, 136n.27
Shaw, Arnold, 133n.6
Shepherd, John, 4-5, 6, 139n.7
Sidran, Ben, 27
Small, Christopher, 43, 52
Small-McCarthy, Robin, 142n.30
Smith, Bessie, 50, 81, 132n.32
Smith, Mamie, 114
Smith, Willie "The Lion," 52
Sollors, Werner, 48, 59, 140n.20, 142n.29
Solomon, Maynard, 22
Sonata Pathetique, 20, 21
"Sonny's Blues," 109
Southern, Eileen, 52
Spencer, Jon Michael, 129
"Spiritual," 35
Stearns, Jean, 134n.7
Stearns, Marshall, 14, 25, 29, 134n.7, 142n.30
Stoddard, Lothrop, 39, 40
Stoller, Paul, 112, 113
Stowe, Harriet Beecher, 65
Sundquist, Eric, 15, 16, 23, 91, 110, 112

Thirteenth Nocturne, 20, 22
Thomas, Theodore, 20
Tin Pan Alley, 39, 42, 46, 52, 59
Toomer, Jean, 32
"Tradition and the Individual Talent," 93
Tripmaster Monkey, 128n.9
"Trombone Blues," 96
Tyner, McCoy, 133n.37

Uncle Tom's Cabin, 65
"Under the Bamboo Tree," 24

Van Vechten, Carl, 49, 50, 136n.25

Walser, Robert, 131n.28
Washington, Bryan, 62, 136n.29
Waterman, Guy, 26
"Wedding March," 21
Werner, Craig Hansen, 139n.9, 140n.13, 142n.30
West, Cornel, 136n.30
"What Did I Do to Be So Black and Blue," 110
Whiteman, Paul, 43-44, 50, 133n.1, 133n.3, 133n.6, 142n.30
Williams, Martin, 26
Williams, Raymond, 141n.26
Wilson, Sondra Katherine, 132n.31
Wilson, Woodrow, 138n.6
Wonder, Stevie, 6
Wonham, Henry, 142n.29
Woolf, Virginia, 111, 112, 113, 118-19, 142n.28
Workman, Reggie, 133n.37

Young, Lester, 138n.2